The 16P
Personality in ~~Depth~~

D0899785

Heather Birkett Cattell

With a Foreword by Raymond B. Cattell

**Institute for Personality and Ability Testing, Inc.
Champaign, Illinois**

APR   1990
ELMHURST COLLEGE LIBRARY

Copyright © 1989 by the Institute for Personality
and Ability Testing, Inc. All rights reserved.
Printed in the United States of America.

ISBN 0-918296-20-X

Institute for Personality and Ability Testing, Inc.
P. O. Box 188, Champaign, Illinois 61824-0188

Cover design by Judy Henderson.

Grateful acknowledgment is made for permission to reprint lines from the following:

From *The Moon and Sixpence* by Somerset Maugham. Published by Doubleday, a division of Bantam, Doubleday, Bell Publishing Group, Inc. and used by permission.

From *A Woman of Substance* by Barbara Taylor Bradford. Published by Doubleday, a division of Bantam, Doubleday, Bell Publishing Group, Inc. and used by permission.

From *The Road Less Traveled* by M. Scott Peck. Published by Simon & Shuster, Inc. and used by permission.

From *The Accidental Tourist,* copyright © 1985 by Anne Tyler Modarressi, et. al. Published by Alfred A. Knopf, Inc., New York and used by permission.

From *All Things Bright and Beautiful,* copyright © 1973, 1974 by James Herriot. Published by St. Martin's Press, Inc., New York and used by permission.

From *An Outline of Psychoanalysis* by Sigmund Freud. Translated by James Strachey. W. W. Norton & Company, Inc. Copyright 1949 by W. W. Norton & Company, Inc. Copyright renewed 1969 by The Institute of Psychoanalysis and Alix Strachey. Used by permission.

From *West With the Night,* copyright © 1942, 1983 by Beryl Markham. Published by North Point Press and reprinted by permission.

Dedication

This book is dedicated to my children, Vaughn, Gary, and Heather Luanne.

Contents

(Concluded on next page)

Contents *(Concluded)*

Foreword

This is a work of science and a work of art. It is science in that it builds on and discusses the now repeatedly confirmed 16 primary source traits found by sophisticated factor-analytic studies here and abroad. It is art in that it distils the experience with the 16PF, on some 900 diverse subjects, of a successful psychotherapist.

The 16PF has been a challenge to conservative psychologists in that, instead of supporting their homegrown subjective conceptions, it presents a set of 16 new constructs from the hand of objective science (new except for the Freudian one of superego). The history of science is a story of having to make constant adjustments to the new—new chemical elements, new elementary particles, new types of stars. The psychology undergraduate has now to learn at least 16 new personality dimensions—but at least that's better than 106 new elements that the young chemist faces.

Here the genius and art of Dr. Heather Cattell clearly show. She makes the dimensions come to life, in recognizable behavior. She shows how an initial diagnostic testing by the 16PF makes the patient, and his or her problems, intelligible. It is strange to remember that until the primaries and secondaries of personality could be mapped for each subject, the practitioner had no better clinical, educational, or industrial systematic framework (except extraversion and intelligence) by which to grasp the totality of the personality. The systematic presentation of dimensions in this book, done with accuracy and charm, will lead the reader happily into a new world of understanding.

RAYMOND B. CATTELL

Acknowledgements

This book became possible because of the contributions made by clients and examinees who shared their insights and personal experiences, clinicians and organizational officials who allowed me access to data bases, authors who gave permission to draw on their fictional creations, students and friends who gave editing suggestions and feedback about content, and the army of researchers that discovered and studied the 16 personality factors. I wish that it was possible to thank each one of you individually, but since to do so would require listing well over a thousand names, I will mention just two: Lucille Medcalf for her patient typing of the manuscript and Mary Russell for her thorough and creative editing.

Chapter 1

Introduction

THE 16PF AS A COMPREHENSIVE MEASURE OF TEMPERAMENT

THE RESEARCH BEHIND THIS BOOK
Description of the Sample
Collection of Data

ABOUT THIS BOOK

INTRODUCTION

The 16PF as a Comprehensive Measure of Temperament

The Sixteen Personality Factor Questionnaire (16PF), originally developed by Raymond Cattell, is a factor-analytically derived questionnaire for personality assessment. Cattell used factor analysis to uncover the deep, basic traits that underlie human behavior. The 16PF scales that he derived measure temperament— a person's characteristic style of thinking, perceiving, and acting over a relatively long period of time and in a wide range of different situations. These personality traits are manifested in a set of attitudes, preferences, social and emotional reactions, and habits. Each trait has its own history, and is derived from a complicated interaction between inherited disposition and learning from experiences. Some traits primarily involve internal regulation of impulses and service defensive or adaptive purposes. Others are maintained by habit or are functionally autonomous. Still others seem to be stylistic responses to the pressure of inner drives. In all, they have a pervasive effect on practically every facet of a person's overall functioning and way of being in this world.

Hippocrates, who is usually credited as being the first observer to recognize temperament as a separate personality dimension, believed it was further divisible into four traits which he described as Sanguine, Choleric, Phlegmatic, and Melancholic, asserting that any person could be assigned to one of them. Although Hippocrates quite accurately described traits that have since been experimentally replicated (and may be related to 16PF Factors A, E, Q_4, and O), he grossly underestimated the number of traits the human temperament subsumes. Other observers after him have also erred in this respect, some having compounded this error by not differentiating between similar-appearing traits that have later proved on experimental analysis to be separate entities.

The test that Cattell developed measures no fewer than 16 temperament traits; these traits, interchangeably called "factors" here, are laid out for convenience inside the cover of this book.[1] Much of what makes people unique comes from the array of possibilities that so many traits afford. As with everything else in nature, whatever exists does so in some quantity or strength, and an individual's particular endowment on these poles is what creates his or her distinctive style.

This book is meant to provide a deeper psychological understanding of the factors that make up this popular instrument. It is also intended to provide a more intensive clinical perspective for interpreting the 16PF than has hitherto been attempted. As such, this book should be useful to helping professionals (such as psychologists, psychiatrists, and social workers, among others) as well as to researchers (especially those in the clinical and personality branches of behavioral sciences).

THE RESEARCH BEHIND THIS BOOK

Description of the Sample

Although this book draws from numerous other research findings, its core is based on my own data, the bulk of which was drawn from interactions with a total of 905 examinees, most of whom were seen in the years between 1978 and 1984. Some I saw only once, but well over 60% I saw for periods ranging from a few months to several years. The largest portion were clients treated either by myself or by other clinical practitioners. Others were encountered in consultation work with clinical and non-clinical institutions such as outpatient clinics, residential substance abuse treatment programs, prisons, and business

---

[1]While it is not the purpose of this book to describe the test development and history in detail, Appendix A does present a brief history of the test. Appendix B describes factor analysis, the statistical technique used to develop the test. Readers interested in the more technical aspects of the 16PF should refer to the *16PF Handbook,* referenced in the bibliography. Further, recognizing that, along with temperament, motivation and ability also influence personality, Cattell developed other instruments. One is the Motivation Analysis Test (MAT), which taps motivational traits by assessing the strength of an individual's drives and emotional attachments. The Culture Fair Intelligence Test measures intelligence by assessing the capacity for perceiving similarities and differences in a series of timed recognition tests, independent of cultural learning. These two tests are discussed in Appendix C. These and other applications of Cattell's multivariate experimental methods will be referred to occasionally throughout the text.

organizations. All were above 18 years of age. References made to children and adolescents in this book were obtained from other observational data bases and sources. Table 1.1 below shows the various sources from which my sample was drawn.

Table 1.1

**Sources of Data Base: Number and Percentages of Examinees
From Each Source
N = 905**

Source	Number	Percent of Sample
Private practice clients (identified clients and their family members/ significant others)	426	47.0
Employees and prospective employees of business organizations	137	15.1
Clients residing in substance abuse programs and their family members/ significant others	206	22.7
Employees of substance abuse treatment programs	42	04.6
Inmates of correctional institutions	38	04.1
Outpatient clients in mental health clinics	31	03.4
Miscellaneous	25	02.7

Mean age of examinees = 29

Collection of Data

The data were collected by multidimensional means. First, I checked each examinee's scores on the 16 factors against direct observations of their behavior. Second, I carefully listened to and recorded all insights, self-disclosures, and associations that the examinees volunteered in response to feedback about their 16PF test results. Third, I drew on available sources of knowledge of the examinees' psychological histories, present life situations, and diagnoses or other clinical material, if relevant. Finally, whenever possible, I watched their social interactions with family members, group therapy members, coworkers, and others.

As the data accumulated, certain regularities of thinking, feeling, and behavior became increasingly associated with each factor. These regularities, which had not hitherto been reported in the literature, aid and extend understanding of the factors and the personality dimensions to which they correspond. This provides a clearer understanding of the human psyche as a whole, and makes important practical discriminations possible. As an example, upon sharing some of these factor associations, colleagues have come to recognize that the making of repetitive mistakes, by clients whose 16PF profiles showed a combination of low scores on Factor B and high scores on Factor H, was due to a mixture of lower intelligence and adventurousness, rather than to a self-destructive motive. Similarly, I have noticed that people who show high scores on Factor A and low scores on Factor I, even though they can be warm and sociable, also lack empathic understanding.

Most of the earlier work in the Cattellian literature stays with facts, derived from data, that have undergone the full complement of sequences involved in the scientific method. This work is unlike some of that earlier work; while it draws heavily on established facts, it includes what should be considered preliminary or hypothetical data, as the conclusions here rest largely on unquantified observations collected by clinical methods rather than by techniques like structured interviews. However, documenting this clinically gleaned data is intended to be consistent with the scientific method, not a break from it. Because these observations were not controlled or qualified, no superimposing structure prematurely selected out pertinent information. Through open-ended questioning, passive observing, and patiently mulling over what was seen and heard, patterns gradually took form for me. Although I have recognized distinct patterns, a full scientific investigation of these patterns must be done before they can be taken as final truths. This cannot be stressed too much, since so much that passes for psychological theory merely represents preliminary conjecture.

ABOUT THIS BOOK

This book contains 18 chapters, of which this introductory chapter is the first. Chapters 2 through 17 each deal with a specific primary factor of the 16PF, from Factor A through Factor Q_4. Chapter 18 deals with the second-order factors, each of which combines several of the primary factors. These second-order factors address some of the broad, predictable patterns of inter-relationships found between the 16 basic scales of the test.

While each of the "Primary Factor Chapters" varies in length, depending on the kinds of information available for each factor, there is a general order within most of these chapters. First, the factor is briefly outlined in terms of the trait it measures. Within this section, age trend, sex differences, and heritability information is presented. Next follows a discussion of the intrapsychic and social characteristics, childhood experiences, and clinical associations of both extreme poles of the factor. (The major exception to this format is the chapter on Factor B. Unlike the others, Factor B is a measure of ability rather than temperament, and so requires a different kind of exposition.)

Here is some useful, general information that will appear across chapters: As can be seen in the profile sheet on the inside cover of this book, each of the 16 personality scales (or factors) is identified by a letter, A through Q_4. In the original research, these symbols were used to label emerging factors until they could be investigated for their psychological meaning. Later, Cattell assigned names to the factors, sometimes creating a neologism where no existing word adequately conveyed the factor meaning. (These neologisms allowed precision in language, and avoided preconceptions and biases that might otherwise have occurred.) However, in recognizing that some practitioners use the neologisms while others simply use the factor "letter" in referring to the factor, this book refers to the factor by its letter, often in combination with the neologism.

A factor's order in the alphabet indicates how broad an area of human personality it represents (or, more technically, the amount of variance that factor accounts for in personality assessment). Generally, factors earlier in the alphabet have a broader influence on personality.

Scores on each of the scales of the 16PF range from 1 to 10 (this is a "sten" scale).[2] Figure 1.1 shows how sten scores are distributed in the general population, and how the sten scale relates to other commonly used scales.

---

[2]The mid-point, or mean, of the sten scale is 5.5; and the standard deviation of this scale is 2.0.

Figure 1.1

Translations from Stens to Standard Scores and to Centile Ranks*

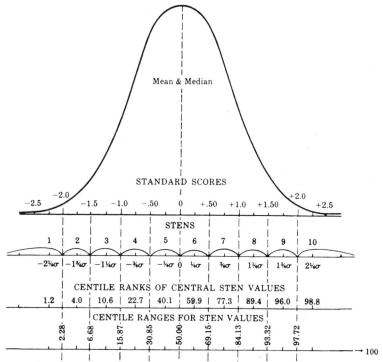

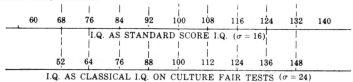

b) In the case of Factor B, Intelligence, it is desirable also to have translations to I.Q.'s on traditional and on culture fair tests, as follows :

60	68	76	84	92	100	108	116	124	132	140

I.Q. AS STANDARD SCORE I.Q. ($\sigma = 16$)

	52	64	76	88	100	112	124	136	148	

I.Q. AS CLASSICAL I.Q. ON CULTURE FAIR TESTS ($\sigma = 24$)

*The term "percentile" is, unfortunately, in more common use than "centile." That the latter is the more logical word should be clear when it is recognized that we are referring to a concept analogous to "decile," "quartile," and "tertile." To speak of "percentile" is just as awkward as to say "perquartile" for "quartile."

Reproduced by permission.

On a sten scale, most people get average scores (usually sten scores that fall in the 4-7 range are considered average). Scores that fall outside the average range occur with less frequency; roughly 18% of the population scores between stens of 1-3;

another 18% scores between stens of 8-10. However, it is these extreme scores (stens of 1-3 and 8-10) that usually are more telling indicators of distinctive temperament traits. Table 1.2 shows how sten scores were distributed in my sample.

Table 1.2

Number and Percentages of Data Base Examinees Scoring in Low, Middle, and High Range for Each Factor
N = 905

Factor	Examinees Scoring Between 1-3 Stens		Examinees Scoring Between 4-7 Stens		Examinees Scoring Between 8-10 Stens	
	Number of Examinees	Percent of Sample	Number of Examinees	Percent of Sample	Number of Examinees	Percent of Sample
A	245	27.1	515	56.9	145	16.0
B	29	03.2	635	70.2	241	26.6
C	302	33.3	494	54.5	109	12.2
E	276	30.4	540	59.6	89	09.8
F	264	29.1	503	55.5	138	15.2
G	159	17.5	566	62.5	180	19.8
H	199	21.9	609	67.2	97	10.7
I	86	09.5	615	67.9	204	22.5
L	75	08.2	529	58.4	301	33.2
M	142	15.6	567	62.6	196	21.6
N	93	10.2	627	69.2	185	20.4
O	91	10.0	538	59.4	276	30.4
Q_1	154	17.0	584	64.5	167	18.4
Q_2	164	18.1	572	63.2	169	18.6
Q_3	233	25.7	512	56.5	160	17.6
Q_4	135	14.9	570	62.9	200	22.0

Sten scores from 8-10 fall at the right of the sten scale, and by convention are referred to as the "plus" or " + " pole of the factor. Sten scores between 1-3 are at the left of the sten scale, and are referred to as the "minus" or " − " pole of the factor. Throughout this book, then, when I refer to a " + " person on a given factor, I mean a person who scored between 8-10 on that factor. For example, an F+ person would have scores at the right of the sten scale on Factor F. Similarly, an H− person would have scores at the left of the scale on Factor H.

Heredity. In the beginning section of each chapter on a primary factor, information is given on the estimated influence of heredity on the trait measured by that factor. This information is given in the form of what is called an H-coefficient. For example, .80 is the heritability coefficient presented for Factor B. This means that 80% of the variance is due to heritability rather than environmental influences.[3] These H-coefficients are taken from *The Inheritance of Personality and Ability* (Cattell, 1982).

Male and Female Differences Throughout the Life Span. This section discusses known age trend data, taken from R. B. Cattell's *Personality and Mood by Questionnaire* (Cattell, 1973). It also discusses relevant sex differences noted in the raw score distributions for men and women on combined Forms A and B of the 16PF. These data are taken from the norm supplement for the 16PF (Institute for Personality and Ability Testing, 1970).

Factor Intercorrelation Tables. Within each section on high and low scores, there is a table that shows the important correlations between scores on the factor pole being discussed and other 16PF factor scores. These correlations are presented so that test interpreters can notice when they encounter a profile in which the factor interrelationships are not in the expected pattern. It is these unusual patterns that can raise questions about how the person expresses these temperament traits that are usually not found together. The typical way of indicating the degree of relationship is through correlation coefficients, which range from −1 to +1, where 0 implies no relationship, and where −1 implies that the two variables are completely related in opposite directions (getting a high score on one scale means getting a low score on another scale, always). Of course, then, +1 would indicate a perfect relationship between variables, where a high score on one scale means getting a high score on another scale. Many 16PF scales are not related; others are more related. In fact, the highest degree of relationship is −.61 and is between Factor C (ego strength) and Factor O (guilt proneness), but typically the relationships fall more in the .20 range. However, even when two scales tend to show an important relationship, the

---

[3]Appendix D explains the methods used to estimate the ratio of heritability over observed variance in 16PF traits.

relationship is certainly likely to vary from person to person, and so should always be independently evaluated in every 16PF profile.

A word about the portraits of high- and low-scoring examinees: I have presented portraits of the contrasting extreme scores, even though the traits measured by the 16PF are normally distributed and, hence, the more extreme scores will occur less frequently. Contrasting the extremes has the instructional advantage of presenting the classical case. Nonetheless, it must be recognized that "classical cases" are rarely encountered outside textbooks, even in medicine, where the term originated. Unadulterated, "pure" extreme scores on a factor are artificial (as Cattell has long recognized by insisting on oblique, correlated factors); one personality variable cannot be isolated from all others. Thus, the reader is asked to be mindful of this artificiality, when I speak of A + (affectothymic), or A − (sizothymic) persons, for example—as if that particular trait alone explained the entire personality. These presentations should be taken for what they are: Galsworthian-like portraits, unidimensional and larger-than-life illustrations of single personality traits.[4]

I have used the 16PF extensively in clinical practice. From my experience with the test, I have developed an understanding of the ways that Cattell's personality traits, as measured by his 16PF, are manifested in human behavior. I hope that this book will impart this understanding in a way that both instructs and simplifies.

---

[4]I am here following the lead of Carl Jung (1928), who presented his formulations on temperament characteristics by calling them Galsworthian-like portraits.

Chapter 2

Factor A: The Warm-Cool Social Orientation

THE CONSTRUCT
Gregariousness

Heredity

Male and Female Differences Throughout the Life Span

HIGH SCORES ON FACTOR A
Intrapsychic Data

Interpersonal and Social Data

A+ and Childhood

Important Correlations Between A+ Scores
and Other 16PF Factor Scores

Clinical Relevance of A+ Scores

LOW SCORES ON FACTOR A
Intrapsychic Data

Interpersonal and Social Data

A− and Childhood

Important Correlations Between A− Scores
and Other 16PF Factor Scores

Clinical Relevance of A− Scores

FACTOR A: THE WARM-COOL SOCIAL ORIENTATION CHARACTERISTICS OF A+ (AFFECTOTHYMIC) AND A− (SIZOTHYMIC) EXAMINEES

Left Score A− (SIZOTHYMIA)		Right Score A+ (AFFECTOTHYMIA)
(Reserved, Detached, Critical, Aloof, Stiff)	vs.	(Warmhearted, Outgoing,* Easygoing, Participating)
Critical	vs.	Good Natured, Easygoing
Stands by Own Ideas	vs.	Ready to Cooperate, Likes to Participate
Cool, Aloof	vs.	Attentive to People
Precise, Objective	vs.	Softhearted, Casual
Distrustful, Skeptical	vs.	Trustful
Rigid	vs.	Adaptable, Careless, "Goes Along"
Cold	vs.	Warmhearted
Prone to Sulk	vs.	Laughs Readily

*Please note that these characteristic expressions of Factor A are ranked in order of their involvement with the factor, just as in their original appearance in Cattell, R. B., Eber, H. W., and Tatsuoka, M. M., *Handbook for the Sixteen Personality Factor Questionnaire (16PF)*. Champaign, IL: Institute for Personality and Ability Testing, Inc., 1970, 1988. The same ranking format will be used for all other 16PF primary and secondary factors in this book. The descriptions are reprinted here with the permission of the publisher.

THE CONSTRUCT

Gregariousness

Factor A measures emotional orientation toward other people, from warmth at the right, A+ (affectothymic) pole to coldness at the left, A− (sizothymic) pole. *Affectothymia* combines the Latin roots "affect" and "disposition." The *"sizo"* in sizothymia, which is also derived from Latin, refers to "flatness." More operationally stated, this factor measures the degree to which contact with others is sought and found rewarding as a primary goal or end in itself, rather than as a means to another goal. When this goal is openly expressed, it is easily recognizable as the gregarious interest shown by persons who enjoy "get togethers" for their own sake and who display a friendly interest in even casual acquaintances. By contrast, its covert expression is often misleading, as it may occur, for example, in hypochondriacal patients who may make frequent trips to their physicians, not because of real illness, but because of the need for social interaction. Other covert examples of A+ (affectothymia) include helping professionals who find work primarily socially rewarding and town newcomers who join churches and service clubs, not so much to further the goals of these organizations, but for the purpose of making friends. On the other side, sometimes less obvious but almost institutionalized into the culture, are those who feign sociability for instrumental reasons, as in the case of salespeople who play golf regularly with business clients, inviting them to the weddings of their children and other intimate family gatherings. All of these instances point out that the primary motive may be hidden in social interactions and that the score a person might achieve on Factor A is not always easily discernable merely through observing his or her behavior.

Factor A makes the largest contribution to the assessment of personality of all the factors in the 16PF. In fact, the factors are named in order of their effect on general behavior. This means that the trait that Factor A measures has a broad influence on personality, and that a given person's endowment on it largely determines whether his or her energy will be directed toward social interaction or focused instead on objects and the inner world of ideas. Although sometimes mistaken for the Extraversion-Introversion dichotomy, it is actually only *one* contributing primary factor to the broader factor by that name, which will be discussed later in Chapter 18.

Heredity

At this time, the genetic component of Factor A has not been established. What is known about its environmental component indicates that it evolves, not only from the more common learning experiences of modeling and reward and punishment, but from the early bondings that occur between caretakers and the child.

Male and Female Differences Throughout the Life Span

Although the standard deviation is similar for both sexes (men, 6.32 and women, 5.91), women as a group score higher on Factor A than men. The mean raw score for women is 22.88 compared to 20.36 for men.[1] This difference, which is statistically significant,[2] has been found to exist across cultural groups tested so far. The conclusion from this finding is that females seem to be, on the whole, more affectothymic (A+), hence more warmly interested in people. But whether this is due primarily to genetic or environmental influences is not at this time clear, as stated above.

It seems that once an affectothymic (A+) or a sizothymic (A−) life position is achieved, it rarely changes in a statistically significant way in response to life events (Cattell, 1973), although it may fluctuate predictably as a consequence of age. Age curve data[3] show that Factor A scores tend to increase steadily until the early 30s, remain constant thereafter for almost a decade, and then gradually decline.

Although there may be some clinical examples to the contrary, my experience is that disappointment and disillusionment generally fail to be manifested by a drop in A+ scores, while, conversely, experience of positive human encounters are not associated with significant increases of A− scores. Thus, a proclivity for being affectothymic (A+) and sizothymic (A−) appears to be acquired early and, once formed, generally remains fixed throughout life. Clinicians should be mindful of the tenacity of these traits, especially sizothymia (A−), since it is often targeted for change in psychological treatment. Though it is a normal trait, it is apt to be negatively evaluated by those clinicians who share the cultural bias towards favoring the gregarious personality, and who, therefore, urge their A− clients to be more sociable and outgoing. Clients who receive these messages tend to become more self-critical, and to feel stressed by their effort to behave in ways inimical to their natural reserve.

---

[1]Male and female group raw score means and standard deviations for Forms A and B for Factor A, as well as all other primary 16PF factors, are taken from Tables 15 and 18—Norms for the 16PF, Forms A and B. Tabular Supplement No. 1, pp. 17 and 20, Institute for Personality and Ability Testing, Inc., Champaign, IL, 1983.

[2]Throughout this text, male and female scores will be reported only when the difference between them is significant at the .001 level.

[3]Information on age-related correlations for Factor A, as well as that for other 16PF factors which will be reported, is taken from Figures 10-13 in Cattell, R. B., *Personality and Mood by Questionnaire*. San Francisco: Jossey-Bass, 1973, pp. 151-154.

HIGH SCORES ON FACTOR A

Intrapsychic Data

In describing A+ persons, I present here the first of the promised Galsworthian portraits. A warm, emotional response for others was the central characteristic noted in the self-reports of the 145 examinees in my sample whose score on the A scale was eight stens or above. These individuals reported that they seldom choose to be alone, preferring the company of others singly or, more likely, in groups; "the more the merrier" was apt to be their motto. If questioned about their values, they described themselves as "people persons" or said they "love people." It is not surprising, therefore, that A+ people prefer group projects over individual competition, and like jobs that emphasize interpersonal contact such as sales, social work, and teaching.

Often, A+ persons also get high scores on Factors F and H. In these cases, it can be difficult to discern, even on the basis of their self-reports, how much of a typical A+ person's style is due to actual affectothymia as distinct from the associated F+ and H+ traits. This difficulty has been overcome in my data since about 50 (roughly 34%) of my 145 A+ examinees had either average or below-average F and H scores, sometimes in combination. This gave them the advantage of reporting on their core affectothymic experience as uncontaminated by these other influences. All expressed warm interest in others and felt themselves to be, in turn, popular and well liked. Even those with below-average F and H scores—and who were therefore somewhat sober and taciturn in the first instance, or shy and retiring in the latter—were able to initiate, recognize, and respond appropriately to a wide spectrum of communications ranging from small talk to sharing intimate feelings.

However, just as all virtues come with vices, especially when carried to extreme, persons who score toward an extreme end on any temperament factor, even if it is the seemingly more desirable pole, are apt to have adjustment difficulties of some sort. This truth was manifested in the A+ examinees in my sample who reported that their dislike of being alone resulted in intolerable feelings of loneliness. Consequently, they avoided being alone. This avoidance of being alone led to various forms of underachievement, since developing intellectual and creative potentials depends largely on reading, practice (such as that required in music), and personal reflection—all activities requiring periods of concentration free from social distraction. The tendency for A+ people to avoid these activities is evidenced in the findings of Cattell and Butcher (1968) and Rothman and Flowers (1970), all of whom examined academic achievement. They showed that in the early school years a positive correlation exists between A+ scores and grade-point average, but at the eighth grade this trend reverses, so that high scores negatively correlate with grades. This negative correlation holds through high school and college. The reversal is best explained by the emphasis placed on classroom participation in grade school, thus favoring the sociable and outgoing A+ students. However, the junior high school years bring a move away from classroom participation and toward added homework assignments. Further, there are social opportunities outside of class at this age. These students naturally prefer the company of their peers to studying alone, thus reducing the likelihood of getting good grades.

Approximately 78 (54%) of my 145 A+ examinees also believed that their dislike for being alone had been responsible for rushing them into premature arrangements not in their best long-term interests, such as a hasty remarriage after the loss of a spouse. However, after viewing their 16PF profiles, I concluded that the actions for about 50% of these examinees could not be totally attributed to their A+ scores, because their profiles showed, in addition to A+ scores, either C− (low ego strength) scores, indicating that they had difficulty in delaying gratification, or extreme F+ (surgency) scores, indicating a proclivity for enthusiastic, sometimes heedless behavior.

Interpersonal and Social Data

Since they are genuinely interested in people and rate interpersonal relations as one of their highest priorities in life, it is not surprising that A+ persons are cooperative, adaptable, concerned, considerate, kind, generous with their time and possessions, and slow to discern and criticize human frailties (Cattell, 1957).

Other research data (Cattell, 1973) suggests that A+ persons find all areas of their interpersonal lives satisfying. They tend to be happy in their marriages, to be devoted parents, and to receive more job promotions than low or moderate Factor A scorers. They also tend to be elected as leaders of small groups, where they are viewed as making socially significant contributions (Cattell & Stice, 1960).

On the less positive side, a consistent finding among my A+ examinees was that their dislike of being alone led many of them to have significant problems at work. Despite their having social skills, even jobs that emphasize interpersonal contact, such as sales, demand that some time must be spent alone in order to fill out reports, keep records, and so on. Particularly, examinees whose profiles also showed $Q_2 -$ (group dependency) scores found that their strong need to maintain social proximity caused them to seek social distractions and to avoid or put off tasks. The result was often tardiness in completing assignments and complaints from supervisors that they socialized too much.

A+ and Childhood

Early social experiences, starting with the bondings of infancy and continuing on through family and peer relationships, strongly shape later social expectancies and attitudes. Therefore, it would be ideal to investigate A+ scores from this perspective, using possibly a longitudinal design and examining such specific variables as the presence, absence, or separation from a caretaker at critical developmental stages. While, hopefully, this study will one day be done, I have presently available only the less finely tuned data of Barton, Dielman, and Cattell (1973), who studied recollections of A+ adults. Their recollections were usually that they had been raised in relaxed homes by parents who used reasoning rather than discipline to control their behavior. This was also typical of what examinees in my data have reported.

As Table 1.1 in the previous chapter indicates, no juveniles were included in my database. Moreover, direct professional contact with A+ children and adolescents has been minimal. Interestingly, what contact I have had has revolved around issues of discipline, when teachers and parents have sought my advice on how to encourage A+ children to persist with task-oriented behavior by eschewing social distractions. My advice has been to use "time-out" procedures, since removal from social stimuli for a short period is proportionate in aversiveness to these children's strong gregariousness needs. Jokes about the lack of aversiveness in banishing children to rooms equipped with stereos, color television sets, toys, and books does not apply to A+ children. For them, these objects, which provide solace for less socially inclined children, are pale substitutes for human interaction.

Important Correlations Between A+ Scores and Other 16PF Factor Scores

Table 2.1 presents important correlations between Factor A scores and other 16PF factor scores. The correlations are based on a group that combines males and females.[4]

Table 2.1

Important Correlations Between A+ Scores and Other 16PF Factor Scores*

Factor Pole	Correlation	Possible Associated Traits Indicated by Correlation
H+ (Parmia)	.38	Adventuresome, Uninhibited, Socially Bold
Q_2 − (Group Dependency)	.37	Group Dependent, a Joiner and Sound Follower
F+ (Surgency)	.31	Happy-go-lucky, Enthusiastic

*In this and similar tables, the correlations reported are among scales, and so are usually higher than among pure factors.

The correlations in Table 2.1 indicate that typical A+ persons are likely to have other traits that accompany their warm, outgoing dispositions. These associations, I must stress, commonly occur but are *not* invariable, so it is important to review the actual profile of each examinee.

A correlation between .20 and .40 for any of the 16PF factor scores is interpretable as a weak but relevant degree of relatedness. A correlation above .40 is interpreted as moderate; a correlation above .60 is considered to reflect a strong association with the corresponding trait. Consequently, in this instance, the correlation of .38 with H+ scores may be interpreted as meaning that A+ persons have some tendency to also be adventurous, uninhibited, and bold. The correlation of .31 with F+ scores means that an A+ person may show some tendency towards being happy-go-lucky and enthusiastic. They may also have tendencies towards dependency, since the correlation between Q_2 − and A+ scores is .37.

[4]The correlations presented in Table 2.1 are taken from Krug, S. E., *Interpreting 16PF Profile Patterns*. Champaign, IL: IPAT, 1981. All other correlations between 16PF factor scores in this book are also obtained from this source.

Clinical Relevance of A+ Scores

There are two adjustment difficulties of clinical significance that A+ persons may experience. The first, which was noted by Krug (1980), is an overriding desire for approval by others, causing them to go beyond usual limits of cooperation and flexibility, and to go on to compromising their standards to those of the reference group. Recognized and often described as being easily influenced, these persons may find themselves in trouble, sometimes with the law. In observing my A+ examinees, it became apparent that those who indulged in this kind of compromise were also apt to seriously discount discordant information that challenged their positive orientation towards their friends.

Similarly, A+ scores are also linked to gullibility, which was the root of the second kind of difficulty I frequently observed in examinees with extreme A+ scores. Even though it is usually more conducive to happiness if the jar of human goodness is estimated as being half full rather than half empty, this characteristic can lead to exploitation by unscrupulous persons. Somerset Maugham in his novel *The Moon and Sixpence* (1984) has written insightfully on this matter by describing the way the obviously affectothymic Dirk Stroeve was treated by his associates:

> His fellow painters made no secret of their contempt for his work, but he earned a fair amount of money, and they did not hesitate to make free use of his purse. He was generous and the needy, laughing at him because he believed so naively their stories of distress, borrowed from him with effrontery. He was very emotional, yet his feeling, so easily aroused, had in it something of the absurd, so that you accepted his kindness, but felt no gratitude (p. 66).

LOW SCORES ON FACTOR A

Intrapsychic Data

As noted earlier, sizothymia is a neologism meaning emotionally flat, in contradistinction to the emotional expressiveness of affectothymia. Almost all my A− examinees recognized their lack of affect as a deficit in social relating. Many described themselves as not easily warming up to people. Their interests focused more on ideas or objects, even animals, than people. They avoided human contact, not because they were shy or felt socially threatened, but because it was simply not rewarding. Indifference is probably the best word to describe their attitudes.

In my sample of 145 A− examinees, I discovered approximately 55 individuals (37%) who scored 1, 2, or 3 on Factor A, but had moderate scores on Factors H and F. Like their affectothymic counterparts, they were able to experience and report on their sizothymia, unconfounded by the similar, subjective reactions produced by other traits. Most notably, these traits are F− (desurgency), H− (parmia), and Q_2− (group dependency), which I will describe in Chapters 6, 8, and 14, respectively.

The lifestyles of my A− examinees showed wider variation than those of their A+ counterparts. Since the many hours that other people spend in social interaction were available to them in great blocks of solitude, I found that choices about how to spend their time, hence their lives, were strongly influenced by their endowment of other traits or the sorts of interests they had developed. For example, a preference for solitude combines particularly well with high intelligence, for working alone enhances concentration and minimizes distraction, leading some of them to achieve successful careers, especially in the sciences. Likewise, I noted this same combination allowed those examinees who were college students to excel academically—since their time and energy were not consumed by social needs. Unfortunately, though, those young persons (who were often referred to as "bookworms" or "egg heads" by their peers) were often friendless. I was concerned that, because they were channeling all their energies into nonsocial activities, they were failing to enter smoothly into the adult world of sexual and peer relations. In younger persons this concern was supported by experimental findings showing a positive correlation between poor adjustment and low A scores in adolescents, especially among girls (Cattell & Cattell, 1975).

Less intellectually inclined examinees in my sample were typically involved with hobbies or were engrossed in their work as substitutes for social involvements. Those uninterested in work or hobbies were hard pressed to structure their time; some spent many hours in withdrawal in front of the television set.

I discovered, but predictably, that A− examinees were generally indifferent to what psychologists call "social reinforcement," as they were not easily induced, by praise or other people's disapproval or dislike, to compromise their standards, views, and values. Depending upon the situation, this inflexibility has advantages or disadvantages. For the scientist in pursuit of truth, or the lone juror locked into a dissenting position, it has obvious advantages. But in many other situations, especially clinical ones, the opposite is true, for it renders ineffective such techniques as peer pressure or social support as instruments of change.

> *Example:* A student discovered that her roommate did not change her untidy behavior in response to criticism. After taking an introductory behavior modification class this student decided to use positive verbal reinforcement to elicit the change she desired. Although her plan was entirely consistent with behavioral principles, she discovered it had not the slightest effect on her roommate, who was as impervious to praise and compliments as she was to criticism. In discussing this failure with me and describing her roommate, I realized she was describing a sizothymic individual for whom social rewards would be relatively inconsequential. Upon my advice, she substituted nonsocial rewards like giving her roommate some of her food every time she noticed her putting her books away or washing dishes, whereupon her behavior began to improve substantially.

Finally, although A− individuals are often considered accurate observers of human affairs, my finding is to the contrary. Although their observations are not colored by the Pollyanna way of thinking of their A+ counterparts, their coolness can produce opposite kinds of perceptual distortions. I noticed that the A− examinees in my sample were inclined to overemphasize the more reprehensible aspects of human nature. Moreover, although their detachment allowed them to recount objective facts, it also led them to overlook the importance of the social and emotional context of the occurrences they observed.

Interpersonal and Social Data

While A− persons may feel only indifference to others, I have noticed that the effect of their cool detachment is apt to evoke, not just indifference, but dislike from those with whom they interact. Frequently, I heard them referred to as "cold fish." Coworkers and other acquaintances sometimes confided that they found conversations, even small talk, arduous with A−

people, due to their lack of sociability and disinterest in human affairs. In my own interactions with them, it became obvious that most of the A− persons in my sample ordinarily preferred exchanges that were ritualistic and in which no affective response was called for, as when the conversation was focused on an impersonal outside activity. On those occasions when they did become talkative, they might have launched into animated, though impersonal, soliloquy about their special interest, which was often highly idiosyncratic.

The interpersonal style described in the above paragraph did not apply to examinees whose profiles showed I+ (premsia) scores along with A− scores. Premsia (I+) is a powerful modulator of A− scores, as I+ is essentially emotional sensitivity and is manifested, among other ways, as an ability for empathetic understanding leading to a tender-hearted social orientation. Persons who show this combination of traits are likely to be kind and sympathetic, though reserved and aloof. (Here Emily Dickinson, the poet, who, despite her finely tuned responsiveness to human emotions, lived a reclusive kind of life, comes to mind as a likely, if rather extreme, example.) These persons are not included in the discussion that follows, which is about A− examinees who achieved moderate or low I scores.

An important question is whether an A− social orientation extends to all people. More concisely, is it possible that, despite being cool and detached to humankind as a whole, A− individuals can form and sustain warm attachments to a particular few?

In attempting to answer this question, I reasoned that if A− persons were warmly disposed toward anyone, it was likely to be their spouses. While the relationship between emotional attitudes to spouses and A− scores had not been the primary or direct focus of any research to date, two studies had touched peripherally on the subject. One of these studies found that A− husbands were less likely to assist their wives in the physical upkeep of their homes (Barton & Cattell, 1972a), which could be indicative of a lack of warmth on the part of these husbands. The other study, conducted by Cattell and Nesselroade (1967), found that differences in A scores between spouses were associated with unstable marriages, but revealed nothing about the degree of emotional involvement on the part of the lower scoring spouse.

To augment this data, I also looked at the spousal relationships of married A− examinees in my sample. My observations suggested that A— spouses, rather than being emotionally involved, exhibited the same detachment to their partners as they did to other persons. Their histories revealed that, although they may have shared the same initial rush of excitement that more A+ persons do in the early stages of romance, as time passed they did not sustain it and eventually came to show more coolness in their marriages than in other relationships. Moreover, in order to preserve a comfortable emotional distance, they were apt to withdraw whenever their partners expressed a desire for intimacy.

I found, in relationships where differences on Factor A were the primary cause of the couple's problems, that marital therapy was invariably initiated by the spouse with the higher A score, who typically complained of their partner's indifference. Typical remarks were: "I feel I am not important." "I feel like I am living with a stranger." "I feel as though I am talking to a stone wall." In different ways, they felt they lived in an emotional vacuum with no intimate exchange of feelings and receipt of few compliments, endearments, or other forms of positive recognition.

The behavior of A— persons and the behavior of others who did not have low A scores but who are simply "turned off" toward their spouses, while strikingly similar, have, of course, very different origins, each requiring an intervention distinct from the other. For this reason, when someone seems cold and distant from his or her spouse, it is helpful for the marriage counselor or therapist to know as soon as possible how that individual scores on Factor A. This information immediately aids in discriminating between a general social orientation versus disillusionment with the marital relationship, as is illustrated in the following example:

> *Example:* A 27-year-old female client, whom I had treated some years earlier for a minor adjustment disorder, consulted me one year after her marriage. She was morose and questioning of her self-worth, which contrasted markedly with my recollection of her as the vivacious and self-confident young woman I had known earlier. She reported that she had become depressed because of her husband's diminishing enthusiasm and emotional involvement toward her, which had now decreased to the point that he showed more interest toward his glass bottle collection than toward her. Assuming that her husband's behavior was due to some lack on her part, i.e., that she must not be sufficiently well

informed, sexually attractive, entertaining, etc., to engage his interest, she had enrolled in self-improvement
courses, revamped her wardrobe, and showered him
with attention. These efforts had not produced the desired result, for her husband's behavior did not change.
Her husband agreed to come in for marital counseling
and psychological testing. His score of 2 on Scale A
showed that his indifference toward her resulted from
his social orientation, not because of any defect on her
part. Her concern now turned to the real issue of how
to share her life with a partner who was by nature cool
and distant.

If the A− spouse was male—and providing the marital relationship followed traditional lines—it was also common for the
wives in my sample to be apologetic about their dissatisfaction,
since their husbands' emotional distancing was not one of the
clearly recognized reasons for marital discord (like, for example,
unfaithfulness, violence, or squandering of the family assets).
Moreover, these wives often doubted the validity of their needs
whenever their husbands spent time in ways that seemed directed to wives' or the children's well-being, like working overtime. Sometimes only in the course of treatment was the real
reason for working overtime revealed, when it became clear that
the husband's work provided an emotionally safe outlet and an
impersonal activity around which to structure time. Often this
fact had not previously been recognized even by the husband, as
he rationalized his absences as being due to a desire to make
extra money for the family. When home, these same men were
commonly involved in some solitary home improvement project
in the garage or other part of the home to which they would
retreat after dinner and on weekends, but would rationalize this
also as being in the service of the family.

Communicating a desire for intimacy to an A− person is
often like describing color to the congenitally blind. I came to
recognize this from the genuine difficulty my examinees had in
understanding the nature of others' complaints about them. Although their responses sounded like alibis, they were more often
reflections of lack of emotional insight. I have heard male
examinees, particularly, who, upon hearing their wives complain,
"You don't pay attention to me," respond with honest bewilder-
ment, "I watch TV with you." I was not surprised to find a tendency in my sample for wives who were more affectothymic than

their A— husbands to act out by nagging and having temper tantrums. As one wife said, "Even a negative response is better than no response at all."

Here I have much to say about A— husbands and little to say about their female counterparts. The reason for this is that although my sample contained approximately 20 couples where the wife's A score was much lower than her husband's, the interactions followed a less clear pattern. When husbands of these women felt rejected or neglected, it was in subtle, hard-to-pinpoint ways that were difficult to describe.

One striking difference between relationships where the A— spouse was the wife, rather than the husband, was that by the time they have sought marital therapy, the husband had frequently become involved in an extramarital affair. In the reverse situation, i.e., when the husband was the low scorer, the wife had usually not entered into an affair but was seeking to understand either why she was not content with the relationship or what was wrong with her.

A— and Childhood

In contrast to their A+ counterparts, who showed a strong tendency to come from relaxed homes where there was minimal punishment, A— examinees tended to report coming from punishing homes (Barton, Dielman, & Cattell, 1973). Occasionally, however, my clinical case histories of A— examinees presented striking exceptions to these trends, indicating that the social orientation of these individuals was not always associated with cold, punitive early socialization experiences.

My most direct observation of the absence of a steady and predictable relationship between home environment and the development of A— traits is regarding autistic children. I have encountered several children with this diagnosis who come from what I verified as warm, affectionate environments, and whose social indifference I can only conclude must arise from their own innate dispositions.

Important Correlations Between A− Scores and Other 16PF Factor Scores

Table 2.2

Important Correlations Between A− Scores
and Other 16PF Factor Scores

Factor Pole	Correlation	Possible Associated Traits Indicated by Correlation
H− (Threctia)	.38	Shy, Timid, Restrained
Q$_2$+ (Self-sufficiency)	.37	Resourceful, Prefers Own Decisions
F− (Desurgency)	.31	Serious, Sober, Taciturn

Table 2.2 above shows the important correlations between A− scores and the scales of other 16PF factors.[5] Just as those presented in Table 2.1 are best construed as indicating the associated characteristics typical of A+ persons, these correlations can be viewed as representing the personality traits that are commonly found in A− persons.

The correlations in Table 2.2 indicate that, in addition to their core sizothymic (A−) traits, persons who achieve low scores on Factor A are also sometimes H− (threctic), i.e., shy, timid, restrained, and F− (desurgent), i.e., serious, sober, and taciturn. They may also be inclined towards being Q$_2$+ (self-sufficient).

Clinical Relevance of A− Scores

Since so many of the adjustment difficulties of A− persons are manifested in disturbed intimate relationships, they have been largely discussed in the earlier section that dealt with the social aspects of sizothymia. What remains to be mentioned here is the relationship of A− scores to various clinical syndromes.

---

[5]The correlations in Table 2.2 represent the obverse of those set out in Table 2.1. Moreover, they are presented as positive correlations between poles, for it is more psychologically revealing to present relationships in terms of what they are, rather than in terms of what they are not.

In my experience, the appearance of an A− score in a profile may signal the existence of some internal psychological disturbance such as depression, psychosis, or a schizoid personality disorder. However, this score by itself is not sufficient to indicate that any of these conditions exists, as they depend on the accompaniment of sizothymia with other traits. Thus, this information is revealed only when A− scores are combined with other factor scores. Because knowledge of these other factors is particularly important for understanding A− combinations, I shall delay discussing them here until these other factors are discussed in the chapters which follow. For example, I will discuss the meaning of an A and E factor combination in Chapter 5, which discusses Factor E.

Chapter 3

Factor B: The Ability to Discern Relationships (Intelligence)

THE CONSTRUCT

Intelligence
Description of the Scale
Male and Female Differences Throughout the Life Span
Interpreting Scores
Clinical Relevance of B Scores

FACTOR B: THE ABILITY TO DISCERN RELATIONSHIPS: CHARACTERISTIC EXPRESSIONS OF B+ (ABSTRACT-THINKING) AND B− (CONCRETE-THINKING) EXAMINEES

Left Score B− (CONCRETE THINKING)		Right Score B+ (ABSTRACT THINKING)
Low Mental Capacity	vs.	High Mental Capacity
Unable to Handle Abstract Problems	vs.	Insightful, Fast-learning, Intellectually Adaptable

The measurement of intelligence has been shown to carry with it, as a factor in the personality realm, *some of the following ratings.* The correlations, however, are quite low.

Apt to Be Less Well Organized	vs.	Inclined to Have More Intellectual Interests
Poorer Judgment	vs.	Showing Better Judgment
Of Lower Morale	vs.	Of Higher Morale
Quitting	vs.	Persevering

THE CONSTRUCT

Intelligence

This factor is indexed B, because it is the second largest in the 16PF contingent. That is, with the exception of Factor A, it represents the broadest influence on the total personality of all the factors included in this test. It is unique among the 16PF factors because, unlike the others, it measures not temperament, but ability. As stated in Chapter 1, an ability trait is unlike a temperament trait in that it does not involve style and tempo. Rather, it involves a capacity to perform, related to a given standard.

The ability Factor B measures is intelligence, which is defined here as the capacity to discern relationships in terms of how things stand, relative to one another. According to Cattell (1987), recognizing analogies and similarities, and being able to classify events and form typologies, are the essential skills involved in this discernment.

Description of the Scale

The scale for Factor B is made up of verbal and numerical items. A typical item might ask the examinee to choose which alternative most logically follows a stimulus word:

Adult is to child as cat is to:
a) **kitten**
b) **dog**
c) **baby**

According to the 16PF Handbook,[1] care was taken by the test authors to construct Factor B items from simple language, and to use familiar references. For some items, the examinee must possess basic information obtained by formal education in order to choose the correct answer. Other items are designed to pick up what in technical terms is called *fluid intelligence*,[2] i.e., cognitive skills that appear to be innate rather than acquired.

As with all other 16PF scales, Factor B is measured in sten scores. However, these scores can be translated into standard I.Q. scores, as illustrated in Fig. 1.1 in Chapter 1 of this book.

Male and Female Differences Throughout the Life Span

Male and female distributions on this scale show similar means and standard deviations. After age 40, scores show a similar, gradual decline for both sexes.

Interpreting Scores

Interpretation of an examinee's B score is largely influenced by the number of forms administered. As Cronbach (1970) has shown, a minimum of 40 items is required to reliably assess intelligence. With the 16PF, one would need to administer all five forms of the 16PF (Forms A, B, C, D, and E) in order to meet this requirement. Despite Karson and O'Dell's (1976) claim that this procedure yields a measure of intelligence that can be assumed to be as accurate as that from most standard tests, for practical reasons such a large scale administration rarely occurs. Typically, only a single scale of 13 items (as in Form A) is used, which provides only a rough estimate, to be treated with caution.

When a person gets a high score on Factor B, the score is more likely to reflect a true measure of intellectual ability for

---

[1]Cattell, R. B., Eber, H. W., & Tatsuoka, M. M. (1970). *Handbook for the Sixteen Personality Factor Questionnaire (16PF)*. Champaign, IL: IPAT, p. 82.

[2]The interested reader will find a more complete explanation of these terms as well as a description of Cattell's Culture Fair Intelligence Test in Appendix C.

two reasons. First, it is not possible to fake high scores unless the test is given in an unsupervised situation where the examinee can obtain the correct answers from other people. Second, the laws of probability indicate that a sten score of 8, 9, or 10 rarely results from chance.

By contrast, there are many instances when average or low scores do not reflect the examinee's actual intellectual ability. These instances are apt to occur in examinees who are educationally disadvantaged or who are depressed, anxious, or preoccupied with their troubles. They also occur when examinees are distracted by environmental stimuli, are wrong in their interpretation of the instructions, or are, for various reasons, not motivated to spend the time figuring out the correct answers. While it is also possible for examinees to intentionally underrepresent their intelligence by faking bad (See Appendix E). This, in my experience and the experience of other clinicians with whom I have discussed this matter, is fairly rare. There are few situations, other than trying to substantiate brain damage in lawsuits, or being conscripted into the work force, in which an advantage can be gained for persons to appear less bright than they actually are. However, rare as this may be, it may be suspected that the examinee deliberately answered incorrectly whenever he or she obtains a *raw* score below three, since even when the items are answered randomly, three or four items should be answered correctly.

Thus, whenever a social history indicates that an examinee should have obtained a high score, it can be profitable to inquire about whatever was going on with that individual during the test-taking situation. This inquiry may uncover information that greatly alters the way the results should be interpreted, not only for the B scale, but for other scales also, since the examinee's feelings at the time could have colored his or her overall response to the 16PF.

Clinical Relevance of B Scores

The benefit clinicians receive from having an intelligence scale included in the 16PF is that it indicates such things as the client's aptitude for abstract thinking, hence whether he or she would most likely benefit from insight therapy or some other form of treatment. Furthermore, since one's level of intellectual ability tends to color judgments, beliefs, and preferences, as well as social behavior, knowing a client's score on Factor B can help predict how that individual's other 16PF traits are likely to be expressed.

For example, in the previous chapter, I discussed the fact that A+ individuals have Polyannic attitudes, disposing them towards being overly trustful and credulous. When an A+ examinee's profile also shows B− scores, indicating that he or she also has difficulty in discerning complex relationships, this individual is more likely to succumb to the persuasion of a clever "con artist" or to be be the target of other forms of trickery. Conversely, another examinee whose profile shows an A+ and B+ combination should be considered less likely to be duped, all other things being equal.

Chapter 4

Factor C: Adaptation to the Environment

THE CONSTRUCT
The Ego: Confusion Regarding the Term and the Construct
Freud's Final Definitive Theory of the Ego
The Ego's Alloplastic Role
The Ego's Autoplastic Role
Heredity
Male and Female Differences Throughout the Life Span

HIGH SCORES ON FACTOR C
Intrapsychic Data
Interpersonal and Social Data
C+ and Childhood
Important Correlations Between C+ Scores
and Other 16PF Factor Scores
Clinical Relevance of C+ Scores

LOW SCORES ON FACTOR C
Intrapsychic Data
Interpersonal and Social Data
C− and Childhood
Important Correlations Between C− Scores
and Other 16PF Factor Scores
Clinical Relevance of C− Scores

FACTOR C: ADAPTATION TO THE ENVIRONMENT
CHARACTERISTIC EXPRESSIONS OF C+ (STRONG EGO) AND C− (WEAK EGO) EXAMINEES

Left Score C − (EMOTIONAL INSTABILITY)		Right Score C + (HIGHER EGO STRENGTH)
(Affected by Feelings, Emotionally Less Stable, Easily Upset, Changeable)	vs.	(Emotionally Stable, Mature, Faces Reality, Calm)
Gets Emotional when Frustrated	vs.	Emotionally Mature
Changeable in Attitudes and Interests	vs.	Stable, Constant in Interests
Easily Perturbed	vs.	Calm
Evasive of Responsibilities, Tending to Give Up	vs.	Does Not Let Emotional Needs Obscure Realities of a Situation. Adjusts to Facts
Worrying	vs.	Unruffled
Gets into Fights and Problem Situations	vs.	Shows Restraint in Avoiding Difficulties

THE CONSTRUCT

The Ego: Confusion Regarding the Term and the Construct

It is not possible to discuss ego strength and weakness without defining the underlying construct which is being measured—namely, the ego. This is not an easy task, mostly because the term "ego" is without a common referent, both in its popular use, and in psychoanalysis. The term, popularly used in such statements as "He has a big ego," means something more akin to the hubris of the Greeks, and in psychoanalysis it is confused with attributes which are unrelated, even antagonistic, to its basic psychological underpinnings. Yankovich and Barrett (1970), who have documented this situation in psychoanalysis, have gone so far as to compare the present state of its ego theory to Ptolemaic astronomy in the Middle Ages. In both instances an existing, complicated system was made even more complex by adding cycles and epicycles to explain each new observation.

Since Cattell's multivariate research based theory of the ego is essentially interlaced with that of mainstream psychoanalysis,

I shall begin this chapter by examining the latter. Doing this requires stripping the construct of its superfluous meaning so that its basic structure can be revealed.

Freud's Final Definitive Theory of the Ego

Contemporary readers of Freud's actual writings are apt to become very confused as to what his theory of the ego actually was. Its evolution followed a circuitous path paralleling his reformulations on the psyche, so the theory was continuously revised.[1]

In the last decade of his life, Freud arrived at his final theory of the ego, which he stated in the *Outline of Psychoanalysis* (1961). This much-quoted and definitive conclusion is both explicit and lucid, and essentially describes the ego as *a set of cognitive and perceptual functions that serve adaptive purposes.*

> Here is the principal characteristic of the ego. In consequence of pre-established connection between sense and perception and muscular action, the ego has voluntary movement at its command. It has the task of self-preservation. As regards external events, it performs that task by becoming aware of stimuli, by storing up experiences about them (in memory), by avoiding excessively strong stimuli (through flight), by dealing with moderate stimuli (through adaptation), and finally by learning to bring about changes in the external world (by activity). As regards internal events in relation to the id, it performs that task by gaining control over the demands of the instincts, by deciding if they are to be allowed satisfaction by postponing that satisfaction to times and circumstances favorable in the external world, or by suppressing their excitations entirely. It is guided in its activity by consideration of the tension produced by stimuli, whether these tensions are present in it or introduced. (p. 15)

-Excerpt reprinted by permission. See acknowledgments, p. *iii*.

---

[1]The literal translation of the term *ego* is the pronoun "das ich," which means "the I" and is a relic of what is generally regarded as the prepsychoanalytic period of Freud's thinking, in which he conceptualized the ego as being co-extensive with the whole person, as did other theorists of that time.

Adaptation is a biological term that can refer to a *state,* which is a relationship between a genotype and an environment that is favorable to the genotype's survival (Hartman, 1939). (I will say more about Hartman shortly.) Adaptation can also reflect a *process* that brings this condition about. It is the second use of the term that Freud refers to in his theory of the ego. In humans, because of the choices afforded them by their advanced levels of development, adaptation as a process occurs in two ways: They can act (1) alloplastically, i.e., changing their environments to meet their needs, and (2) autoplastically, i.e., changing themselves in order to survive or live more harmoniously with exogenous conditions. Essentially good adaptation requires the use of these two actions and proper judgment about which is more appropriate for a given situation. Incidentally, this understanding is not confined to behavioral scientists. St. Francis of Assisi, for example, articulated the essence of good adaptation with a succinct simplicity in his famous prayer:

Give me the courage to change the things I can change,
The serenity to accept the things I cannot change,
And the wisdom to know the difference.[2]

Since Freud delineated his ego theory so late in his career, its further extension and clarification was left to his daughter, Anna Freud, and his colleague, Heinz Hartman. Although each focused on different aspects of the ego (Anna Freud focused on its defensive, i.e., changing of self, hence autoplastic role; Heinz Hartman focused on its alloplastic, i.e., changing of environment, role), their findings together form a unified theory of human adaptation.

The Ego's Alloplastic Role

Hartman's monogram, *The Ego and the Problem of Adaptation,* though less popularly known than Anna Freud's *The Ego and the Mechanisms of Defense,* is probably regarded among psychoanalysts as an equally important contribution to ego

---

[2]This prayer has come to be known as the Serenity Prayer and is the credo of men and women in Alcoholics Anonymous and other 12-step programs who, one day at a time, attempt to avoid unnecessary frustrations that would tempt them to return to their former maladaptive ways.

theory. His basic formulation is that alloplastic adaptation is brought about by the ego's cognitive and perceptual functions' being oriented towards the environment, according to an innate predetermined psychological scheme of ". . . anticipating the future, orienting our actions according to it, and correctly relating means to each other." (p. 43) In other words, the ego in this role acts as an evolutionarily shaped pattern of behaviors, that function to overcome the obstacles that humans inevitably encounter as they attempt to sustain their lives and meet their needs. An analogy to this action of the ego is the inborn predisposition for humans to use verbal symbols. Speech evolves quite naturally, independent of coaching or tutoring, in normal circumstances.

In teaching, I find it aids my students' understanding when I say that the ego works in a problem-solving capacity, and then define what I mean by *problem* and *problem solving*.

Problem. A problem occurs, from a psychodynamic point of view, when a person has a need (for simplicity, I use the word *need* to include terms like *desire, wish,* and *want*) for which the environment offers no automatic effective means for its satisfaction. This is either because none is immediately available, or because satisfying this need would conflict with the meeting of others more basic to that person's survival or ultimate overall satisfaction. Absolutely essential to this definition of problem is that a need exists, for without a need no satisfier is required. To use an everyday kind of example, being unable to travel to a certain location presents no problem to a person with no need to go to that destination.

Problem solving. Problem solving describes a response made for the purpose of satisfying a need. Most problem solving calls for a synthesis of the ego's interpretative and synthetic capacities. That is, problem solving requires anticipation, judgment, planning, reality testing, memory, and self-regulation. It also requires the ability to integrate novel experiences and new knowledge in such a way as to provide the best probability of incurring healthy survival, and maximizing overall satisfaction. Moreover, a good solution to a problem, in addition to effectively satisfying the presenting need, will not produce other problems, i.e., create situations that frustrate or endanger the satisfaction of other needs that are ultimately equally important, or even more so, than the one being satisfied.

I can now link Cattell's sequential model of alloplastic adaption (Cattell, 1979) to Hartman's. Cattell's ego theory is also dynamic. It postulates that, since human personality fundamentally stems from the pressure of innate drives seeking satisfaction, the ego is a problem-solving structure that mediates between needs and the environment. However, Cattell goes further than Hartman by explicitly hypothesizing that the ego, to solve problems, normally operates according to four distinct sequences that are outlined below:

Ego Sequence 1. Recognition of tension signifying existence and strength of inner need. Since problem solving is, by definition, the process of satisfying a need, it must necessarily begin with the recognition that a need exists. Hence, in this initial sequence, the inner tension signaling the underlying need is perceived. This perception may occur either as a direct, one-to-one isomorphic sensation, say as in thirst and fluid deprivation or boredom and stimulus deprivation, or by the internal discomfort that accompanies conflicts between feelings and, therefore, needs.

Ego Sequence 2. Generating options for satisfying needs. After the need has been recognized, questions arise about how, where, and when to satisfy it. The satisfaction of needs, whether they are for food, security, or even self-esteem, customarily require interacting with the physical or social environment. Consequently, in this second sequence, one's perceptual processes shift away from an inner to an outer focus, so that one is aware of available options and actions to take on the environment in order to satisfy the need.

Effective operation of this sequence requires frustration tolerance. This means that, rather than relieving tension by accepting the first seemingly reasonable, need-satisfying option that presents itself, one should continue to delay satisfaction until alternative options are generated and considered. Osborne's (1963) research on brainstorming speaks specifically to this point, as it demonstrated that the larger number of potential choices perceived, the greater the likelihood of making a superior choice.

Ego Sequence 3. Selection of best option for satisfying need while preserving safety and long-term well-being. Here an option for meeting the perceived need is selected by weighing it against each other alternative as to how successfully it may satisfy the presenting need and how the consequences of its implementation are likely to impact on other needs. In this respect, a good decision requires reality testing, along with the eliminating of any option that jeopardizes a need, or needs, potentially more important than the one presently seeking satisfaction.

If no suitable options are perceived, good adjustment requires that the need remain unsatisfied. When this option is exercised, the ego turns from its alloplastic to its autoplastic mode, utilizing defense mechanisms, or other strategies, to make the loss more bearable. This allows one to forego the psychological disorganization that normally accompanies the grief this involves.

Ego Sequence 4. Implementation of the selected options. The final sequence is actually the solving of the problem, because it is only after the decision is *implemented* that the need is satisfied.

The process of implementing the option usually brings new frustrations, as it is common that, in the process of meeting one need, the satisfaction of other needs (like the need for rest or relaxation) must be sacrificed. Moreover, since the inner tension aroused by these other needs often eclipses that of the original need, this sequence also requires patience and persistence in pursuing the original goal.

Research supporting the existence of the four ego sequences. The sequences delineated above passed from their original inception as hypothetic intervening variables into experimentally validated factors through Birkett's 1980 experimental findings. Birkett's experiment involved 122 male and female subjects, drawn from different cultural and ethnic groups, who were tested by both objective and self-report instruments for a total of four and one-half hours. A factor analysis performed on their test results confirmed, just as Cattell had earlier predicted, the existence of all four sequences as separate factors, correlating with the high pole of Factor C. Thus, even though, in real life (as the reader's own introspection will agree), these sequences may overlap and transect one another and their actions go more or less unnoticed, they remain the basic human problem-solving strategies. It is certain, therefore, that any C − examinee will show some deficit in one or more of them.

The Ego's Autoplastic Role

I return now to the ego's second, autoplastic role. In this role, the ego serves adaptive purposes by enabling persons to alter their own psychological responses rather than altering their environments, in order to cope with frustrations and delays in gratification. To recapitulate to the words of St. Francis, they "accept the things that cannot be changed." Disappointment, anger, fear, and other unpleasant emotional states, if sufficiently intense, can be so disorganizing to cognitive and perceptual processes that the ability to solve problems rationally and to interact safely with the environment becomes impaired. In terms of the ego sequences, this dysphoria is revealed in the familiar clinical picture of confusion about the nature of feelings (Sequence 1); rigid and narrow perceptions regarding the range or availability of options for reducing distress (Sequence 2); indecisiveness, or unrealistic decision making (Sequence 3); and poor behavioral control (Sequence 4).

Altogether, from the perspective of the ego's autoplastic role, there are three ways human beings defend themselves against psychological disorganization, in tolerating both permanent and temporary frustrations. These are (1) by using defense mechanisms, (2) by using palliatives, and (3) by adopting a stoic mental attitude. Let us consider each one in turn.

Defense mechanisms. I have already alluded to Anna Freud's *The Ego and the Mechanisms of Defense* (1946). In this monogram, she described the actual conditions under which defense mechanisms can be observed as behaviors, rather than postulating their existences by inferences deduced by psychoanalytic theory. Moreover, she produced testable hypotheses which have been experimentally confirmed by Cattell and Wenig (1952), as well as by many other researchers.

Briefly, Anna Freud concluded that, when people perceive a threat to their self-esteem or personal safety (which, since these are the most fundamental of human needs, might lead to experiencing debilitating levels of dysphoria, fear, guilt, depression, etc.), they may partially or totally block conscious recognition of these perceptions from awareness. She proposed that defense mechanisms, to some extent, are used by everyone, and that they become pathological only under the following conditions: (a) when they either assume a primitive or neurotic form, (b) when they are used in inappropriate contexts, and (c) when they grossly distort perceptions to the point that they endanger the person's safety or undermine effective interaction with the environment.[3]

Palliatives. The second autoplastic mode persons use to defend themselves from experiencing potentially disabling levels of painful affect is by the use of palliatives. In contradistinction to defense mechanisms, which are used unconsciously and automatically, palliatives are the *intentional* things people do to make themselves feel better, without changing the relationship between themselves and their environment, in order to solve the problem at hand. They include such strategies as going to a movie, to "take their minds off their troubles," taking a walk to cool down, and cheering themselves up by compensating themselves with some special treat after a disappointment. As with defense mechanisms, palliatives are adaptive only when they are appropriate for the context in which they are used. Persons who resort to venting their anger by displacing it onto others, eating and drinking excessively, or spending money, even though they temporarily reduce their dysphoria through these outlets, usually ultimately create additional problems that are sometimes worse than those of the dysphoric effects which they are ameliorating.

Stoic mental orientation. While an unpleasant affect in the form of unrelieved inner tension characteristically accompanies an unsatisfied need, it can be compounded by surplus dysphoria according to how the situation is assessed by an individual's particular belief system. This point has been demonstrated by

---

[3]Defense mechanisms are unlike the other autoplastic modes of adaptation, since they operate outside of awareness. They also differ from these others in that they operate by misperceiving and distorting reality. On first consideration, these characteristics seem paradoxical to the ego's problem-solving role, which supposes that the more accurately reality can be reflected by the thinking and cognitive processes, the more precisely and efficiently it can be influenced. In clarification of this paradox, I am indebted to Monat and Lazarus (1979), who studied persons who undoubtedly, from his description, would have performed well on the C scale if they had been tested by the 16PF. These researchers found that, although these persons used coping strategies that involved disavowals of reality such as denial, distancing, and humor, they did so in a way and in a context that did not interfere with their using appropriate problem-solving actions. For example, they did not deny or distort facts when faced with symptoms of a life-threatening illness such as early signs of cancer, which required immediate medical attention, but rather distorted the implications of having that disease by being overly optimistic about the outcome. By giving themselves hope and reducing fear without resorting to delusions or gross misrepresentations of reality, they were able to continue to function effectively.

exponents of cognitive modification techniques who have amassed substantial evidence showing that those individuals who accept such immutables as death, loss, aging, illness, etc., as inevitable parts of their lives suffer less dysphoria than others who somehow expect that they should be exempt from the laws of the universe.[4] Ellis (1975), for example, states in the plainest and most simple language:

> ... The world has great difficulties and injustices—but you don't have to whine or make yourself furious about them. This in no sense implies that when things don't go the way you want them to go, you should not try to change them. Of course, try! But when you find things unchangeable—as on many occasions you will—don't wail or upset yourself about this. (p. 122)

It is important, as Ellis notes, that, although a stoic mental orientation implies an acceptance of life's difficulties, this does not mean passivity. Attempts to change what initially *seemed* immutable obstacles have fueled many social, technical, and scientific advances, and have unquestionably aided human adaptation individually and collectively.

Discernment of whether an alloplastic or autoplastic response is best suited for a given situation. Despite having mapped out a taxonomy of ego components, there remains one unanswered question regarding flexibility. It is still not clear what is involved in the ability to correctly discern the context most appropriate for an alloplastic or autoplastic response. This core characteristic of a strong ego is a phenomenon which has long puzzled observers of human nature. Socrates observed, for example, over 2,500 years ago, that there are certain individuals "who manage the

---

[4]This same theme has been elaborated on by Peck (1978) in his popular book, *The Road Less Travelled*. He wrote:

> Once we truly know life is difficult—once we truly understand and accept it—then life is no longer difficult. Because once it is accepted, the fact that life is difficult no longer matters.

> Most people do not fully see this truth that life is difficult. Instead they moan more or less incessantly, noisily or subtly, about the enormity of their problems, their burdens, and their difficulties as if life were generally easy, as if life *should* be easy. They voice their belief, noisily or subtly, that their difficulties represent a unique kind of affliction that should not be and that has somehow especially been visited upon them, or else upon their families, their tribe, their class, their nation, their race, or even their species, and not upon others.

circumstances which they encounter daily, who possess a judgment which is accurate in meeting occasions as they arise and rarely miss the expedient course of action."

Given that intelligence is defined as the ability to make accurate discriminations, I initially contemplated that it was involved for this component of ego strength. Further reflection, however, clearly reveals that it was not. It is true that some people with high intelligence manage their lives well. However, historical examples (such as Rousseau and Cellini), clinical case histories, and ordinary everyday social experiences clearly indicate that this is far from always being so. Intelligence is not proportionate to amount of ego strength. Furthermore, although there is a positive correlation between intelligence (B+ scores) and ego strength (C+) in the general population, it is small in magnitude. Moreover, about 60 percent of my C+ examinees had only modest intellectual endowment, but nonetheless exercised enviable judgment and expediency in conducting their practical affairs. Given all of this, it continues to be a yet-unanswered question as to just how the strong ego responds correctly to contextual cues.

Having now concluded my description of the ego, readers will notice that I have failed to include references to traits like self-image and capacity for object relations, which are generally regarded as two of its central components. This omission is due to the discovery, by repeated factor analysis, that these traits are not part of Factor C or ego strength, but are part of other factors— Q_3 (self-sentiment), in the first instance, and, in the second, a combination of several factors, but mostly A and I. Their place in personality will be discussed in later chapters.

Heredity

That individuals differ in ego strength is due to their particular learning experiences and to their genetic endowment. Research evidence indicates that much of the variance of ego strength (.41) is due to heredity.

Male and Female Differences Throughout the Life Span

The group means for Factor C are approximately the same for men and women (men, 32.96 and women, 33.26), but with a slightly higher, even though insignificant, standard deviation for women's scores (women, 7.87 and men, 6.72).

Age curves follow similar patterns for both sexes, starting to rise after their 10th year of life and continuing thereafter until their 40th year, when they slowly begin to decline.

In addition to these chronological variations, C scores also change predictably with certain life events (Cattell, 1973). They show increases with marriage and with church participation. They also increase among those who are taking medically prescribed tranquilizers, possibly due to their palliative effect.

On the other hand, decreases in C scores occur with chronic illness and disability. Possibly, these decreases reflect the disorganization that occurs in perceptual and cognitive functions when people are anxious or depressed, especially for protracted periods. The decreases may also reflect the stresses that result from coping with increased obstacles to meeting needs which people normally encounter when sick or disabled.

HIGH SCORES ON FACTOR C

Intrapsychic Data

The ego's strength and efficiency is most clearly subjectively experienced and objectively observed while persons are either actively involved in solving their problems or dealing with their frustrations. And, since it operates according to problem-solving sequences, or with dysphoria-avoiding strategies (defense mechanisms, palliative behavior, or calling forth a stoic attitude in times of trouble), my interest focused mainly on how C+ examinees actually acted under these types of conditions.

What I discovered was that C+ examinees in my sample showed seven characteristics which set them apart from their lower scoring counterparts. These characteristics are listed below. Each of the 109 examinees showed at least five of these characteristics and no less than 28% showed all seven.

Stoic mental orientation. I have already mentioned a stoic mental attitude as a core characteristic of ego strength. This tendency showed itself in all 109 of my examinees. They had a philosophy which accepted that effort, frustration, and loss are inevitable parts of life. As a consequence of this philosophy, they avoided unrealistic expectations, which in turn minimized disappointments. It also allowed them to plan ahead to meet emergencies, misfortunes, and eventualities that were forseeable. For example, they typically made wills and had adequate insurance plans and financial savings.

Formulation of problems in concrete and specific terms. Regardless of their level of intellectual ability, there was a strong tendency among C+ examinees to grasp the meaning of most problems, usually by reframing them in simple terms. Rather than getting intimidated by abstractions, they attempted to reduce them as much as possible into familiar and manageable concepts using what is recognized as "common sense."

The kind of questions they asked when confronting problems were reminiscent of Kipling's (1940) poem:

> Keep six honest serving men
> (They taught me all I know);
> Their names are What and Why and When
> And How and Where and Who. (p. 677)

Appropriate sense of timing. An acute sense of timing was manifested by a disproportionate number of my C+ examinees, when compared to those with lesser scores. This was shown by their allocation of sufficient time to their priorities, and their being neither hurried nor slow paced in their daily activities. Free from time pressure, they also bridged between present and future time zones by taking care to safeguard future options. Although this characteristic occurred in about 50 to 60 percent of my sample, it was not unanimous.

Acknowledgement of problems without undue delay. Confronting a problem usually involves some effort or foregoing of pleasure, and it is often for this reason that many individuals tend to procrastinate. C+ examinees characteristically responded promptly to surfacing problematic situations and lived their lives according to a "stitch in time saves nine" philosophy. This characteristic shows itself most conspicuously in clinical C+ examinees who made up about 68% of the sample. Not one of them entered therapy with chronic neglected problems as many clients are apt to do. Although this freedom from procrastination was a widespread characteristic, it, like an appropriate sense of timing, was not invariant in the sample.

Lack of perfectionism. By perfectionism, I do not mean a striving for excellence. Rather, I mean an attempt to comply with impossible, superhuman standards which are therefore unreachable and which doom aspirants to feelings of inadequacy and self-denigration. Even my clinical C+ examinees, on the whole, were free from this human error so frequently seen in therapy and in counseling clients. Consequently, they did not create unnecessary frustrations for themselves by setting unreachable goals. Similarly, they did not demand of themselves that they solve problems with computer-like precision, i.e., making the one decision that would maximize their overall satisfaction. Instead, they were content with choosing between life's imperfect alternatives.

Self-acceptance. Especially in comparison to low and moderate scorers, it was typical for C+ examinees to engage in less self-blame and criticism. They tended to maintain positive self-orientations. This, in part, seemed to result from their ability to correctly discern the limits of their own control or responsibility.

It also stemmed, however, from their ability to use defense mechanisms judiciously. Although they distorted reality, they did so in the service of preserving their self-images and sense of self-worth. This was in marked contrast to C− examinees, who also distorted reality, but in ways that ultimately produced negative, rather than positive, self-orientations.

Preparation for stressful events. I asked C+ examinees what they did while anticipating unpleasant events. Since three examinees were, at the time of the interviewing, preparing to undergo serious surgery and two had a terminally ill loved one, I was able to obtain introspections of present experience as well as recollections about how they had coped with past ordeals.

Examinees said that, once they accepted that a forthcoming unpleasant event was inevitable, they prepared themselves, first of all, by rehearsing for it, and second, by generating helpful thoughts. Many referred to this latter strategy as "giving myself a good talking to," which involved reflecting on certain beliefs that were implicit in their stoic mental orientations.

A C+ person explained how he coped with his anticipation of a painful medical procedure that he regularly had to undergo about every four weeks. He said, "I remind myself there are 720 hours in an average month and that being physically uncomfortable during one of them isn't a bad ratio. I am not going to let worrying or negative feelings about one hour spoil the other 719."

Interpersonal and Social Data

When I hear someone who is admired for being reliable, realistic, and having "good emotional control," and then later am able to test that person with the 16PF, I invariably find that he or she has superior ego strength. Consequently, I have frequently come to be able to predict that a person will obtain a C+ score just by hearing things that others say about that person.

Since C+ persons are *not* apt to be moody, impulsive, or panicky in emergencies, it is fortunate for the general public that C+ scores are found in the group norms of firefighters, police officers, pilots, flight attendants, judges, anaesthesiologists, and school bus drivers. Other occupational groups that show C+ scores are Lutheran clergy, politicians, social workers, biologists, chemists, geologists, dental assistants, electricians, psychiatric technicians, kitchen workers, machine operators, life insurance agents, retail counter clerks, sales representatives, finance managers, nursing administrators, store managers, education administrators, school counselors, and special education teachers.[5]

According to the 16PF Handbook, an above-average Factor C score in a group indicates a high level of general morale. Therefore, C+ persons would be ideal companions for facing ordeals, especially those that are uncomfortable and dangerous. Especially, they could be relied upon to tolerate deprivation, solve problems, and not make unrealistic demands. There are numerous historical examples of individuals who maintained good interpersonal relations and positive outlooks during inordinately dangerous and uncomfortable undertakings. Had they been tested, they most likely would have shown C+ scores.

On a more prosaic note, I found that my C+ examinees were generally appreciated as companions on life's more ordinary undertakings. I have heard them described by coworkers, family members, and friends as wearing well over time and with rough treatment. Unless they have other personality traits that complicate their ego strength, they make particularly good marriage partners, since they deal well with the frustrations and challenges of raising children, growing old, and the unpleasant twists that normally beset life's journey.

---

[5]Rieke, M. L., & Russell, M. T. (1987). *Narrative Score Report User's Guide.* Champaign, Illinois: IPAT, Appendix B.

Some years ago a 41-year-old widow with two sons, one 12 and the other 7, consulted us because she loved two men, but for different reasons, and could not decide which one to marry. One was outgoing, witty, and fun loving. Obviously, to me he was A+ (affectothymic), B+ (intelligent), and F+ (surgent), but, from her description, was somewhat low on ego strength. The other, on whom the 16PF profile was available, had only average scores on Factors A, B, and F, but obtained a C score of 8. Although she knew she would not have as much fun, she chose the latter, but rather regretfully.

Recently, I reencountered this woman, but this time in a social situation. She told me about the personal misfortunes that had fallen upon her in the intervening years. She had, for the past three years, been caring for her mother, who was suffering from Alzheimer's disease, and her younger son had been seriously involved with drugs. She confided how glad she was that she had chosen her present husband, as she appreciated his ego strength and his qualities of calmness, good sense, and ability to handle crises. She believed, quite correctly, I thought, that she would not have weathered her difficulties so well with the other former suitor.

As well as making good spouses, I have noted that my C+ examinees, because they are relatively free from neurotic symptoms, are firm, consistent, and reasonable parents. However, their ego strength alone does not qualify them as ideal parents, for it does not mean they are always warm and loving (these qualities are associated with other factors). Sometimes when their ego strength is accompanies by certain other traits, they come to be resented by their children, who see them as lacking in ordinary vulnerability to human feelings and as handling their lives too systematically. One parent fitting this description was nicknamed "The Machine" and another "The Computer" by their respective families. Still another was named Mr. Spock after the Star Trek TV character. All of these examinees had A− (sizothymia), F− (desurgency), I− (harria), and M− (praxernia) scores. Having taken on the negative aspects of the traits signified by these scores, these C+ examinees were stiff and critical (A−), sober and taciturn (F−), tough-minded and emotionally insensitive (I−), and lacking in imagination and governed by practical concerns (M−). They impressed me as having a robot-like quality. Fortunately, such individuals are somewhat rare, since in the general population, C+ scores are not highly correlated with scores on these factors.

C+ and Childhood

Although heredity has been shown to contribute significantly to the acquisition of ego strength, environmental experiences also play an important role, especially those that occur in childhood. The research on this matter is sparse. What is reported in the Cattellian literature is only that C+ scores are rarely seen in people who grew up in a matriarchal type of home environment. Often, C+ is associated with a parental tendency to use reasoning rather than punishment (Cattell, 1973).

Since it is synonymous with mental health, ego strength has been recognized and studied in regard to its development, even though it is usually referred to by other names (such as emotional maturity or stability). Theorists Ellis (1975), Winnicott (1964), and Bandura (1973), to name just a few, are in remarkable agreement about the experiences that impact favorably on its development. These experiences include: receiving consistency in reward and punishment contingencies, being exposed to manageable levels of stress and frustration, being allowed to experience natural consequences arising from one's behavior, being permitted to exercise age-appropriate levels of initiative, and receiving firm but kind discipline.

Given the unanimity and face validity of these findings, I was shocked to discover that they did not have application to the childhood experiences of most of my C+ examinees.

With only 16 exceptions, all other of 109 C+ examinees reported having had difficult childhoods, many having been subjected to the same kinds and levels of stress that usually antecede psychopathology. Some had lived with an emotionally disturbed, schizophrenic, or alcoholic parent, or had parents whose relationship to each other was clearly dysfunctional. Others had been rejected, physically abused, or raised under a variety of conditions that could be expected to distort their perceptions of reality and to undermine their self-confidence and their ability to behave competently.

Later on in this chapter, Table 4.3 illustrates the relationship between superior ego strength and high percentages of negative childhood experiences in the sample.

Two other studies parallel my case histories that link high levels of ego strength with such unlikely origins: the longitudinal studies of Anthony (1975) and Garmenzy (1976). In independent studies, Anthony and Garmenzy each documented numerous instances of children who, just like my C+ clients, demonstrated strong adaptive qualities despite being brought up in difficult, sometimes horrendous environments. The example below, reported by Garmenzy, is fairly typical of the kinds of experiences C+ examinees revealed.

> As an example of how these children both master the environment and rearrange their responses for emotional coping, Garmenzy tells the story of an eight-year-old girl whose father died and whose depressed mother did not prepare a lunch for her to take to school. After attempting to scavenge some things out of the refrigerator for lunch, she decided to make herself a "bread sandwich" by putting two pieces of bread together which looked similar to the well-made sandwiches other children brought to school.

Note in the example above the use of both alloplastic and autoplastic responses. The child behaved alloplastically, by meeting her needs (for having something to eat and for not being conspicuous when sitting down to eat with the other children). She also behaved autoplastically, by giving a special name, "bread sandwich" to the two pieces of bread, a palliative which helped her feel better about there being nothing between them.

I am still at the time of writing trying to identify the specific environmental variables that might be operating to allow children to develop ego strength despite such obvious obstacles. What I have uncovered so far, though tentative, agrees with the proposition voiced by both Anthony and Garmenzy that children in this position (1) have had somewhere in their backgrounds a good relationship with an adult (even if not their parent), (2) have been challenged by their environment to develop coping methods children in more ordinary circumstances are never required to develop, and (3) although the stressors seem formidable, are able to deal with them, even though to do so probably requires stretching their skills to near capacity.

Important Correlations Between C+ Scores and Other 16PF Factor Scores

The five correlations between C+ scores and other 16PF factor scores are presented below in Table 4.1.

Table 4.1

**Important Correlations Between C+ Scores
and Other 16PF Factor Scores**

Factor Pole	Correlation	Possible Associated Traits Indicated by Correlation
O− (Untroubled Adequacy)	.61	Self-assured, Complacent, Placid, Secure, Serene
Q_4− (Low Tension)	.59	Relaxed, Tranquil, Unfrustrated, Composed
Q_3+ (Strong Self-sentiment)	.40	Controlled, Exacting Will Power, Socially Precise, Compulsive
H+ (Parmia)	.39	Adventurous, Uninhibited, Socially Bold
L− (Alaxia)	.38	Trusting, Accepting Conditions

The largest correlation in Table 4.1 is between C+ scores and O− (untroubled adequacy) scores. O− scores are indicative of self-esteem, and a correlation of this magnitude indicates that a strong ego usually fills its defensive role of protecting the self-image. From interview, I have discovered that, although C+ individuals do have strong defenses, they are usually of the more mature variety, e.g., suppression and humor rather than repression and projection. The absence of the last-mentioned defenses is also supported by the association of C+ scores with L− scores. (The minus pole of Factor L signifies an absence from projection. Here, perceptions of other people are not distorted for the purpose of maintaining a personal self-orientation.)

The large correlation (−.59) with Q_4− (low nervous tension) scores probably reflects need satisfaction. The lesser correlation (.40) with Q_3+ scores indicates that investment in oneself seems to be related to emotional stability.

Finally, the correlation with H+ (parmia) suggests something about how the typical C+ person interacts with the environment. Parmia refers to a bold, adventurous orientation. Sometimes, persons with high ego strength tend to demonstrate these characteristics, rather than to be timid or retiring.

Clinical Relevance of C+ Scores

Since the indication is that an ultra-strong ego seems to generally arise out of childhood disadvantages similar to those that many of my C − examinees said contributed to their maladaption, one might wonder whether this ego strength might be built on quicksand. This seems possible, especially in view of the fact that the ideas and decisions that went into its early formation occurred when the individuals involved were neuropsychologically immature and lacked experience. These considerations suggest, therefore, that any examinee whose C score is 8 or above may show a loss of ego strength later in life.

Some indirect support for this possibility is suggested by research on the adjustment history of individuals who, as a consequence of being raised by alcoholic parents, were subjected to extreme stress. Many of these individuals showed outstanding ego strength in childhood but later became poorly adjusted. Research on adult children of alcoholics is replete with examples of nine-year-olds who cooked breakfast, dressed their younger siblings, and then did a couple loads of laundry before going to school, where they distinguished themselves by making good grades and maintaining excellent interpersonal relations, but who later as adults showed neurotic symptoms.

My own practice contains a fairly large number of clients who show this pattern. Though currently depressed, anxious, or dependent on drugs or alcohol, their histories indicate they had previously attained exceptionally good levels of functioning. One may surmise that, although they now show only moderate or low C scores, it is possible that, had they been tested earlier, they would have been in the superior range.

What I have just described is "after the fact" information. Since I have not encountered any C+ examinees whose ego strength degenerated during the period of time I was in contact with them, I have no direct observations about a "pseudo" form of ego strength. Nor do I know for sure if this phenomenon could be picked up through psychological testing as changes in Factor C scores. But if it could, I speculate that a mental status exam of such examinees would reveal the absence of a stoic mental attitude and the presence of immature forms of defense mechanisms. Consequently, their 16PF profiles might show excessively low scores on Factor O (unrealistic self-esteem) and possibly high scores on Factor L, indicating that they were using unusually strong distortions to maintain their positive self-image and to project their inner conflicts outwards.

I have so far found this constellation of C+ L+ O− scores in 10 examinees, all of whom, incidentally, were family members of identified clients. As a result, they were included in family therapy sessions, but had not sought therapy for themselves. Since none of these clients wished to obtain deeper levels of self-understanding, I did not have the opportunity to analyze their ego structures for confirmation of my hypotheses.

In relating what I have just said here, and in previous sections, to practical clinical application, I advise clinicians to inquire, of anyone achieving a C score of 8 or above, whether he or she had an unusually difficult childhood. While ego strength formed under such conditions may be entirely sound, it may, on the other hand, be precipitous and therefore liable to crumble under the pressures of adult life. The possibility of whether or not this is so should nevertheless be considered on an individual basis. Soundness may, in particular, be questioned whenever it is observed that ego functions are maintained by particularly strong or immature defense mechanisms, or when the client has an unrealistically positive self-image.

LOW SCORES ON FACTOR C

Intrapsychic Data

To score only 1, 2, or 3 stens on the C scale, items must be endorsed to say that one *often* loses control over feelings, tolerates frustration poorly, and gets easily upset. Therefore, unlike most other people who only occasionally respond in these ways, C− examinees report that this is their usual mode of experience. It follows that these individuals are usually fairly unhappy and dissatisfied.

Like the C+ counterparts in my sample, the C− examinees reported different variants of subjective experience. Each of these variants, which will be discussed below, suggests a primary origin in a particular ego sequence. In most cases, the variant was associated with specific patterns of 16PF scores.

Variant 1. Ego Weakness: Primary association either with overly strong defenses or discounting of feelings. Some C− examinees complained chiefly of being out of touch with their feelings. They also demonstrated this by being confused about what they actually wanted, either in the moment or from their lives as a whole. This failure can best be interpreted as arising from a dysfunction in the first ego sequence, since its function is to assess and identify the nature and strength of inner needs.

The 16PF profiles of examinees with this complaint usually showed one or two score combinations. One was made up of markedly lower scores on Factor O (untroubled adequacy) and high scores on Q_4, in addition to the C− scores. The other combined I− scores with C− scores.

The subvariant showing a C− O− Q_4+ combination indicated that, although the defense mechanisms were filling their intended purpose of maintaining self-esteem and freedom from guilt (as indicated by the O− scores), the repression which sustained this positive self-orientation was incomplete, as revealed in the nervous tension reflected in Q_4 scores. My interviews with examinees showing C− O− Q_4+ suggested that they were denying the existence of important needs and feelings that were personally unacceptable for some reason or another. Commonly, they were overly socialized individuals who also showed extreme G+ or Q_3+ scores.

The C− I− pattern proved difficult to interpret in my early days of working with the 16PF. Examinees whose profiles showed this combination showed a mental orientation similar to the stoicism characteristic of ego strength. With more experience, however, I eventually discerned reasons I will explain later in Chapter 9 (on Factor I) that I− (harria), although it also shows itself as a hard, realistic orientation, differs from stoicism in that it is based on repression of feelings and absence of personal reflection, rather than on a philosophy.

Variant 2. Ego Weakness: Primary association with failure to adequately consider available alternative courses of action. C− examinees who were dysfunctional in this second ego sequence were able to identify their needs, but then found it hard to generate a sufficient range of potential alternatives about how they could satisfy their needs. (For reasons I have already noted, it is desirable that persons generate an adequate number of alternatives in order to increase their chances of making good choices.) The 16PF profiles of these examinees tended to divide them into two pattern types. The first pattern shows C− and F+, the second shows C− F−. C− and F+ people were sufficiently fluent in their thinking to be capable of generating a wide choice of alternatives, but rarely proceeded to do so since their tendency towards being eager (which is another F+ [surgent] characteristic) prompted them to act on the first appealing idea that occurred to them.

An acquaintance who is C − and F + almost drowned when surfing. I knew he was a poor swimmer and was mystified as to why he went surfing. He later explained that he had been sitting by the beach feeling bored when someone invited him to go out on his board. "I didn't think it through, but it seemed like such a good idea at the time," he said.

C − examinees who show F − scores in their profiles, in keeping with their F − scores, share narrow and constricted thinking that makes it difficult for them to generate an adequate number of possible choices for meeting their needs. Consequently, they often felt themselves "stuck" or "not knowing what to do" when confronted by unfamiliar situations calling for novel and imaginative problem-solving responses. Therefore, they attempted to meet their needs by using a routine and limited repertoire of low-risk, familiar familiar responses. Unfortunately, however, as this solution left many needs only partially satisfied or seriously compromised, these examinees were usually depressed, as well as liable to have moments of unexpected behavior when internal pressures built up.

A C − F − client had for several months wanted to meet a woman who regularly lunched at a restaurant he frequented, but the only way he could think of to do this was by having a friend make the overture for him. The friend refused and told him he should do it himself.

Since he could not think of an alternative for meeting the woman, my client despaired. However, he continued to see her in the restaurant several times a week and the longing increased. One day he surprised himself and her by sitting down at her table and blurting out his feelings for her. She complained to the manager, who asked him to leave. It was shortly after this incident that the client entered therapy.

Variant 3. Ego Weakness: Primary association with poor timing. Fairly commonly, I observed that my C − examinees tended to respond to situations either too quickly or too slowly. When this behavior was primary, it, too, was divisible into two subvariants which both seem to involve functions located in the ego's decision-making sequence (Sequence 3).

Some examinees who tended to make quick decisions did so without adequately considering the consequences of their acts.

This group is unique among the other ego dysfunction groups, because I have not been able to associate it with a distinct pattern of 16PF scores. Although their behavior seemed to originate in desurgency (the C− F− subvariant described above), closer analysis revealed that these examinees were rather rigid individuals who made "snap decisions" because of their intolerance for ambiguity.

Other examinees often arrived at decisions too late to be implemented, since the deadlines for exercising them had been passed. Examinees with this tendency vacillated, wavering back and forth between alternatives, as Hamlet does in his "To be or not to be" soliloquy. Sometimes they referred to themselves and were referred to by others as "always missing the boat."

Typically, profiles of examinees showing this variant of dysfunction showed I+ scores. High Factor I scores indicate emotional sensitivity, manifested by a tendency to make responses based on subjective reactions (rather than objective facts) and by an unwillingness to accept the harsher realities of life. Undoubtedly, these characteristics make decision making difficult, especially since people often have to choose between imperfect alternatives and also have to tolerate the loss which inevitably follows the selection of one course of action over another.

Variant 4. Ego Weakness: Primary association with failure to take action. Clinical practice is replete with individuals who, after executing the first three sequences of problem solving—i.e., identifying a need, thinking of ways to gratify it, deciding upon a course of action—habitually fail to implement it. Although they may know precisely what they could do to live more satisfying lives, they fail to act accordingly. Clues for explaining their failure are often found in their 16PF profiles, which in my experience almost always show C− scores combined with at least one of the following scores: Q_3- (low self-sentiment), H− (threctia), or E− (submissiveness). The C− and Q_3- combination suggests examinees who are not interested in maintaining socially approved self-concepts, and who are not motivated to carry through with their plans.

C− scores combined with H− (threctia) scores suggest examinees for whom "the spirit is willing but the flesh is weak." A high score on Factor H, as we shall see in Chapter 8, involves constitutional overreactivity to both physically and socially threatening stimuli. Examinees showing this variant become easily trepidated and are apt to retreat from implementing decisions that require boldness and risk taking.

On profiles in which C− scores are combined with E−, the examinees are apt to give way to the wants and needs of others at the expense of gratifying their own. Since I have identified, not just one, but several reasons for underlying unassertive behavior, this subvariant requires even further analysis along the lines to be discussed in Chapter 5 on Factor E.

What has been laid out above is not meant to be an exhaustive list of ego weakness patterns. They are simply patterns that have shown themselves as reliable trends in my collected data.

Interpersonal and Social Data

Given the core characteristics of low ego strength, e.g., moodiness, changeability, lack of realism, and emotional instability, I was not surprised by the negative responses evoked by C− persons in my sample. Since C− behavior can be so disruptive to close interpersonal relationships, I have seen a fairly large number of C− clients in family therapy. Family members most commonly complained of feeling "let down" by their undependability or capriciousness, or being confused by their moodiness and unpredictable "temper tantrums." Often the most healthy responses that adult family members could make was to avoid relying on the C− person as much as possible. This strategy was less satisfactory for children, since it pushed them to be prematurely self-reliant.

> A 10-year-old boy was brought into family therapy. His mother's 16PF profile showed a C score of 2. His father had an average C score, but was detached and passive. The parents complained that the boy didn't "mind them," which turned out to mean "not minding" his mother, as she was the only parent who gave him directions. Contrary to what the parents asserted, I discovered that this boy was not rebellious. He had learned to handle his problems alone. For example, if he complained of such things as being bullied by another boy, his mother would overreact, exacerbating the problem. He had also learned to avoid disappointment by not asking her to attend school functions, for in the past she would often promise to attend them and change her mind at the last moment. Although it seemed to me that he had adopted the most adaptive response

possible in the situation, I wondered if in adulthood he would be able to enter into trusting, mutually dependent relationships.

Low ego strength is not always readily conspicuous. Presumably because their conscientiousness compensated for their lack of ego strength, I heard fewer complaints about C− examinees whose profiles showed G+ (superego strength) scores. Moreover, ego strength deficits seemed often to go completely undetected in those who, in addition to G+ scores, had B+ (higher intelligence) and N+ (shrewdness) scores. These individuals successfully portrayed a socially poised image that belied their tendencies towards moodiness, lack of realism, and other C− traits.

Cattell (1973) reported on the occupational groups in which C− scores are found. These include accountants, clerks, farmers, artists, professors, and employment counselors. He reasoned that persons with weak egos might gravitate to these kinds of jobs because they were fairly routine and did not usually call for responding to crises or unexpected demands. I have also noted that my C− examinees functioned best in routine kinds of jobs, and I have recommended these jobs to other C− examinees seeking vocational guidance. Although I have had a few—about 35—examinees with very low scores who were in decidedly nonroutine occupations, such as nursing and police work, all reported that they were suffering from work-related stress.

C− and Childhood

Deficiencies in ego strength, as the genetic research has shown, result from both an hereditary endowment and environment. Especially influential is the exposure to early environments that normally promote the ego's proper unfolding and growth.

The only clear research finding between developmental variables and C− scores comes from retrospective self-reports. These reports indicate that a disproportionate number of persons with low scores were raised in matriarchal families (Cattell, 1973). Added support for this finding was provided by the recollections of my C− examinees, a disproportionate number of whom reported that they did not have enduring early relationships with strong father figures. I can only speculate that these findings indicate that traditionally there is something in the father's parenting style that is more conducive to fostering ego strength.

Table 4.3

Frequency of Negatively Rated Childhood Experiences Reported by High, Moderate, and Low Scale C Scorers
(N = 140)

Negatively rated childhood experience	Low 63 (45%) examinees obtaining 1-3 stens	Average 48 (34%) examinees obtaining 4-7 stens	High 29 (21%) examinees obtaining 8-10 stens
1. Habitual discounting of personal perceptions or feelings. (Example: Child says, "I am angry," and the parent responds, "No, you are not. You are tired.")*	48 (76%)	18 (37%)	12 (41%)
2. Impulsive or irresponsible behavior by one or both parents.	52 (82%)	30 (62%)	19 (34%)
3. Inconsistency in reward and punishment contingencies.	41 (65%)	21 (43%)	18 (36%)
4. Excessive use of physical punishment or criticism.	41 (65%)	20 (41%)	15 (31%)
5. Control of child by evoking excessive levels of fear. (Example: The child is consistently warned that if it doesn't act in such and such a way it will be subjected to excessive punishment or be abandoned.)	50 (79%)	26 (54%)	17 (58%)
6. Frequent and especially unpredictable altercations between parents or parent and other significant person.	44 (69%)	23 (47%)	20 (68%)
7. Parental rejection or neglect manifested as lack of support or disinterest in child's welfare or achievements.	49 (77%)	17 (35%)	21 (72%)
8. Excessive punishment for mistakes and unrealistic emphasis on perfectionism.	54 (85%)	26 (54%)	18 (62%)
9. Pressure to act in accordance with external standards of rightness or wrongness, or what is most congruent with maintaining a desired self-concept while neglecting consideration of realistic consequences.	47 (74%)	30 (62%)	22 (75%)

10.	Parents attempting to foster excessive dependency on their approval.	39 (61%)	34 (70%)	17 (58%)
11.	Being subjected to double binds (being damned if you do and damned when you don't).	48 (76%)	22 (45%)	15 (51%)
12.	Overprotection that denies the child opportunities for learning to solve problems or deal with frustrations appropriate to its age level.	39 (61%)	16 (33%)	10 (34%)
13.	Protection from the logical and environmental consequences of its behavior.	54 (85%)	22 (45%)	9 (31%)
14.	Not being taught certain skills necessary to being able to function effectively either because of the unavailability of a suitable teaching adult or because the adults in the child's life were themselves deficient in these skills.	46 (73%)	15 (31%)	23 (79%)
15.	Parents performing tasks for the child which the child is capable of doing for itself, e.g., doing its homework.	38 (60%)	14 (29%)	8 (27%)
16.	Parental behavior that imparts an expectancy to the child that it should not be required to exert itself, delay gratification or do without anything it wants.	12 (19%)	17 (35%)	2 (6%)
17.	Being exposed to excessive levels of stress for two or more protracted periods during childhood.	44 (69%)	10 (20%)	22 (75%)

45% examinees scoring 1-3 stens, 48% scoring 4-7 stens, and 21% scoring 8-10 stens.

*The term *parent* is used above to include not only actual parents, but parent surrogates and other primary caretakers.

In addition to having lacked paternal influences, C−examinees routinely reported that, as children, they had other kinds of negative childhood experiences. I noticed that these experiences occurred with far less frequency in examinees who obtained *moderate* scores, e.g., between 4 and 7 stens on the C scale. Table 4.3 below lists these experiences, together with the frequency with which they were reported by a subsample of low-scoring and moderate-scoring examinees. Also, the table includes the frequency with which these same experiences were reported by C+ examinees. When the frequency scores of this last group of examinees is compared with those of the other two groups, it will be seen that on most variables, C+ people's experiences are closer to C− than to moderate scorers. This suggests a curvilinear relationship between levels of ego strength and negative childhood experiences, as indicated in an earlier section of this chapter.

It was only towards the end of collecting the self-reports of my C− examinees that the similarity of their recollections with many of the C+ examinees' became obvious. Therefore, the frequencies in Table 4.3 are tabulated on only 140 of the total number of 905 examinees. The early recollections provided material that was later formally organized into the structured questions posed to subsequent examinees for obtaining the data presented above. While the 17 variables which are enumerated are by no means meant to be an exhaustive list of the early environmental associations influencing the various levels of ego development, they are presented as reliable trends.

Important Correlations Between C− Scores and Other 16PF Factor Scores

Table 4.2 presents the important correlations between C− scores and the scores of other 16PF factors. Like the A− scores in Table 2.2, these correlations are actually the same as those for the right side of the pole, but the text is now transposed to show the relevance to the left-sided pole—a format which will also be followed in the ensuing chapters.

All of the correlations in Table 4.2 join with C− scores in completing the second-order anxiety pattern, to be detailed later in Chapter 18. The highest correlation (.64) is with O+ (guilt proneness). It indicates that often, when the ego strength is low, the ego has failed in its important role of maintaining a positive self-concept. The ego has also failed to ward off the dysphoria that follows from the negative self-evaluation that is reflected in a high O score. The second correlation, which is almost equal in magnitude, is with Q_4+ (ergic tension) scores. This large correlation (.59) indicates that, in addition to experiencing these noxious feelings, C− persons also often suffer from nervous tension.

Trailing the O− and Q_4+ correlation values come $Q_3−$ (low self-sentiment) at .40; H− (threctia) at .39; and L+ (protension) at .38. Respectively, these correlations indicate difficulty in maintaining an adequate sense of personal identity, timidity, and projected insecurity. These traits, along with those delineated in the paragraph above, show that C− persons often experience other anxiety symptoms besides those associated primarily with low ego strength.

Table 4.2

Important Correlations Between C− Scores and Other 16PF Factor Scores

Factor Pole	Correlation	Possible Associated Traits Indicated by Correlation
O+ (Guilt Proneness)	.61	Apprehensive, Self-reproaching, Insecure, Worrying (Strong tendencies)
Q_4+ (Ergic Tension)	.59	Tense, Frustrated, Driven, Overwrought (Strong tendencies)
$Q_3−$ (Low Self-sentiment)	.40	Undisciplined, Self-conflict, Lax, Follows Own Urges, Careless of Social Rules (Moderate tendencies)
H− (Threctia)	.39	Timid, Threat Sensitive (Moderate tendencies)
L+ (Protension)	.38	Suspicious, Hard to Fool (Moderate tendencies)

Clinical Relevance of C− Scores

A score of 1, 2, or 3 on Factor C should alert the clinician that the examinee is adjusting poorly to life. This is true, even when the scores on other factor scales show that other traits involved in self-direction and control, such as a high score on Factor G (superego) are substituting for some of the ego's functions.

Because they are related to physical illness, C− scores are important from a medical standpoint. For example, Sherman and Krug (1977) found that C− scores are more indicative of medical risk than any other factor scores in the 16PF contingent. Krug and Sherman (1977) discovered that C− scores were associated with many diseases, especially those involving the cardiovascular system. In yet another study, Calsyn (1977) found C− scores to be associated with chronic back pain.

From a more purely psychological standpoint, C− scores, in addition to being the second largest contributor to the second-order anxiety pattern, have been shown to be associated with clinical diagnosis (Cattell, 1973). The exception is an antisocial personality disorder, where C+ scores correlate somewhat positively with the Psychopathic Deviation Scale (Pp) of the Clinical Analysis Questionnaire. The reader may wish to turn to Appendix C for a description of this instrument.

In addition to the Psychopathic Deviation scale, the Clinical Analysis Questionnaire includes 12 pathology-oriented scales, including 7 related to depression. C− scores correlate positively with the pathological ends of all these scales except Agitated Depression, D_3, which is manifested as excitement-seeking behavior that serves as a diversion from depressed feelings.

Given these CAQ associations, as well as the entry of C− scores into the second-order anxiety pattern, the probability is high that any examinee showing C− scores may also be anxious, depressed, or psychotic. It is probably for this reason that Karson and O'Dell (1976) warns clinicians that C− scores are indicative of a poor clinical prognosis. Since C− scores occur so often in the profiles of the majority of persons receiving psychiatric treatment, this observation would have ominous implications if it were not that they sometimes reflect an adjustment disorder, e.g., an acute reaction to some recent loss or trauma, rather than always indicating a fixed, ongoing pattern of characterological maladaptation.

Clinicians should be advised to review the history of an examinee whose C score is 3 or less, to determine if any of these conditions is suggested. Those in whom C− scores indicate true ego weakness have typically interacted poorly with their environments throughout their lives. By contrast, those who are suffering from only some transient disorganization of their ego functions demonstrate having sustained higher levels of competence for substantial periods of time.

Chapter 5

Factor E: Control and Deference in Human Relations

THE CONSTRUCT

Dominance and Submissiveness

Assertiveness as Distinct from Dominance

Heredity

Male and Female Differences Throughout the Life Span

The Influence of Physical Stature on Intelligence

Cattell's Confidence Ratio Theory

HIGH SCORES ON FACTOR E

Intrapsychic Data

Interpersonal and Social Data

E+ and Childhood

Important Correlations Between E+ Scores and Other 16PF Factor Scores

Clinical Relevance of E+ Scores

LOW SCORES ON FACTOR E

Intrapsychic Data

Interpersonal and Social Data

E− and Childhood

Important Correlations Between E− Scores and Other 16PF Factor Scores

Clinical Relevance of E− Scores

The Frustration Underlying E− Scores

Alcoholics and Narcotic Addicts

FACTOR E: CHARACTERISTICS OF E+ (DOMINANT) AND E− (SUBMISSIVE) EXAMINEES

Left Score E− (SUBMISSIVENESS)		Right Score E+ (DOMINANCE OR ASCENDANCE)
(Obedient, Mild, Easily Led, Docile, Accommodating)	vs.	**(Assertive, Aggressive, Competitive, Stubborn)**
Submissive	vs.	Assertive
Dependent	vs.	Independent-minded
Considerate, Diplomatic	vs.	Stern, Hostile
Expressive	vs.	Solemn
Conventional, Conforming	vs.	Unconventional, Rebellious
Easily Upset by Authority	vs.	Headstrong
Humble	vs.	Admiration Demanding

THE CONSTRUCT

Dominance and Submissiveness

Factor E measures the amount of control people either submit to or exercise over others in their interpersonal relationships. Cattell did not invent neologisms for this factor, simply referring to dominance at the E+ pole, and to submissiveness at the E− pole, for the behavior subsumed by these poles matches what is commonly understood by these terms. In classroom discussions, students quickly grasp the meaning of E+ and E− poles when I illustrate them with the 1970s television characters Archie and Edith Bunker. The contumacious, aggressive Archie describes the E+ (dominance) pole and his wife, the appeasing, accommodating Edith, the E− (submissiveness) pole.

As can be discerned from the personality clashes between Archie and Edith, Factor E is one of the factors where the mean is truly golden, as either extreme is disruptive to interpersonal relationships. Thus, the middle road, assertiveness, by avoiding these extremes, offers the best chance for all-around social satisfaction.

Assertiveness as Distinct from Dominance

On first thought, *assertiveness* may seem more descriptive of the E+ pole, but as I define this term, in acknowledgement of its territorial origin, it means protection of one's boundaries and extensions of self, time, possession, priorities, etc., from invasion, without encroaching on the right of others. Obtaining average scores on the E scale indicates that the examinee has enough flexibility to behave assertively, although these scores do not measure assertiveness per se. (Generally, a shift towards the mean occurred in E− examinees, but not in E+ examinees, when both types had successfully completed one of the Assertiveness Training Workshops currently so popular.)

Having defined assertiveness, I now distinguish it from *dominance,* with which it is frequently confused. Dominance, as measured by E+ scores, is expressed as the wish to obtain a higher status, in order to subjugate and direct others to goals not of their choosing. It is distinct from assertiveness because it implies aggression rather than self-protection.

Heredity

Dominance and submissiveness are roles as well as traits, and interdependent ones at that. Neither can occur in an interpersonal vacuum, since to behave dominantly requires that someone respond submissively, and vice versa. Since the genetic contribution to Factor E is only .18, heredity plays a minor part in determining whether a person will assume a dominant or submissive role in his or her relationships. Rather, this determination involves a complex interaction of situational, attributional, and physiological variables, of which gender is usually the most important.

Male and Female Differences Throughout the Life Span

The group mean score on Factor E is significantly higher ($p < .001$) for men ($\overline{X} = 26.71$) than for women ($\overline{X} = 21.39$). It is noteworthy that this difference of means is one of the largest in the 16PF. However, these data were collected in 1978, and future standardizations of the 16PF may show changes on Factor E, since it, more than any other factor, reflects those traditional male/female behavior style differences which have been most targeted for change in recent years. Even so, I recognize that biological tendencies are important. I cannot ignore the many studies dating from those by Seward (1941) and Beach (1948), and including many thereafter, which show that dominant behavior is influenced by hormonal factors, specifically by the amount of male hormone.

Life span measurements of E scores show that the trend for both sexes is to become increasingly dominant in early life, and then to decrease in dominance thereafter. These scores also have a moderate standard deviation in adults (men, 6.37 and women, 7.22), indicating that there is not a wide range of individual differences along the dominant/submissive continuum of behavior.

The Influence of Physical Stature and Intelligence

Stature is often also important in determining if one will lean towards assuming either a dominant or submissive style, as physical strength has been the traditional means by which human beings have enforced their dominion (Gillis, 1982). While a correlation between physical size and dominance continues to persist in the social life of children, for adults living in a technological society during the last few decades, intellect has replaced physical stature as a means of obtaining social status. Unintelligent people are rarely allowed the luxury of behaving dominantly, according to Karson and O'Dell (1976), who have noticed that they rarely find low B (intelligence) scores with high E scores in the same profile. My observations essentially agree with those of Karson and O'Dell, the exception being in the male prison population, where a return to more primitive means of interpersonal control is common. More explicitly, "might is right" tends to be the prevailing philosophy among the incarcerated males whom I have treated.

Cattell's Confidence-Ratio Theory

A somewhat different way of looking at dominance and submission is according to Cattell's Confidence-Ratio Theory (Cattell, 1972), which proposes that people will act dominantly largely by the degree to which they have the confidence to pit themselves against opposition. This theory puts more weight on the influences of the current situation, since it allows for continuous self-readjustments based on a changing assessment of one's competence, as well as comparisons between oneself and other subgroup members. For example, an increase in dominant behavior would be expected when a person leaves a group in which his intelligence score is in the 50th percentile and enters another in which it is in the 90th percentile. Some empirical support for this position comes from findings that E+ scores have been shown to increase with other situational changes, such as job promotions and geographical relocations, but decline with chronic illnesses and the other vicissitudes of life (Cattell & Barton, 1975; Cattell, Barton & Vaughan, 1973).

Finally, despite what has been said above about role relationships, confidence, and social and gender comparisons, the fact remains that, because dominance and submissiveness are traits, a large number of persons show tendencies toward behaving dominantly or submissively, no matter what subgroup they happen to be in or which role expectation is placed upon them. It helps us to understand this phenomenon if we remember that people respond to their perceptions of reality rather than to reality itself, and that these perceptions are shaped through past experience and do not readily alter, even in response to here and now actualities. More frequently than dominance, I have observed the rigid perseverance of submissive behavior, even when it was not being rewarded. I originally expected that persons who behave this way have had their attempts at healthy self-assertiveness strongly punished, usually in childhood, but as I shall explain later this was not borne out in my data.

HIGH SCORES ON FACTOR E

Intrapsychic Data

Cattell (1957) has described the high E scorer as being boastful, conceited, aggressive, pugnacious, vigorous, forceful, egotistical, and insensitive to social disapproval. Additionally, he or she may be sarcastic, bluffing, upbraiding, and quarrelsome. Karson and O'Dell (1976), in summarizing these characteristics, described these persons as those "who enjoy dominating and controlling others as well as criticizing them, like being in command, enjoy meeting challenges, feel superior to others, and do not mind forcing his ideas on other persons."

Given this description, it is little wonder that Archie Bunker comes so easily to mind. However, to avoid confusion, it is important to separate out Archie's core E+ characteristics from the superfluous trappings of naivete and grandiosity, which are added for comic effect. In real life, the 89 E+ examinees in my sample usually showed their dominance more subtly, even though their mindset was similar, in that they were strongly opinionated and intolerant of views contrary to their own.

Also, like Archie, the thinking of these examinees was rigid. This rigidity seemed to have its emotional origin in the denial of others as independent actors outside of their control, which led them to not fully distinguish between external reality and their own self-will. When E + examinees did see others as independent actors, it was as obstructions to be overcome. I was intrigued to find that this observation fits nicely with the psychoanalytic idea of infantile omnipotence. In extreme instances, the attitude I have just described was manifested in manic behavior. In nonpathological behavior, it came through in the examinees' choice of imperatives, such as when they instructed others that they have to, and need to, do such and such a thing. One examinee who obtained the maximum sten score of 10 on Factor E was fond of telling others: "This is what you *will* want to do, of course."

It was usual for the dominant attitudes of E + examinees to extend beyond the interpersonal sphere to situations, events, and ideas which either challenged their frames of reference or were not in keeping with their desired outcome. This gave them reputations, not only for stubbornness, but for getting things done. I have heard those with very high scores say: "This is the way it will turn out, because I have made up my mind that that's the way it will be." This was said even when the outcome was obviously dependent on riding roughshod over others, or even in circumstances beyond their control.

Eight of the introverted E + examinees (a little less than 10 percent of my sample) displaced their dominance away from social relationships and onto objects and ideas. It was common for these individuals to use expressions like "mastering" a skill or subject, or "conquering" a new intellectual frontier or "getting their teeth" into some problem or other. More than their extraverted counterparts, these dominant introverts were likely to make valuable social contributions.

Interpersonal and Social Data

Dominance in relationships is mostly expressed in the frankly aggressive style of Archie Bunker. Sometimes, however, it is sometimes in other forms, like the stereotype of the so-called smothering mother who is "only trying to help" as she attempts to control the lives of those around her.

Because they are by nature controlling, and unaccepting, it is not surprising that the marriages of dominant persons are often unstable (Cattell, 1972). The specific form the marital difficulties assumes depends largely upon where the spouse stands on the dominance-submission continuum. E − spouses, although seemingly accommodating, often show resistance in ways that are so subtle that they befuddle their dominant partners. But more will be said about this later, during observations of E − examinees.

When both spouses are dominant, there is often open conflict, at least initially. The solution is usually for each to channel their interests in noncompetitive directions, maintaining a "hands off" position in respect to each other's particular domains.

> *Example:* A couple, both with ceiling E + scores, harmoniously coexisted for 30 years until the husband retired and insisted upon helping his wife with the household chores. They were divorced six months later, despite marital therapy, but living apart they were able to maintain a close friendship.

In marriages in which one spouse has a moderate score, the E + partner often complains about the other's unreasonableness (translated into the other not seeing things his or her way). But if the spouse declines to submit and resolutely retains an assertive position, the high-E spouse will either modify his or her behavior over time, or will leave the relationship to find "someone more reasonable" (in other words, more submissive).

E + individuals do tend to become leaders of groups, but not as often as they wish. When they are elected, it is frequently because of their own striving and inclination to take charge rather than because their leadership is solicited. Their leadership style is especially autocratic, except in instances when the group is composed of similarly dominant individuals. This situation requires that a lively democratic process be worked out (Cattell & Stice, 1960). Poor followers, they are often disruptive to the group, being not adverse to raising objections and even heckling. When they are intelligent and have high moral standards, however, they may constructively serve as devil's advocates.

Not surprisingly, E + scores are found in successful salespeople, especially those in jobs which require ability to bring pressure on customers in closing contracts. Athletes, judges, artists, writers, anaesthesiologists, group psychotherapists, pharmacists, psychiatrists, biologists, physicists, psychologists, scientists, computer programmer consultants, mechanics, realtors, administrators, and managers also have been found to obtain high E scores, but there is no information on whether these scores predict success in those professions (Cattell, et al., 1970).

E+ and Childhood

Dominant youngsters, because they have not yet learned to adapt to social codes, tend to exhibit this trait in its frank and primal form. The *Handbook for the Children's Personality Questionnaire*[1] (the juvenile equivalent of the 16PF) reports that E+ children may be disobedient, headstrong, self-willed, and may sometimes show signs of antisocial behavior. They may initiate verbal and physical attacks and teasing of other children, show disobedience to authority, react insensitively, and are ready to infiltrate and take command of groups. It is also reported that, in the classroom, these children are not receptive to most teaching methods that require students to be docile and passive. Their teachers consider them to be headstrong and difficult to control. Although they do not do well academically, even after they have left high school and continued into college, this trend reverses in those who go on to attend graduate school, where students then become rewarded for dominant, rather than submissive, behavior.

Undoubtedly, early learning experiences must play a significant part in acquiring a predilection for dominance, since, as I mentioned earlier, the genetic contribution has been found to be only trivial. In this regard, the negative correlation of −.21 between the E+ scores and emotional attachment to parental home (as measured by the Home Sentiment Factor on the Motivation Analysis Test), suggests that persons who achieve high scores on Factor E generally may not have grown up in happy homes. This hypothesis supports Barton, Dielman, and Cattell's (1973) findings that their subjects, who obtained E+ scores disproportionately, reported that their parents were strict and authoritarian. Given what is known about modeling (Bandura, 1973), one may surmise that their parents were role models for dominant behavior. And, though their status as children did not allow them to retaliate against their parents, E+ examinees did "take it out on" their peers or even younger siblings. My own findings make me further surmise that these youngsters enjoyed behaving

---

[1]Porter, R. B., Cattell, R. B. (1979), & IPAT Staff. *Handbook for the Children's Personality Questionnaire (CPQ)*. Champaign, IL: IPAT, p. 27.

dominantly as a compensation for the powerlessness felt vis-a-vis their parents.

> *Example:* One 46-year-old male who scores 10 on the E scale attributed his dominant behavior to "taking after" his father. He elaborated by saying: "Although I never once spoke back to him, because his word was law in the house, I learned how to boss any other kid around who would let me. I felt so powerless at home; it was nice to feel powerful outside."

This kind of historical data is interesting, as it gives some support to Sweney's proposition, in a personal communication to Krug (Krug, 1980),[2] that high E scores are actually best interpreted as indicating a defensive maneuver. This means that aggressiveness and stubbornness may mask feelings of covert inferiority, attack being considered the best defense.

Important Correlations Between E+ Scores and Other 16PF Factor Scores

Table 5.1 below represents the important correlations between E+ scores and other 16PF factor scores.

Table 5.1
Important Correlations Between E+ Scores and Other 16PF Factor Scores

Factor Pole	Correlation	Possible Associated Traits Indicated by Correlation
H+ (Parmia)	.31	Venturesome, Uninhibited, Socially Bold
F+ (Surgency)	.29	Happy-go-lucky, Enthusiastic
Q_1+ (Radicalness)	.29	Experimenting, Liberal, Critical, Open to Change
L+ (Protension)	.24	Suspicious, Hard to Fool, Distrustful, Skeptical
G− (Low Superego Strength)	.23	Expedient, Disregards Rules, Self-indulgent
N− (Naivete)	.22	Forthright, Unpretentious, Genuine but Socially Clumsy

---

[2]Krug, S. (1980). *Clinical Analysis Questionnaire Manual.* Champaign, IL: IPAT, p. 24.

As associated personality characteristics, these correlations tell us about a personality structure that might be seen in persons with E + scores. The highest correlations are with H + (parmia) at .31; F + (surgency) at .29; and Q_1 + (radicalness) at .29. This pattern is one of boldness, exuberance, and radical-mindedness, possibly rebelliousness. The small but significant correlation of .24 with L (protension) indicates a tendency towards defensive projection. The correlation of .23 with G − (low superego strength) means that the morals of E + persons may not be well aligned with mainstream cultural values. Finally, the .22 correlation with N − (artlessness) suggests these definitely formidable qualities will not be veiled by a veneer of politeness and tact.

Clinical Relevance of E + Scores

I have already touched on the clinical aspects of dominance, in discussing the kinds of interpersonal difficulties that are often engendered by E + persons' controlling, extrapunitive, and un-empathetic behavior.

However, from the point of view of requiring treatment, it is axiomatic that those persons who are on the receiving end of these behaviors are those who suffer. Table 4.1 in the CAQ Manual (Krug, 1980) shows positive correlations between E + scores and the "well-being" side of all of the CAQ depression factor scales (with the sole exception of Factor D_3, which measures freedom from agitation). From these findings, it may be concluded that dominant (E +) persons feel little, if any, discomfort about their behavior. Rather, they derive pleasure from giving orders, expressing their displeasure, issuing challenges, and so on.

It is also axiomatic that dominant behavior is stressful. Even though E + people do not dislike themselves for behaving as they do, they must exert unusually large quantities of effort to stretch the limits of their control, overcome obstacles, and respond to frustrations head-on. For this reason, though they may not get depressed, 45 people (more than 50% of my E + sample) admitted to stress-related symptoms.

Moreover, though unfortunately they rarely seek treatment under such circumstances, it seems to me that dominant persons have the greatest need for psychological assistance whenever they must acknowledge their powerlessness, because for them this is the ultimate insult. When they find themselves impotent to change situations by their usual means, my observations indicate that they are at risk of resorting to last-ditch and desperate efforts. Consequently, I believe that it behooves clinicians who treat individuals with excessively high E scores and who are required to acknowledge their impotence in a situation, to carefully evaluate their potential for dangerousness to both others and themselves. From my personal experience, I have noted males, whose E + scores combine with other factor poles indicating poor internal restraint; namely, C − (low ego strength), G − (low introjection of conventional values), F + (surgency), and Q_3 − (lack of concern for maintaining a socially approved self-image), are particularly prone to violent reactions when threatened with loss. Each of six male prisoners serving time for so-called "crimes of passion" showed this pattern when I tested them on the 16PF during their incarceration. All had physically injured their estranged wives or girl friends, or other men who were romantically involved with these women. They unanimously described having an "If I can't have you, nobody will," orientation while committing their offenses.

No common pattern existed, however, on the 16PF profiles of six E + examinees whose violence was directed towards themselves in the form of both attempted and completed suicides. Their case histories indicated that they were behaving in accord with what Levine (1982) noted when he wrote: "Suicide may be an attempt to take control over what otherwise seems an uncontrollable situation—the only alternative to complete defeat." (*p.* 215).

> *Example:* A man, whose score on Factor E I knew to be 10 (he had been previously tested along with his staff when he was the co-owner of a business organization to which a colleague and I had once provided consultation), lost his hard-fought court battle against his former business partner and was ordered to make financial remunerations. Vowing he would rather die than pay, he killed himself before the date set ordering him to comply.

The final, clinically relevant observation I have made regarding my E + examinees is that they did not cope well, even with normal grief situations. That they should experience difficulty in this regard is hardly surprising, given the finality of death and the state of utter helplessness in which it places the dead person's survivors. Readers familiar with the work of Kübler-Ross and others know that grief is a psychological process, the resolution of which requires working through several distinct stages. One of these stages is characterized by relinquishing the belief that the death could at least have been preventable if only certain things had been done or avoided. This belief represents an underlying attempt to regain a sense of control over important aspects of one's life. It was entirely predictable for me to discover, in my interviews with grieving E+ examinees, that many were stuck in this stage of the grief process, which they showed by stubbornly and erroneously attributing responsibility to others for the deaths of friends and family members. They were particularly apt to become litigious with physicians and hospitals, or hostile towards some other intimate of the deceased. Since forsaking these animosities also involves relinquishing their underlying belief about the controllability of events, helping E+ persons move through their grief presents a difficult and delicate task for clinicians.

LOW SCORES ON FACTOR E

Intrapsychic Data

In comparison to dominant persons, who are more apt to adjust their behavior according to the situational context, I discovered that the behavior of E− examinees altered less across situations, because it seemed to be more responsive to inner demands rather than to environmental cues. Specifically, this meant that they generally did not alter their behavior according to their position on the pecking order, but continued to behave deferentially to all—even to their subordinates—regardless of the appropriateness of the situation. I conjecture that this difference exists because dominance is challenged by competition, whereas submissiveness, by its very nature, is usually not.

In examining the interior experience of my 276 E− examinees, it became clear that the emotions and ideas that caused them to behave submissively were very different from the shyness underlying the minus pole of Factor H. Although the characteristics associated with E− and H− poles are often lumped together under the rubric of unassertiveness, I was able to directly observe their differences from the self-reports and behavior of E — examinees whose profiles showed high or moderate H scores. Unlike their E — and H — counterparts, E — scorers with high or moderate scores on Factor H did not wish to avoid attention, but behaved deferentially, usually out of a desire to be liked. They believed that others would be hurt, angry, or in some way offended if they should refuse a request or present a contrary opinion. Some even had a phobic response towards anger, believing that, if they should elicit an angry response, they would find it intolerable. Depending upon their degree of self-esteem, they saw themselves as being either "too sensitive to hurt others' feelings," or "gutless." They tended to applaud themselves for the former and berate themselves for the latter. Both orientations led them to avoid conflict by acquiescing to the wishes, whims, and wants of others. Ironically enough, others were then imbued with a control which may have been neither desired nor solicited.

Interpersonal and Social Data

Submissive, dependent, and considerate, E — scorers typically make few demands; instead, they accommodate to the wishes of others. In their interpersonal relations, as it has already been mentioned, they are guided by an overriding desire to avoid conflict, which is often accompanied by an effort to please and win approval.

While these obsequious and self-effacing qualities may be gratifying in waiters, they may be less so in persons from whom others expect intimacy and shared initiative. But as with their dominant counterparts, the specific reactions which are elicited depend, of course, upon the personality structures of these others, especially their own tendencies towards being dominant or submissive. For instance, an E + and an E — person can collude in a complementary homeostasis, but the latter may not be treated with respect, as the dominant other may come to agree with the E — person's self-evaluation of being unimportant.

Many of my observations of E — examinees have been in the context of marital counseling. Here, I have observed that, when their marriage partners had average E scores and therefore little or no desire to assume dominant roles, their unwillingness to express themselves or to take stands or make decisions led to much frustration. Thus, partners often come to resent having to take so much responsibility for the direction of the relationship, and, moreover, become dissatisfied with the emotional super-ficiality which inevitably exists in any relationships where feel-ings, values, and opinions are not honestly exchanged, even though this is done to avoid discord. It was not uncommon for submissive spouses in my sample, people who had been paragons of accommodation, to be abandoned by their partners. In a post-mortem analysis of the marriage, the abandoning partners often guiltily confided, "I was bored. He/she had no personality of his/her own."

I sometimes found marriages in which both partners had E − scores and were behaving submissively towards each other. Be-cause neither acted dominantly, the relationship floundered for want of a direction. Thus, with time, one partner might start to behave dominantly. If this did not occur, the couple's solution was to look for an external source of guidance, such as can be found in religious dogma, or an older relative, who then becomes accepted as the regulator of their relationship. Consequently, these relationships tend to become rule bound and ritualistic, lacking the intimacy that comes from open confrontation and negotiation.

Submissiveness and Childhood

I am not at this time prepared to present hypotheses about the early environmental influences which predispose persons toward developing the traits subsumed under the E − pole. In addition to failing to uncover any solid research findings that might ex-plain this development, I have to date not discerned any trends in the reported histories among my 276 examinees whose E scores were 3 and below.

The interesting fact is that, if anything characterizes the recollections of these examinees, it is their diversity. This diver-sity was unexpected in a trait with such a small genetic compo-nent. Usually, when most of the variance of a trait is attributable to environmental influences, it is common to find similar early molding experiences in the persons who show it.

Some E − examinees described their parents as being domi-nant. Conversely, others described their parents as being as sub-missive as themselves. Still others described parents who seemed to be assertive to an average degree. Variables significant in early development, like birth order, the family's social economic status, and the child's physical stature relevant to its peers, also revealed no consistent trends relevant to E − scores in adults.

Given what I have said above, and what I will later say, about the many distinct variants of unassertive behavior reflected by E− scores, my colleagues and I are presently looking into the possibility that the diversity within my sample is actually a composite of several kinds of developmental histories, each related to a particular variant.

Important Correlations Between E− Scores and Other 16PF Factor Scores

Table 5.2 below lists the important correlations between E− scores and scores on other 16PF factors.

Table 5.2

Important Correlations Between E− Scores and Other 16PF Factor Scores

Factor Pole	Correlation	Possible Associated Traits Indicated by Correlation
H− (Threctia)	.31	Shy, Timid
F− (Desurgency)	.29	Sober, Taciturn, Serious
Q_1− (Conservatism)	.29	Conservative, Respecting Traditional Ideas
L− (Alaxia)	.24	Trusting, Accepting Conditions, Easy to Get Along With
G+ (Superego Strength)	.23	Conscientious, Conforming, Moralistic, Staid, Rule Bound
N+ (Shrewdness)	.22	Astute, Polished, Socially Aware

What becomes immediately apparent in comparing the correlations in Table 5.2 to their obverses in Table 5.1 is that, from the perspective of maintaining smoother interpersonal relations, submissive individuals should usually fare better than their dominant counterparts when this correlational pattern is present. However, further reflection on the meaning of these correlations (with the exception of N−) indicates that the pattern is at the submissive individual's expense. Here is a picture of someone who will not "buck the system," and who has a decided lack of joie de vivre. Joylessness would be suggested by the H − correlation (.31), as it indicates shyness and timidity, and the F − correlation (.29), which indicates overinhibition leading to a subdued, cautious life orientation. The correlations with Q_1 − (.29), L − (.24), and G − (.23) are, respectively, interpretable as having difficulty with change, having a trusting acceptance of prevailing conditions, and introjecting conventional values. Altogether, this pattern of factor correlations tells of a willingness to defer to cultural standards, even if they go against one's own best interest.

Clinical Relevance of E − Scores

E − scores are characteristic of the neurotic or self-defeating profile. In my clinical work, I have uncovered no fewer than five distinct variants of unassertive behavior, each being associated with E − scores and a corresponding pattern of other 16PF scores. I was surprised and gratified to find that these variants agreed remarkably well with those outlined by Bloom, Colburn, and Pearlman (1975), who labeled them as: (1) The Sufferer, (2) The Uninvolved, (3) The Saboteur, (4) The Seductress, and (5) The Wet Blanket.

Table 5.3

Sample of 276 E − Examinees Divided Into Five Variants of Unassertive Behavior*

	Number of Examinees	% of Examinees
Variant 1. The Sufferer	96	35
Variant 2. The Uninvolved	36	14
Variant 3. The Saboteur	74	26
Variant 4. The Seductress	28	10
Variant 5. The Wet Blanket	10	3
Unclassified	30	10

*Terms for these variants taken from Bloom, Colburn, and Pearlman (1975).

Though Bloom, et al., described these five variants in terms of their appearance in women, I have found that they apply equally well to men. In the descriptions that follow, I will identify them according to the rubrics found by Bloom, et al., retaining the term "seductress," for example, even though "seducer" would be more exact.

Variant 1. The Sufferer (or Good Boy/Nice Girl Style): E − (submissiveness) with G − (low moral conformity) score pattern. Another word for sufferer in this context would, of course, be "martyr." Exactly 96 (35%) of my examinees showed behavior classifying them into this variant. All showed an immature sense of morality similar to Kohlberg's (1964) "Good boy/nice girl" orientation. I shall explain in Chapter 7 (on Factor G) that examinees with this moral orientation see goodness as synonymous with socially rewarded behavior.

These examinees had a strong, sometimes unarticulated belief that human relationships should be governed by equity. In particular, they expect that their subordination of desires to the desires of others should be appreciated to a degree equal to their sacrifice. Paradoxically, often the obverse occurred. Instead of being appreciated, their self-denial had the effect of inviting others to take them for granted. In such cases, they become indignant. Their recitations of "after all I've done for you" show how carefully they have "kept count." Particularly, they were likely to settle for other people's feeling guilty, in the absence of appreciation in equity to their sacrifices.

Variant 2. The Uninvolved (or Tense, Easily Upset Style): E − (submissiveness) with C − (ego weakness) and Q_4+ (nervous tension) score pattern. The 36 tense, submissive examinees with weak egos, who exhibited this variant, made up 14% of my E − sample. Many described themselves as having a pervasive subjective feeling of "walking on egg shells," a sense supported objectively by their Q_4+ (tension) score. All admitted they greatly feared conflict, and, to avoid it, they passively allowed others to make decisions which sometimes negatively impacted their lives. Conciliators, they were quick to "smooth things over," and were much given to underevaluating, or even denying, the existence of their own wants and needs, as their weak ego strength $(C −)$ scores indicated.

However, the tension that these examinees felt often proved to be difficult to contain. It was often expressed in angry, unpredictable outbursts, e.g., slamming doors, breaking dishes, or what is popularly called "letting off steam," in the manner of Fibber McGee's closet (alluded to in the CAQ Manual). When directed towards people, these outbursts were often displacements, in which the anger was diverted from its real target, usually an authority figure, to a low-status person or someone without sufficient power to retaliate. Sadly, this was often a child. Parents I was treating, who unpremeditatedly abused their children during sudden fits of rage, fell into this variant.

Variant 3. The Saboteur (or Passive-Aggressive Style): E − *(submissive) with* L+ *(protension) score pattern.* What is described here is the well-known passive-aggressive style that is so often found in many seemingly agreeable individuals, but which is actually a manifestation of their unassertiveness. The L+ scores indicate that, underlying their unassertiveness, is social insecurity and suspiciousness. From discussions with the 74 examinees in my sample who exhibited this variant (26% of my E − examinees), I discovered the following predictable sequences linking their cognition to their behavior. (1) They assume that others would be resentful if they expressed contrary wishes and opinions. (2) Having attributed this reaction to others, they then come to see themselves as being externally restrained from expressing their feelings or doing what they want, which, in turn, makes them feel angry. (3) Afraid that their anger will be detected, they act in accordance with the expectations of these persecutors, as they are so perceived, while at the same time procrastinating, forgetting or expressing their anger in other indirect ways in the hope it will not be detected.

Often these examinees were accused of being "two-faced" when their passive-aggressive behavior was expressed in the form of obliquely obtaining the support of others by gossiping and sharing their resentment. Typically, they did this while still maintaining a noncomplaining and even a cordial front to persons about whom they complained.

Variant 4. The Seductress (or Shrewd Manipulator Style): E − *(submissiveness) with* C+ *(ego strength), and* N+ *(shrewdness) score pattern.* Here, low E scores combine submissiveness with C+ (ego strength) and N+ (high shrewdness). The 28 examinees in my sample who showed this combination (10% of the E − examinees) proved to have self-control and to be astute observers of human nature. They especially noticed ways that they might use particular situations and other people's vulnerability to their own advantage. Spurning making direct requests, they used pleasantness, sometimes flattery and compliments, to obtain favors and privileges. Rather than getting into angry exchanges, they subscribed to the philosophy "Get even, not angry."

Traditionally, this variant of submissive behavior has been seen as stereotypically feminine. Given women's lack of legitimized power through the ages, there may be some historical validity for this stereotype, especially since shrewd manipulation carries the least risk towards getting what one wants without creating disharmony. However, since inequitable power relations are not limited to traditional marriages, this variant can be present in any situation where one person is somewhat dependent on the magnanimity of another.

> *Example:* James Herriot's autobiography of his experiences as a country veterinarian in the 1930s recounts his partner Siegfried's passive but shrewd style. After overhearing Herriot's angry expletives over a client's aggressiveness, Siegfried explained how he reacted to similar situations: "After all, the people who come in here provide us with our bread and butter and they should be treated with respect.
>
> "Oh, I know some are not as nice as others but you must never let them irritate you. You've heard the old saying, 'The Customer is always right.' Well, I think it's a good working axiom and I always abide by it myself.
>
> "Well, I will let you into a little secret." His smile took on a roguish quality. "If a client is rude to me, I simply charge him a little more. Instead of getting all steamed up like you do I tell myself that I am putting ten bob on the bill and it works like magic." (p. 318-319)

Despite the example just cited, I expect this variant will be ultimately damaging in most cases, because it involves downright deception and fails to address major issues, such as the need for mutual respect in close interpersonal relationships. Some examinees combined this variant of submissive behavior with traces of passive aggression (Variant 2) and had a strong potential for entering into violent discord in their relationships. I have frequently seen these proclivities in sexual relationships where one partner was financially dependent on the other.

Variant 5. The Wet Blanket (or the Socially Jaundiced Style): E − (submissiveness) with A − (detached) and F − (pessimistic) score pattern. This variant, shown by only three examinees (10% of the sample), is characterized by low A and F scores in addition to E− scores. This triad indicates that, besides a wish to avoid conflict (E− scores), there is general coolness towards people (A− scores) and a dour, gloomy view of life (F− scores). The low A and E scores, when appearing together, indicate that the examinee is socially withdrawn and is suffering from what Karson and O'Dell (1976) describe as the "burned child" syndrome, i.e., a turning away from people because of painful childhood experiences. The appearance of F− scores with A− and E− scores reveal that this withdrawal has an abrasive quality. Thus, in contradistinction to persons exhibiting the other four styles, the examinees who showed this variant made little or no effort to be pleasant about their compliance. Not asking for what they wanted, they remained silent. If they spoke, it was generally to draw attention to a problem or to criticize the decisions or plans made by another. They failed, however, to offer any solutions or alternative course of action.

The Frustration Underlying E− Scores

The outcome, common to all of the variants (with the possible exception of #4, The Seductress or Shrewd Manipulator style) was that the examinees felt extremely vulnerable because they had to rely on others to discern their wishes. Consequently, since mind reading is a very unusual talent, they were likely to have many unmet wants and needs.

Therefore, it is not surprising, given what has been said, that Karson and O'Dell (1976) have found that E− scores are often accompanied by suicidal tendencies, especially when certain other factor scores appear. These additional factors might include F− (dourness), O+ (low self-esteem), Q_1− (lack of critical thinking), and Q_4+ (tension). While Karson and O'Dell are concerned about this pattern as a turning in of frustrations upon the self, I have focused instead on the underlying deprivation experiences. In treatment, rather than teaching clients to vent their anger, I emphasized the need (1) to correct the misbeliefs that have supported their submissiveness, and (2) to aid them in acquiring assertive behaviors, so that they can meet their needs by healthy negotiation, or can protect themselves from others' trespasses.

Alcoholics and Narcotic Addicts

Low E scores are found in group profiles of neurotics and alcoholics (Krug, 1980). The low scores in the latter group may provide some further support for the reputed passivity in those who abuse alcohol. Parenthetically, it is interesting to note that narcotic addicts, in contradistinction to alcoholics, do *not* show low scores, a finding which makes sense in view of the active lifestyle ordinarily required to maintain this expensive habit.

Chapter 6

Factor F: The Exuberant and Somber Orientations

THE CONSTRUCT
Surgency and Desurgency
The Natural and Adapted Child Dichotomy
Heredity
Male and Female Differences Throughout the Life Span

HIGH SCORES ON FACTOR F
Intrapsychic Data
Interpersonal and Social Data
F+ and Childhood
Important Correlations Between F+ Scores
and Other 16PF Factor Scores
Clinical Relevance of F+ Scores

LOW SCORES ON FACTOR F
Intrapsychic Data
Interpersonal and Social Data
F− and Childhood
Important Correlations Between F− Scores
and Other 16PF Factor Scores
Clinical Relevance of F− Scores

FACTOR F: CHARACTERISTICS OF F+ (SURGENT) AND F− (DESURGENT) EXAMINEES

Left Score F − (DESURGENCY)		Right Score F + (SURGENCY)
(Sober, Taciturn, Serious)	vs.	**(Enthusiastic, Heedless, Happy-go-lucky)**
Silent, Introspective	vs.	Talkative
Full of Cares	vs.	Cheerful
Concerned, Reflective	vs.	Happy-go-lucky
Uncommunicative, Sticks to	vs.	Frank, Expressive, Reflects
Inner Values	vs.	the Group
Slow, Cautious	vs.	Quick, Alert

THE CONSTRUCT

Surgency and Desurgency

The natural exuberance of children is curbed and sometimes extinguished by the pressures of socialization. Factor F measures the degree to which this primal exuberance persists into adulthood. Its high F + pole represents high spiritedness, insouciance, change seeking, and exhibitionism, while subduedness, caution, and self-effacement are represented by its F − pole. Interestingly, although it is the highest contributor to temperament in children and adolescents, it is only the sixth largest in adults.

Observationally, the behaviors associated with Factor F are difficult to distinguish from those of Factor A, as both sets of behaviors appear superficially as an outgoingness/withdrawal continuum of social behavior. However, underlying this apparent similarity are contrasting focuses of orientation. Factor A measures interest in people, while Factor F measures interest in self, especially in self-display. For F + scorers, people are primarily valued as audiences and sources of stimulation.

The Natural Child/Adapted Child Dichotomy

The reader familiar with Transactional Analysis may find it helpful to think of Factor F's surgent/desurgent polarities in terms of the natural child and adapted child constructs described originally by Berne (1960). Surgency (F +) corresponds with the natural child, who is exuberant and irrepressible; this manifests itself in adulthood as a happy-go-lucky, enthusiastic, and spontaneous attitude toward life. By contrast, the F− pole (desurgency) is represented by the adapted child, whose natural impulses have been inhibited through hard experience and socialization. The careful conformist is the adult version. Berne believed that whether the natural or adapted child predominates in an adult's personality largely depended upon early personal history, an idea fitting nicely with Cattell's (1973) formulation that a given score on Factor F "indicates the degree to which the examinee has succumbed to an environmental training in general inhibition."

Heredity

A certain inherent predisposition is required, however, for succumbing to environmental influences that are inhibiting, as Factor F contains an extremely strong genetic component. (The heritability coefficient here is .65.) This fact is well recognized by parents who have observed varying degrees of tractability among their children even under the same molding conditions. The psychological basis of this genetically transmitted component may be in the brain's frontal lobe, as there is some evidence that this is the locus of inhibition. Examples that support frontal lobe involvement are the increase in surgent behavior following frontal lobotomies and decreases in inhibition while drinking, as this part of the brain is affected by alcohol ingestion.

Male and Female Differences Throughout the Life Span

The means and standard deviations on Factor F are similar for both sexes (male mean = 28.40 and standard deviation = 7.45; and female mean = 26.57 and standard deviation = 7.35).

F scores for both sexes also enter into two second-order factor patterns: introversion vs. extraversion and emotionality vs. tough poise (cortertia). In their contribution to the former, F scores rank third; in the latter, each makes a similar small contribution.

Longitudinal data thus far accumulated show that F scores fluctuate differently throughout the life span of males and females. While, in childhood, females appear to be less surgent than males, their scores on Factor F increase rapidly in their mid-teens, until in their late teens, when their scores briefly peak above those of males. But, starting about the 20th year, as the scores for both sexes begin declining, they fall below male scores again. The decline in female scores plateaus around age 40, whereas, for men, the scores continue to decline steadily.

HIGH SCORES ON FACTOR F

Intrapsychic Data

The two attitude statements which my sample of F+ examinees were most likely to agree with were "do what comes naturally" and "variety is the spice of life." These attitudes were expressed in their behavior as lacking inhibitions and enjoying attention. They also expressed themselves by speaking freely and frankly about their feelings, and they actively sought out high-stimulus situations.

What was also apparent was that the thinking of these examinees was of the divergent (extensive) vs. convergent (intensive) style described by Guilford (1967). This showed itself in their conversations; they rarely got fixed on one idea but instead fluently generated new associations, discovering several ways of looking at the same thing, and moving swiftly on to the next topic. In my initial interviews, I mistook this quickness of thought for distractibility. Now, I have concluded that it is, rather, an untutored ability to "brainstorm," in the sense described by Osborn (1963), as an ability to generate ideas in quick succession while withholding censorship. (As mentioned earlier, this kind of thinking and behavior can be induced artificially by the disinhibiting effect of alcohol.)

These observations fit well with Krug (1980), who stated that exhibition and looking for change is the quintessence of surgency. Moreover, this statement agrees with self-reports of surgency that appear elsewhere in the literature, which note that F+ people say that they have more friends than most people, that they are sexually expressive, and that they enjoy parties. Their histories also often reveal that they left home early and have since moved frequently.

Because of their self-centeredness, surgent persons may appear narcissistic; but, unlike narcissim, surgency does not arise from a retreat into self after being bitterly disappointed in others. Rather, it is the vestige of the primordial condition when every child experienced itself as the center of the universe. In this regard, Cattell (1973) has judged the poet Walt Whitman as the personification of surgency. These surgent qualities are expressed in his ebullient, sensuous, optimistic, and self-absorbed poetry, as is illustrated in the following line:

I celebrate myself, and sing myself.[1]

Like children, surgent individuals can show much enthusiasm for work, providing it is of their choosing. It is understandable that they are attracted to, and do well in, jobs that require variety and excitement. For example, high scores have been found in pilots and flight attendants, sales people and managers. For my part, I have discovered F + scores in entertainers of all types, especially comedians. The three stand-up comedians my colleagues and I have tested with the 16PF all had F scores of 10.

Also understandably, Cattell (1957) reported that F + individuals do not do well in long-term undertakings, and that high F scores are somewhat negatively correlated with academic success. Based on observations of my sample of examinees, I explain these findings as being due to their tendency to quickly respond to whatever engages their interest, only to have their love of variety lead them to abandon it just as quickly, if boredom or a new interest catches their fancy. Dilettantism such as this often leads to being a "jack of all trades and master of none," and my examinees demonstrated this by commonly being good starters but poor finishers. Many were able to point to a large trail of unfinished projects as well as a history of a series of ever-changing, all-consuming passions. Among one's acquaintances and in everyday life, F + individuals are often recognizable as the faddists who are perennially involved in a series of new and ever-changing interests.

Since ego weakness (C −) is also frequently manifested as a failure to stay with undertakings, it is not surprising that F + (surgency) is sometimes confused with this trait. The difference is that, in the case of a weak ego, such failures are usually due to a low frustration tolerance. By contrast, in surgency, they are

---

[1]Walt Whitman (1959). In J. E. Miller (Ed.), *Complete Poetry and Selected Prose*. Boston: Houghton Mifflin.

due to a divergent thinking style. In other words, the interests of F + people are associative and therefore not deeply penetrating; it is no wonder they fade quickly. Perseverance requires a working against the F + person's natural inclinations. It also requires a heavy drawing on at least one of the intrapsychic controls: C + (ego strength), G + (superego), or Q_3 + (self-sentiment). My examinees who showed low scores on these factors as well as F + scores, consistently reported difficulty in controlling their behavior.

Interpersonal and Social Data

Because they enjoy attention, have a quick sense of humor, and are at ease in conversation, F + individuals are sought out as persons with whom to have fun and to play. They are usually quite entertaining, but may wear thin the patience of others by their constant insistence on being center stage. Also, there is a limit to the number of ideas they, like all human beings, can generate.

F + people's liking for change and variety frequently shows itself in their romantic relationships. They fall easily and ardently in love, but depart when the novelty fades. This is probably why they are inclined to bachelorhood and to marry later than F − (desurgent) people. Even if married, they are apt to behave independently and have more outside contacts and activities that exclude partners. Clinicians often see their jilted lovers, who seek treatment because they are hurt and bewildered by their F + partner's seemingly inexplicable way of falling out of love. Clinicians also often see the current lovers of F + people; these partners are bewildered because they get so little real emotional nurturance from these seemingly warm and outgoing persons. Usually, it is only in retrospect that it is remembered that he or she was a much better talker than listener, and far more able to receive attention than give it.

The capacity of F + people for meteoric relationships is revealed, not only in their romances, but in all kinds of other relationships as well. Many of the F + examinees in my sample were known for their swift and usually vivid entrances into the lives of their acquaintances; these entrances were often matched by equally vivid departures. It was not unusual for them to completely drop out of sight and not keep in touch with their former best friends.

The observations just delineated owe much to the 78 examinees in my sample who had F scores of 8 or above but only low or moderate A+ scores, so that I was able to see F+ (surgency) in its unadulterated form. Fortunately, these examinees are in a minority, since in the general population F+ and A+ scores are correlated. So, it is common for the F+ person's natural self-centeredness to be somewhat tempered by genuinely warm social interest.

In an F+ profile that has low A scores but pronounced Q_2- (group dependency) scores, the test interpreter can be reasonably sure that, though outgoing, the examinee can be extremely self-serving. Not only is he or she basically cool, but the Q_2- scores indicate a strong need for support and the need for the reassuring presence of others, rather than indicating a genuine need for attachment. In such instances, F+ persons can be extremely seductive, as others may misperceive their behavior as A+ behavior (i.e., warmth and caring). Yet it is not necessarily true that these persons misrepresent themselves. Most of my F+ examinees gave little self-analysis to their motives. They were unaware of the personal needs that motivated their social behavior, and thought of themselves as much more warmly oriented to people than they indeed were.

F+ and Childhood

The research evidence is that high scorers on the F scale, relative to their low-scoring counterparts, were as children either overindulged or subjected to fewer social inhibitions (Barton, Dielman, & Cattell, 1973). This finding was further supported by the self-reports of my F+ examinees, although some also reported that they had been pressured to be socially inhibited, but resisted these pressures.

My direct observations of F+ children are generally limited to counseling teachers, who sought advice on how to control these children in classroom situations. (These observations were not actually included in my sample.) In looking into the reinforcement contingencies regarding their behavior, I discovered that the classmates of these F+ classroom clowns enjoyed the diversion from routine that they provided, giving them enough mirthful attention to offset their other, negative responses. Actually, F+ children are often regarded with contempt by their peers who label them as "show offs" and accuse them of "hogging the show."

Sometimes F+ children who were brought to my attention were incorrectly thought to be hyperactive. However, F+ (surgent) behavior is quite different from hyperactive behavior, as the latter comes from an attempt to relieve tension rather than to focus attention on oneself. This latter quality is actually measured by Factor D, excitability (Cattell, H., Tomakawa, S. A., DeRega, F., & Cattell, R. B., 1985). Excitability as a factor is found only in children and adolescents, but not usually in adults, unless they are showing pathological manic behavior. Factor D is described in more detail in the *Children's Personality Questionnaire Handbook* (1985) and the *Manual and Norms for the High School Personality Questionnaire* (1984).

Important Correlations Between F+ Scores and Other 16PF Factor Scores

Table 6.1

Important Correlations Between F+ Scores and Other 16PF Factor Scores

Factor Pole	Correlation	Possible Associated Traits Indicated by Correlation
H+ (Parmia)	.45	Bold, Venturesome, Uninhibited
Q_2 – (Group Dependence)	.36	Group Dependent, A "Joiner" and Sound Follower
A+ (Affectothymia)	.31	Outgoing, Warmhearted, Easy Going, Participating
E+ (Dominance)	.29	Aggressive, Stubborn, Competitive
N – (Artlessness)	.22	Forthright, Unpretentious, Genuine but Socially Clumsy

Table 6.1 presents five correlations that include three with factor poles that combine with surgency to make up the second-order extraversion factor. High scores on Factor F are correlated with H+ scores (.45), with Q_2 – scores (.36), and with A+ scores (.31). F+ persons, therefore, are often extraverts. This means that, besides being surgent, they are also likely to be bold and thickskinned (H+), dependent on the support and presence of

others (Q_2-), and warmly sociable ($A+$). The other correlations, which do not enter into this extraversion pattern, are with $E+$ scores (.29) and $N-$ scores (.22). These additional correlations suggest some tendency towards dominance and outspokenness.

When this entire pattern is met, the person that is portrayed here is someone most people will recognize. He or she is often described as "the life of the party." Psychotherapists often like to include one or two of them in therapy groups to vitalize the process, despite their tendency to monopolize sessions and draw attention to themselves.

Clinical Relevance of F+ Scores

Some clinical associations have been established for surgency. The most clinically significant is that $F+$ scores, in combination with certain other 16PF factor scores (which will be discussed later), indicate that conflicts are likely to be externalized (Krug, 1980). Krug's statement is empirically supported by the correlation of $F+$ scores with D_3- (agitated depression) and P_p+ (sociopathic deviation), in the Clinical Analysis Questionnaire. $F+$ scores are also routinely found in persons suffering from hysterical disorders, especially when conversion symptoms are involved. I anticipate that they would also be found in manic depressives, if they were tested during the manic phase of the disorder.

Also clinically significant is Karson and O'Dell's (1976) proposition that $F+$ persons are inadequately socialized. This proposition is somewhat supported by the research of Pumfrey and Ward (1971), who found $F+$ scores in adults and youngsters who violate society's norms and rules. However, in the 16PF analyses I have conducted so far, I have found that I am only able to predict asocial kinds of behavior in those examinees who, in addition to $F+$ scores, had low scores on at least two of the three self-control factors: C (ego strength), G (superego), or Q_3 (self-sentiment). Over time, I found that examinees who did not have normal-to-high scores on at least one of these factors were like fast cars without brakes, for they had no way of halting their exuberance, and so ultimately landed in trouble.

At the very least, examinees whose F score is 8 or above should be considered as having a potentially unreliable or flighty side to them, even if other control factors are average or above average in magnitude. Moreover, since the scores are referenced upon a mean age of 30, and since scores usually decline with age, the older the examinee, the higher this potential.

LOW SCORES ON FACTOR F

Intrapsychic Data

Cattell (1957) suggested the "dour Scot"—serious, cautious, taciturn, respectable, somewhat colorless, and with a wry sense of humor (if he or she has one at all)—as the caricature of the person scoring at the low pole of Factor F, the essence of which he views as "a sobering inhibition formed by experiences of punishment and failure."

Desurgency is not so much a retreat into self as it is a cautious life orientation. Subjectively, it is felt as an anticipation of difficulties, fear of making mistakes, and hesitancy to take risks, explaining perhaps why F− individuals are late to leave home as young adults and why, throughout their lives, they move less often than their F+ counterparts. Customarily, my F− examinees perceived their cautiousness as a sign of their good adaptation or ego strength, as would be measured by C+ scores. They are mistaken in this perception, since it does not arise from the realistic prudence based on responsiveness to discrimination cues that C+ examinees show, but is based on pessimistic distortions and a general inhibition of spontaneity and liveliness.

Usually, F− examinees recognized their inhibition and, when it led them to behave in accordance with conventional moral standards, interpreted this aspect of their desurgency as good superego control. However, here too they were mistaken. The well-developed superego inhibits behavior to avoid internal moral censure, while desurgent inhibition is rooted in fearful adaptation to the environment. In the following chapter, which describes Kohlberg's developmental model of moral behavior, it will be proposed that desurgency may probably best be viewed as avoidance of punishment, which is a primitive form (Stage 2) of moral development.

Other observations of my examinees confirmed that these persons are not only careful in speech and behavior, but in their thinking processes also. In contradistinction to their surgent counterparts, they do not generate associations fluently and rapidly. Instead, they move from thought to thought ponderously, critically, checking and rechecking for possible mistakes. It is not surprising, therefore, that F− scores appear in group profiles of scientists of all kinds, including biologists, physicists, geologists—all occupations that require careful, plodding mental work. Since the thinking of F− persons is deep, it can be extremely creative when combined with superior intelligence. Cattell (1973) cited Darwin as someone who showed this combination of qualities. Other occupational profiles that show F− scores are for artists, employment counselors, clergy, engineers, psychiatric technicians, janitors, kitchen workers, machine operators, mid-level managers, plant foremen, education administrators, university administrators, and university professors.

Although I discovered that a combination of F− and B+ scores on a profile reliably predicted an examinee's intellectual success, he or she typically had a restricted range of interest. But what that person lacked in range he or she usually made up for in depth.

> *Example:* Studs Terkel, in his book *Working,* interviewed a 57-year-old stonemason who had steadily pursued his craft since he was 17. After lengthy discussion about stone, its variations and uses, and the history of stonemasonry since prehistoric times, the stonemason said: "Stone is my life. I daydream all the time, most times it's on stone." Later he described his concentration on his work. "If I got some problem that's bothering me, I'll actually wake up in the night and think about it. I'll sit at the table and get a pencil and paper and go over it, makin' marks on paper or drawin' or however . . . this way or that way." (pp. 17-22)

Comments about knowing "more and more about less and less" are probably based on such extreme examples of F− (desurgent) behavior. F− people report that they find little to talk about in situations that call for general conversation, and that they often feel ill at ease in social gatherings for precisely this reason, although they are not necessarily shy.

Interpersonal and Social Data

Role relationship is an important variable in deciding whether F− persons are appreciated or depreciated. For example, they are likely to be appreciated by supervisors because they are usually responsible and take their work seriously. On the other hand, they do not seem to be appreciated as leaders, as can be surmised by the infrequency with which they are elected to leadership roles (Cattell & Stice, 1960).

One study that catches the ambivalence that others feel toward F− behavior demonstrated that military officers with F− scores received high ratings for their effectiveness from superiors and officers alike, but were not rated as good battle companions. The reason for the latter rating, one can surmise, is that they lack cheerfulness, a sense of humor and conversational skills, all of which would heighten the morale of their fellow soldiers.

I have noted that, in more ordinary social situations, F− examinees were often the proverbial wet blankets, seldom laughing and talking, yet quick to notice what could go wrong. They are not the types most people would enjoy meeting at a party. One group therapist complained that, at one time, she had the misfortune of having six of a seven-member therapy group with F− scores of 3 or less. Eliciting responses from them was some of the most exhausting clinical work she had ever done. It took several months for her to be persuaded to run another series of groups.

Because of the complexity of the marriage relationship, I have noted F− persons tend to elicit substantial amounts of intrapsychic conflict in their spouses. In counseling situations, the spouses commonly express appreciation for their F− partners' seriousness and careful handling of the couple's affairs, while resenting the sense of heaviness, even gloominess, which so often accompanies it. It is not uncommon for these spouses to find outside sources for fun and entertainment, not necessarily of a sexual nature, while at the same time feeling guilty for feeling bored with their "good" man or woman.

F− and Childhood

F− children are not favorites among peers, and are rated as secretive and daydreamers. They are prone to nailbiting (Guinouard & Rychlak, 1962), which may be a reaction to the stress of the childhood socialization process, since there is evidence that these children come from strict homes and have been disproportionately exposed to such harsh realities as chronic illnesses and unfavorable childhood conditions (Cattell, 1972).

I have had several opportunities to directly observe children I knew to have F− scores. Superficially, their demeanor was difficult to tell apart from the social aloofness shown by A− (sizothymic) children or the diffidence shown by H− (threctic) children. But, on closer analysis, I invariably uncovered that, under their subdued and quiet manner, was a very sober orientation to life. This was true regardless of whether they came from functional or dysfunctional families. Unless teachers and parents worried that they were "too quiet," they were often referred to as "the one we don't have to worry about," as these children did not get involved in the kinds of exploits and adventures that more spirited children got into.

Of course, to dismiss the behavior of an F − child so cursorily is a mistake. In my sample, F − adults who had formerly been desurgent children usually recalled that they had deep feelings which they did not usually discuss with others. They also felt that they had had to cope with realities that were too advanced for their years.

F − scores correlate significantly with all of the seven depression poles of the Clinical Analysis Questionnaire (CAQ) scales except for D_3 (agitated depression). D_3 measures an "acting out" form of depression which, as I mentioned earlier, correlates with F + scores. F − scores also correlate with the right pole of the Ps scale (psychological inadequacy) of the CAQ. This scale measures a sense of hopelessness and helplessness which is often involved in psychoticism as well as depression.

Thus, although desurgency is not in itself depression, the quietness and seriousness of F − clients is apt to be initially misinterpreted as a sign of depression, even by clinicians. Clinicians may also interpret the thinking style of these persons as being obsessional because of their narrow concentration. However, upon careful listening, it is possible to distinguish between these two styles, as F − (desurgency) lacks the "broken record" repetitiveness characteristic of obsessional thinking.

Important Correlations Between F − Scores and Other 16PF Scores

The factors shown in Table 6.2 to correlate with Factor F − all relate to the second-order Introversion factor. F − persons, therefore, are often introverts, just as their F + counterparts are often extraverts. In other words, F − scorers can also be timid, self-sufficient, and reserved, as well as serious and quiet. The two remaining correlations in Table 6.2 are with E − scores (.29) indicating unassertiveness, and N + scores (.22) indicating tactfulness and forethought in responding to others. The picture that arises of the examinee whose profile shows all five of these correlations in addition to F − scores, is of a socially aloof and self-reliant individual who has limited involvement with others, but who takes care not to be socially offensive.

Table 6.2

Important Correlations Between F− Scores and Other 16PF Factor Scores

Factor Pole	Correlation	Possible Associated Traits Indicated by Correlation
H− (Threctia)	.45	Shy, Timid, Threat Sensitive
Q_2+ (Self-sufficiency)	.36	Self-sufficient, Resourceful, Prefers Own Decisions
A− (Sizothymia)	.31	Reserved, Detached, Critical, Aloof, Stiff
E− (Submissiveness)	.29	Humble, Mild, Easily Led, Docile, Accommodating
N+ (Shrewdness)	.22	Shrewd, Polished, Socially Aware, Calculating

Clinical Relevance of F− Scores

Desurgent clients without any diagnosable psychopathology are often seen in clinical practice. It is usual for them to seek treatment, complaining that they "can't loosen up and have fun" or they "take everything too seriously." When treatment is successful, it is rewarding to see these persons begin to enjoy themselves and to witness the visible rejuvenation that occurs in their faces and body postures.

In this regard, however, I must stress one crucial point. Before proceeding to modify F− (desurgent) behavior, clinicians need to consider, not only the client's F scores, but also the C (ego strength), G (superego strength), and Q_3 (self-sentiment strength) scores also. When a client's scores on these self-control measures are low, it is certain that he or she is relying on F− behavior, and is displaying a cautious, pessimistic outlook, to keep out of trouble. Consequently, it is most important that at least one of these other agencies of control (the ego, superego, or self-sentiment) is able to restrain rash behavior, before introducing any disinhibiting strategies into the treatment. Irreverent remarks about psychological treatment turning neurotics into sociopaths are probably referring to instances in which this consideration was neglected.

Chapter 7

Factor G: The Content and Action of Moral Values

THE CONSTRUCT

The Superego

Guilt

Origin of the Superego

The Superego's Progressive Reorganizations:
Piaget and Kohlberg

Congruence Between Factor G and Kohlberg's Fourth
and Fifth Stages of Moral Development

Superego in Action: Conscience and Conscientiousness

Heredity

Male and Female Differences Throughout the Life Span

Summary

HIGH SCORES ON FACTOR G

G+ Scores and Motivational Distortion

Intrapsychic Data

Interpersonal and Social Data

G+ and Childhood

Important Correlations Between G+ Scores
and Other 16PF Factor Scores

Clinical Relevance of G+ Scores

LOW SCORES ON FACTOR G

Important Correlations Between G- Scores
and Other 16PF Factor Scores

G- Scores and Variants of Superego Development

G- Scores and Motivational Distortion (Faking Bad)

FACTOR G: CHARACTERISTICS OF G + (SUPEREGO STRENGTH) AND G – (LOW SUPEREGO) EXAMINEES

Left Score G – (LOW SUPEREGO STRENGTH OR LACK OF ACCEPTANCE OF GROUP MORAL STANDARDS)		Right Score G + (SUPEREGO STRENGTH OF CHARACTER)
(Disregards Rules, Expedient)	vs.	**(Conscientious, Persistent, Moralistic, Staid)**
Quitting, Fickle	vs.	Persevering, Determined
Frivolous	vs.	Responsible
Self-indulgent	vs.	Emotionally Disciplined
Undependable	vs.	Conscientious, Dominated by Sense of Duty
Disregards Obligations to People	vs.	Concerned about Moral Standards and Rules

THE CONSTRUCT

The Superego

Krug (1980) and Karson and O'Dell (1976) both call this factor "conformity," focusing on its alignment with conventional moral standards. I reject this label as being not sufficiently comprehensive, preferring, like Cattell, to call it superego, after the Freudian construct by that name, even though further multivariate experimental research is needed to show, conclusively, exactly how well these two constructs match.

Meanwhile, however, my less formal clinical observational methods have convinced me that Factor G represents a construct similar to the Freudian superego, as it measures an internalized set of rules which has both *content* and *action*. Its content is made up of cultural mainstream values.

With only ideational content, the superego would remain passive—a mere museum of intellectually endorsed ideals. Its ideals, however, achieve *action* when they powerfully restrain self-satisfying impulses, or put duty before personal gain. In this *action,* it resembles an omnipresent overseer, dispensing disapproval whenever its rules are broken and approval when its rules are followed.

Guilt

Guilt is the normal response to the superego's disapproval. Though the dictionary defines guilt as an act or state rather than a feeling, numerous clinical examples, as well as my own personal introspections, place me on the side of the popular view that guilt also refers to a feeling. This feeling occurs specifically in recognition of one's wrongdoings, and can easily be differentiated from neighboring feelings such as shame and self-doubt.

However, despite their close association, guilt does not reside in Factor G, but is tapped by the high $(O+)$ pole of Factor O (guilt proneness). This pole, as shall be discussed in Chapter 13, reflects, not only the negative feelings people have about themselves in regard to their culpability, but the full spectrum of their negative self-evaluations about their competence, worthiness, and social value. The relationship between Factors G and O is shown in Diagram 7.1 below.

Origin of the Superego

According to psychoanalysis, the superego comes into being as a result of incorporating outside agents. Internalization is the technical term that describes this psychological phenomenon, which evolves from the innate proclivity to identify with other humans who are admired or who have authority over us.

Also, according to psychoanalysis, the original content of the superego forms between the child's third and sixth year, when the child identifies with its opposite-sexed parent in order to resolve its Oedipal conflict. In identifying with the parent, the child introjects the parent's values and makes them his or her own. If this is so, it is fortunate for the moral progress of humankind, as Cameron (1963) observes, that superego contents do not generally stay fixed at that time, for this early identification and introjection is based then on whatever the child *perceives* as his or her parent's prevailing attitudes towards good and bad and such trivial matters as cleanliness, freedom from accidents, care of furniture, toilet habits, and learning correct procedures. And even when the focus of the parents' concerns are more sophisticated, the child's ability to reason is limited, leading to distortions

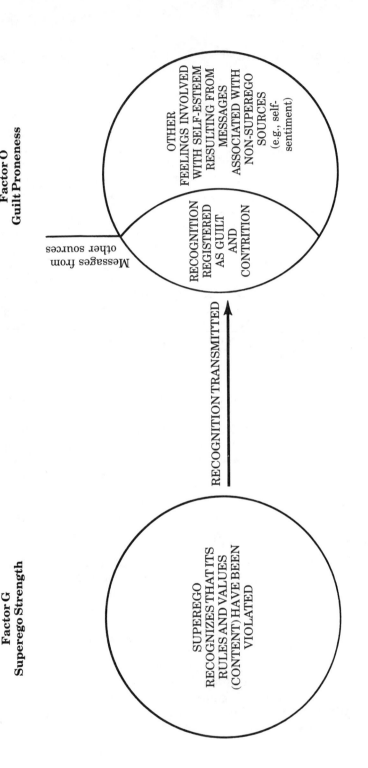

Factor O
Guilt Proneness

OTHER FEELINGS INVOLVED WITH SELF-ESTEEM RESULTING FROM MESSAGES ASSOCIATED WITH NON-SUPEREGO SOURCES (e.g., self-sentiment)

RECOGNITION REGISTERED AS GUILT AND CONTRITION

Messages from other sources

RECOGNITION TRANSMITTED

Factor G
Superego Strength

SUPEREGO RECOGNIZES THAT ITS RULES AND VALUES (CONTENT) HAVE BEEN VIOLATED

Diagram 7.1. Relationship Between Factors G and O

and misinterpretations. Moreover, as Cameron also observes, parents, being neither impeccable nor infallible, impart their own idiosyncratic biases as well as cultural wisdom.

The Superego's Progressive Reorganizations: Piaget and Kohlberg

When moral development proceeds normally, the superego does not stay fixed in childhood, but instead undergoes progressive reorganizations in which outmoded notions are discarded, as more abstract values become incorporated. These progressive reorganizations have been extensively studied by two psychologists. The first was Piaget, who, in his groundbreaking book *The Moral Judgement of the Child* (1965), reported his conclusions that moral development begins with an interaction between the human organism's native structure and universal structure; it then progresses to higher levels where the child solves moral dilemmas that it had been unable to solve at lower levels.

Kohlberg is the second psychologist to study this progressive reorganization.[1] Elaborating and extending Piaget's observations, Kohlberg (1964) delineated the following seven states of moral development, each one of which builds on the preceding one.

Stage 1. Hedonistic Orientation. Good is defined as what is liked and wanted.

---

[1] Kohlberg's method of assessing the level of moral reasoning is to present stories embodying various moral dilemmas and examine the child's reasoning about them. One of the most well known of these stories is presented below:

> A woman near death needed a drug that a local pharmacist had recently discovered. It had been expensive for the druggist to make, but he was charging for the drug at a substantially higher price than it had cost him to make the drug. The woman's husband, after trying desperately to raise the money from friends and acquaintances, could only get together a fraction of what the pharmacist was charging for the drug. The husband pleaded with the druggist to allow him to pay later, or to sell the drug cheaper, as his wife was dying. But the druggist insisted on getting all of the money up front, saying that he had discovered the drug through his own efforts and thus was entitled to the money from it. So the man became desperate and broke into the pharmacy to steal the drug for his wife. Here, the moral dilemma is whether the husband should have broken into the store to steal the drug for his wife? (Longstreth, 1974).

Stage 2. Punishment/Obedience Orientation. Goodness is equated with avoidance of punishment by unquestioned obedience to authority.

Stage 3. Naively Egoistic Orientation. Goodness is obtaining rewards by equitable exchange of favors.

Stage 4. Law and Order Orientation. Goodness is conformity to established social order for its own sake and also to avoid censure.

Stage 5. Contractual Legal Orientation. Goodness is concern for social welfare by accepting democratically arrived at individual rights.

Stage 6. Principle Orientation. Goodness is defined by broader universal principles.

Stage 7. Cosmic or Infinite Orientation. Goodness is fulfilling one's purpose in the universe by furthering what is in the best interest of the cosmos.

The stages set out above involve a progression wherein concerns shift from immediate authority figures, usually parents or parent surrogates, to nonpersonal abstractions. In this sense, the stages reflect an ever-expanding set of references, flowing from the original parent-child relationship to a wider immediate social circle, and then, finally, to the cosmos as a whole. They can also be seen, motivationally, to be shifting away from conformity out of fear of punishment or out of social reward-seeking and shifting toward virtue as its own reward.

Congruence Between Factor G and Kohlberg's Fourth and Fifth Stages of Moral Development

I am not ready to completely accept Kohlberg's stages as pure superego representations, as I suspect that a factor analysis would reveal that they contain elements of Factor Q_3 (self-sentiment). However, as it is clear that States 4 and 5 are congruent with the ideals of the constitutional politico-legal system of the United States, I accept these two as generally corresponding to the same form of conventional morality measured by Factor G. This factor, however, contains, in addition, various remnants of the Protestant Puritan ethic, such as a belief in the virtue of hard work. Stated differently, the Factor G scale taps the content of only one of several sets of superego values, but it is the one endorsed by the majority of Americans and northern Europeans. There are other superego values which the G scale does not tap, as shall be illustrated later.

The Superego in Action:
Conscience and Conscientiousness

Having delineated its *contents,* let us now consider what the G scale reveals about how the contents take active form. Here, I start by saying that, on this point, I part company with the psychoanalytic position, which proposes that the superego's contents are transformed into an image of an ideal self, which then calls forth guilt whenever behavior is either incongruent with this image, or is in danger of becoming so. The basis of my rejections is that investigations of the 16PF factors, including my own, have found that the ideal self dwells in the camp of Factor Q_3 (self-sentiment) and not in the superego, as psychoanalysis proposes. Instead, I believe that the active side of the superego is simply a drive. This explanation is based on evidence from Motivation Analysis Test and 16PF correlational research, which has consistently shown that the superego has a dynamic property with both conscious and unconscious roots. Consequently, the superego motivates persons as do other drives, such as sex, hunger, and parental protectiveness. Moreover, like other drives, it is experienced subjectively by (*a*) its magnitude and (*b*) degree of conflict with other drives.

As Cameron (1963) notes, the actions of the superego are well known and referred to in everyday language as conscience and conscientiousness. Its first action, conscience, as Cattell (1973) points out, has been referred to since antiquity, beginning with the Hebrew prophets and the Greek dramatists. By definition a conscious experience, conscience is felt when superego contents, as manifested in our moral values, come into conflict with other incompatible personality elements, usually hedonistic desires. We then experience an inner demand to resolve the conflict by rejecting these desires.

Conscientiousness, which is the other superego action, is less keenly felt, maybe scarcely noticed. Here, rather than being oppositional, the superego leads and guides behavior. In this form it has received less attention than conscience, precisely because it lacks the drama and poignancy of a moral choice.

Heredity

The heritability component of Factor G is low (.12), which means that most of the superego's development is due to exposure to environmental conditions.

Male and Female Differences Throughout the Life Span

In both sexes, Factor G has strikingly similar standard deviations (men, 5.78; women, 5.61) and means (men, 26.88; women, 26.44). Also, in both sexes, G scores show similar increases with age. These increases, however, follow a somewhat different pattern, indicating that, in men, superego strength accelerates after 20, reaches its peak at 40, and remains consistent thereafter; whereas, with women, the peak is reached earlier.

These statistical data, indicating, as they do, similarities between male and female superegos, appear contrary to the findings of naturalistic studies which indicate moral development proceeds differently for each sex. These studies begin with Freud (1946) and were continued by Piaget (1965) and Kohlberg and Cramer (1969), and more recently, and probably most compellingly, by Gilligan (1982). Gilligan and her coworkers investigated, in a series of well-conceived and carefully conducted interview studies, the relationship between moral reasoning and resolving moral conflicts, as related to making personal choices like having an abortion. Her findings led her to agree with earlier theorists that males arrive at adulthood with a more acute legal, contractual sense than females, who emphasize context rather than formal rules and abstract definitions of justice in resolving moral dilemmas. She did not see the quality of one form of moral reasoning superior to the other but, rather, as different but equally satisfactory ways of reaching conclusions.

At first glance, therefore, it seems that these sex differences might be reflected by a higher ratio of males than females obtaining mid-range or high scores on Factor G, since, as noted earlier, it measures a legalistic contractual moral code which goes more easily with men's rather than women's moral reasoning. However, this congruence does not occur, and in explaining this fact, it should be remembered that Factor G reveals only orientation and not the actual reasoning that underlies it. For example, although equal numbers of men and women report that they would feel compelled to intervene in potentially violent disputes between their neighbors, their reasons may be quite different.

Summary

Before continuing to a discussion of the factor poles, I will conclude this section by summarizing my theory of Factor G with the following six points.

1) The basic trait Factor G targets correspond structurally to the Freudian superego, for it has action as well as content.

2) The superego's action restrains and prompts certain kinds of behavior; it is subjectively experienced as conscientiousness and as conscience.

3) As an internalized set of moral ideas, the content of the superego as measured by Factor G seems to approximate Kohlberg's fourth and fifth stages of moral development, as well as incorporating elements of the Protestant ethic.

4) Therefore, it measures those ideals and moral principles endorsed by the majority of people in contemporary American and northern European culture.

5) Males and females score similarly on Factor G, indicating that both sexes endorse the same moral ideals, even though their underlying styles of moral reasoning may be somewhat different.

6) There are other moral systems which are not tapped by Factor G. Thus, examinees with other moral systems may obtain low G scores, as psychometrically they are being compared to persons who endorse mainstream cultural ideals.

HIGH SCORES ON FACTOR G

G+ Scores and Motivational Distortion

Because they represent the ideal virtues of our culture, scale items for Factor G are thought to be susceptible to faking, i.e., motivational distortion, by persons who have something to gain by presenting an impression of themselves as being more conventionally moral than they really are.

> *Example:* The 16PF was administered to a group of 12 prisoners as part of a screening procedure to determine their suitability for release from prison into a highly desirable, low security, treatment community. The prison psychologist was puzzled to find that every one of these men—all of whom had extensive histories of antisocial behavior—achieved Factor G scores of 9 or 10. Only later did he discover that the test administrator allowed the men to take the test in their respective cells, where the G scale items were answered by a committee of cellmates. This occurrence was before inclusion of the faking scales into the 16PF scoring format.

Karson and O'Dell (1976) go into the motivational distortion problem in some depth, pointing out the resemblance of Factor G scale items to the lie scale items on the MMPI. The MMPI lie scale items present such inordinately high, even superhuman, moral standards that persons who positively endorse a substantial number of them can be strongly suspected of misrepresenting their behavior.

The conclusion reached by Karson and O'Dell is that, as with the MMPI lie scale, it would be rare to find anyone but professional moralists, e.g., clergy, obtaining high G score by telling the truth. If one follows this line of reasoning, G + scores should be considered cheating scores. However, my experience leads me to disagree. I found, in my data, 90 instances of examinees who scored 8, 9, or 10 on the G scale. These people had no reason to fake their responses, and their behavior was entirely congruent with what they reported about themselves.

The discussion that follows is based largely on what I learned from these examinees, since I regard their extreme G + scores as truly reflecting their underlying moral dispositions.

Intrapsychic Data

Let me stress that the felt presence of the superego as an internal agency of control is not limited to those who obtain high G scores; it is also felt in some form and to some degree by those who have moderate and even low scores, even though the latter are responding to different sets of moral values than the G + person.

Conscience, which, as I have already said, is the superego's most conscious manifestation, is experienced as passage from passivity into activity and has been likened by Cameron (1963) to a sleeping giant which awakens from its sleep whenever its rules are about to be violated. He writes:

> It feels almost as if a wise, more mature, righteous personage had been awakened to judge us, or approve or criticize, to dictate how we ought to act or speak or think. Once the conflict of interest has been settled and after an approved choice has been made, the righteous giant seems to go to sleep again. (p. 197)

Contrary to what I had initially supposed, my G + examinees said that they rarely felt the giant awake. Upon examining their behavior, I have concluded that this is probably because it rests secure in the knowledge that there is little danger of its rules being violated, for these examinees reported having little conflict. For them, major battles had been fought and won and their superegos coexisted comfortably with old enemies who had either been transformed and rehabilitated (sublimation) or enemies securely impressed in the deep dungeons of their psyches (repression).

Conscientiousness, rather than an activated conscience, turned out to be the hallmark of my G+ examinees. If conscience is felt as the giant's accusations, conscientiousness is felt as adaptation to its presence. That this adaptation is usually felicitous is supported by the negative correlation between G+ scores and the 16PF second-order anxiety pattern, especially with Factor Q_4 (emotional tension) scores.

From our discussions, I have concluded that these examinees experienced their conscientiousness as a heightened awareness of whatever is conventionally considered good or bad. Their interests were strongly drawn to moral concerns, and their actions were close to being unquestioning responses to the dictates of their internalized moral ideals. Unlike persons with strong egos (the C+ scorers discussed in Chapter 4, whose actions were based on their assessments of consequences), for G+ people, moral absolutes provided the guide for their behavior. In instances when their behavior was not completely in accord with these moral absolutes, or when the validity of their beliefs was brought into question, I noted that they were apt to rationalize. This relation between superego strength and rationalization is what Cattell and Wenig (1952) also discovered in their study on predicting defense mechanism preferences from 16PF traits.

Interpersonal and Social Data

Their inner insistence on conforming to conventional moral standards makes G+ individuals the kind of people Karson and O'Dell (1976) propose that one likes to hire for responsible jobs. In addition to being responsible, they are usually high achievers, sometimes overachievers. This is reflected in the fact that G+ scores have the highest correlation with academic and work-related achievement of any trait after intelligence (Rothman & Flowers, 1970; Cattell & Butcher, 1968; Barton, Dielman, & Cattell, 1972). Other research shows that high scores are found among accountants, airline pilots, flight attendants, mechanics, judges, nurses, pharmacists, police officers, fire fighters, musicians, time-study engineers, business executives, and all other careers requiring either self-discipline and/or precision.

Given what has been said so far, what initially seemed paradoxical was my finding that others' reactions to G+ examinees were mixed and sometimes extraordinarily complex. In unraveling these reactions to my examinees, I discovered that persons with strong superegos are often viewed as parent figures, thereby evoking some of the ambivalences that were once felt toward parents. I see these ambivalences as being rooted in the dual role parents play, as both nurturing and controlling figures, and in the nature of human beings to welcome nurturing but to resent control. Strong-superegoed persons fit the projection of nurturing parents because their sense of duty causes them to sacrifice their time and money for the welfare of others. Not surprisingly, therefore, my G+ examinees were sought out by others in times of trouble. To the perpetually troubled, their support was often indispensable. The fly in the ointment was that, although they might be appreciated in moments of panic or distress by more ordinary persons whose troubles are sporadic, they were found stodgy and boring once the crisis was over.

Interpersonal control was the other parental trait others tended to mistakenly attribute to my G+ examinees. The truth is that persons with strong superegos often do not wish to assert more interpersonal control than other persons in the general population. (In fact, Factor G is negatively correlated with Factor E.) This misperception was probably due to their modeling of what is virtuous and noble in our society, against which less conventionally moral persons find themselves measuring their shortcomings and then attempting to behave in ways that make the discrepancies less obvious. This phenomenon is easily observable at social gatherings when clergy or other custodians of public morals are present. On these occasions, persons self-censure their remarks and show other signs of being constrained by the external circumstances. Even clinicians may recognize something similar in their own behavior when working with clients who have strong superegos, since these parental-type projections may intrude as countertransferences.

Example: A psychiatric intern who had worked well with other clients assigned to him reported that he felt uncomfortable in working with a particular client whose score on Factor G turned out to be 9. The intern reported that he continuously sought this client's approval throughout the therapeutic sessions and that he "felt small" in relationship to him, even though both were of the same age and stature.

In regard to their romantic alliances, I found that a disproportionate number of G+ examinees in my sample had formed symbiotic unions with persons who possess none of their virtues but, rather, who possess their conspicuously absent vices, such as irresponsibility. I have found this phenomenon occurring in examinees whose socially reprehensible, albeit human, qualities I suspected were repressed rather than sublimated. This is similar to the Jungian "Shadow," where the renounced becomes a disowned but fascinating preoccupation.

The relationships formed in these instances were either based on rescuing or persecuting, though in the G+ person's mind they were thought to be helpful. The 23 relationships I have found to date and have classified as this type involved G− men and G+ women and never vice versa. All these strong, moralistic women were involved with irresponsible and morally immature men whom they tried unsuccessfully to reform.

> *Example:* Kiley (1983) cleverly notes that Peter Pan, the boy who refuses to grow up, and Wendy, the woman who seems always to have been an adult, are the fictional equivalents of the real-life strongly superegoed woman and irresponsible man combination. In J. M. Barrie's original story,[2] Peter Pan cavorts with his friends in never-never land and seems free of the restraint of conscience and convention. Wendy continuously and unsuccessfully tries to reform him by reprimands and by playing a protective mother figure. Practically all marriage counselors will recognize this couple among their clientele.[3]

I have consistently observed that the most harmonious unions for my G+ examinees were undoubtedly with persons with similar scores. Although these couples may not have much fun, they show deep mutual understanding and respect.

---

[2]Barrie, J. M. (1978). *Peter Pan, or the Boy Who Would Not Grow Up.* New York: Charles Scribner & Sons.

[3]For a clever clinical analysis of Barrie's work and its relevance to understanding relationships, the reader may wish to consult Kiley, D. (1983). *The Peter Pan Syndrome.* New York: Avon.

Moreover, they make meaningful social contributions. For example, couples such as these have long swelled the ranks of the Christian mission field (see Michener's *Hawaii*[4] for some sensitive, semifictional portraits). Historically, American homesteads were also founded by pioneering couples with this kind of moral fiber.

The most difficult kind of relations for my G+ examinees were typically encountered with their teenage children. These relationships can be unusually traumatic. These examinees generally had taken their parenting seriously, showing the same conscientiousness in their parental role that they did in others. Having carefully trained their children "in the way they should go" (Proverbs), G+ parents are often sorely disappointed when their children become adolescents who express views that depart from those they have been taught. This, of course, even aside from teenage rebelliousness, is almost inevitable, for no generation exactly replicates the moral standards of its predecessor.

On their part, the teenagers have strongly conflicting feelings, experiencing guilt on the one hand for their parents' disappointment and, on the other, anger toward their parents for their rigidity. There are few clinicians in general practice whose clientele does not contain a number of adults who have still failed to solve this conflict.

I discovered that those young persons who were not strong enough to tolerate the disappointments of their parents, continued to endorse the same moral values of their parents. In my opinion, these values were held by default. They were not arrived at through the young persons's own moral growth. This fact is worth mentioning, because I noted that these individuals also obtained extreme G+ scores. However, according at least to my experience, these scorers are a minority within the ranks of examinees who achieve high G+ scores.

G+ and Childhood

The superego in adulthood differs in content, if not in action, from its earlier forms, for only in adolescence, when cognitive processes have fully developed, does the mature superego appear. High-scoring adolescents whom I observed stood out from their contemporaries. In my observations, their moral caliber was also

---

[4]Michener, J. (1953). *Hawaii*. New York: Random House.

easily recognized by their parents, teachers, and peers. Parents reported that they found these youngsters more circumspect than their contemporaries about their choice of companions and that they appeared to do less experimentation with sex, drugs, and alcohol. Teachers reported that they were persistent and willing to follow rules. Finally, their peers saw them as natural leaders because they were fair in their competition and displayed an interest in promoting the common good rather than seeking personal gain. All these direct observations fit remarkably well with what is reported by Cattell and Cattell (1975).

The study by Barton, Dielman, and Cattell (1973) is informative on the kind of parent-child relationship that generally precurs strong superego development. They found that parents of these individuals, especially fathers, tended to be well educated and were not overly strict. Nor were they preoccupied with perfectionistic details. They used praise and reasoning, instead of punishment or bribery, as incentives for good behavior. Above all, these parents showed warm feelings, which were reciprocated by their children.

This describes exactly the kind of parent-child relationship that would be expected, given what is known about modeling and identification. These parents seem to provide both attractive role models as well as the kinds of methods that behavior modification theorists have found to be most useful in helping children incorporate desirable standards of conduct.

Important Correlations Between G+ Scores and Other 16PF Factor Scores

To get more of a sense of the typical G+ person, let us look at the traits that are apt to accompany a strong superego, as shown by the three correlations in Table 7.1. The highest correlation, which is .44, is with Q_3+ (self-sentiment) scores. This relationship indicates, just as would be expected, given that G+ scores measure a conventional form of superego, that a G+ person is likely to be invested in maintaining a socially approved self-image. Conventional tendencies are also reflected in the lower correlations with Q_1− (conservatism) and E− (submissiveness) scores. Q_1− scores indicate satisfaction with traditional values and the status quo, and E− scores indicate a willingness to accommodate the needs of others.

Table 7.1

**Important Correlations Between G+ Scores
and Other 16PF Factor Scores**

Factor Pole	Correlation	Possible Associated Traits Indicated by Correlation
Q_3+ (Self-sentiment)	.44	Controlled, Exacting Will Power, Socially Precise, Compulsive
Q_1- (Conservatism)	.27	Conservative, Respect for Traditional Ideas
E− (Submissiveness)	.23	Humble, Mild, Easily Led, Docile, Accommodating

Any person who demonstrates a triad of G+, Q_3+, and Q_1- tendencies is a recognizable type. Here we have the solid citizen, a bit of a "stick in the mud," maybe, as he or she is slow to change. This person provides a stabilizing force in society who, above all, can be relied upon to do the culturally "right thing."

Clinical Relevance of G+ Scores

A popular but mistaken belief, based incidentally on the misinterpretation of psychoanalytic theory, is that persons with strong superegos are anxious and guilt ridden. The empirical evidence is that a strong superego, as measured by Factor G (i.e., one that has matured and is based on the conventional morality), does not predispose toward anxiety or guilt feelings, since there is no relation between G+ scores and the second-order anxiety factor, or with Factor O (guilt proneness) scores.

Since the kind of superego strength that G+ scores measure is typically manifested in behavior that is rewarded by society, it follows that, for the most part, it leads to good social adaptation. Moreover, it can compensate for deficiencies in other functions. For example, it can aid social adjustment in C− (weak ego strength) persons who might otherwise have severe problems with day-to-day living.

However, on the other hand, I discovered a relatively small number of instances—40 to be exact—of examinees whose strong superego values caused them to have adaptation difficulties. This occurred because they were unable to reconcile conflicts between superego values and ego (security and life satisfaction) goals. The basic difference between the superego and the ego is that, whereas the ego operates on the premise that deeds, beliefs, and ideas are not in themselves good or bad but only in their results, the superego operates on the aesthetic principle that virtue or the absence of it lies in the thing itself. This can lead to rigidity or categorical thinking, however, for it disregards the contexts in which people behave.

> *Example:* In marital therapy, an averagely intelligent woman whose 16PF scores showed her as being heavily endowed with superego strength, but poorly endowed with ego strength, was outraged to discover her husband had told her an innocuous lie. Her husband's motive had been to protect her from needless suffering at a time when she was already coping with excessive stress. She seemed incapable of appreciating that he had been guided by concern and operated without malice. Failing to appreciate the purpose the lie was intended to serve, she categorically denounced all lies as reprehensible.

Superego inflexibility can even threaten physical health by contributing to stress, according to Krug (1980). He reports that G+ scorers may find it hard to modify their self-imposed rules and so work hard, drive themselves to meet deadlines, get little sleep, and allow little time for rest and relaxation.

Finally, there was an adjustment difficulty of a different sort that many of my colleagues and I have observed in G+ examinees whose profiles showed extreme F+ (surgency) scores. This combination is a sign that the examinee has not succeeded in integrating the parts of his or her personality. Here, all the restrained, persevering, other-centeredness and rule-bound superego qualities are combined with those of the untamed natural inner child with all of its impulsive, self-centered, freedom-loving qualities. The result is continual vacillation and the struggle to reconcile internal inconsistencies. Fortunately, this is a somewhat unusual combination. F+ and G+ scores do not correlate in the general population and, as we have said, for the mature G+ person, battles of this sort have typically been fought and won.

LOW SCORES ON FACTOR G

Important Correlations Between G− Scores and Other 16PF Factor Scores

In contradiction to the uniform meaning of their opposite pole counterparts, G− scores can be interpreted as reflecting several superego variants, ranging from immature to highly evolved forms of moral development. What all variants do have in common, however, is that they bespeak of superego systems that are not aligned with conventional standards or right and wrong. In addition, the unconventionality of G− examinees is somewhat apt to be manifested, not only in their morals, but in other areas of their personalities, as is suggested by the correlations in Table 7.2 below.

Table 7.2

Important Correlations Between G− Scores and Other 16PF Factor Scores

Factor Pole	Correlation	Possible Associated Traits Indicated by Correlation
Q_3− (Low Self-sentiment)	.44	Undisciplined Self-conflict, Lax, Follows Own Urges, Careless of Social Rules
Q_1+ (Radicalism)	.27	Experimental, Liberal, Free Thinking
E+ (Dominance)	.23	Assertive, Aggressive, Stubborn, Competitive

Table 7.2 shows a strong correlation of .44 with Q_3− (lower self-sentiment) scores and a weak but significant correlation of .27 with Q_1+ (radicalness) and E+ (dominance) scores. Q_3− scores indicate a low investment in maintaining a socially correct self-image; Q_1+ scores indicate a liberal, rather than traditional, approach to life, and E+ scores point to a need for getting one's own way. It may be, therefore, that G− examinees are often neither deeply connected with the cultural mainstream, nor willing to accommodate to values they do not believe in.

G− Scores and Variants of Superego Development

In my opinion, interpreting a G− score presents the most difficult challenge in the whole 16PF contingent, because it can have several distinctly different meanings. These meanings are presented in Table 7.3 below.

Table 7.3

Various Psychological Interpretations of G Scores of 3 and Below*

Psychological Interpretation		Number and Percentage of Examinees in Each Category	
		Number	Percentage
Motivation Distortion (Faking Bad)	Examinee may have internalized the morals of the mainstream culture but presents self as not having done so.	23	14
Amorality	Examinee has failed to internalize moral values.	28	18
Moral Immaturity	Examinee still holds to moral values internalized in childhood. Contents of their superegos have not undergone the progressive reorganizations leading to the acquisition of mature moral standards.	67	42
Non-Conventional Moral Standards	Examinee has internalized moral standards but they are either of a subgroup or are idiosyncratic and not those of the mainstream culture.	39	24
Post-Conventional Superego	Examinee has moved beyond conventional morality and holds standards not tapped by G scale.	2	2

*Based on sample of 159 examinees.

All but one interpretation, "faking bad," reflect different variants of superego forms. Due to there being no common social, subjective, or historical denominator among them, each will be discussed separately. With each, I will briefly describe the particular variant, with suggestions, based on my sample of G– examinees, on how it might be distinguished from other variants.

Because these suggestions are based on preliminary findings on a fairly small sample, they remain at this time tentative. Therefore, the test administrator, in assigning G− scores to a particular variant, should consider carefully, case by case, how well it fits an examinee's history, present life situation, and behavior.

G− Scores and Motivational Distortion (Faking Bad)

Lying or lack of self-awareness are the two reasons why some examinees may endorse G scale items so as to show less moral conformity than actually exists in their standards and behaviors. This distortion, which can be intentional or unintentional, is called *faking bad,* which is the presenting of oneself in an unfavorable light, as opposed to presenting oneself in a favorable light (faking good). I strongly suspect that 23 examinees in my sample answered G scale items so as to appear less morally conforming than they actually were.

Intentional role distortion, i.e., lying about lack of moral conformity, is rarely encountered in most settings in which mental health clinicians or organizational psychologists work. In my sample, I discovered it only in the prison population and, even there, only among inmates who "run" the prison, i.e., had informal authority. In this role, lacking conventional moral standards is sometimes considered highly desirable and affords higher status.

> Billy, one of my clients who patterns himself after the notorious Billy the Kid, faked his 16PF responses to obtain a low G score. In fact, he had some rather conventional moral values, which I discovered later after he helped quell a prison riot. Until that time, in order to maintain a "don't fool with me or you will be sorry" posture, he carefully maintained an antisocial, or (to use prison jargon) "bad" image.

The second form of motivational distortion is actually misnamed, as it occurs without intention and is without a conscious goal. Arising out of distorted insight, it is seen rather frequently in ordinary office practice and mental health clinics. I have found it particularly in depressed clients whose self-depreciation often led them to grossly underestimate their levels of moral behavior. Exaggerating and overgeneralizing their pecadillos, they come to see themselves as behaving immorally. Due to this finding, I have learned to question G− scores in depressed patients, preferring to examine them closely in context of the full 16PF profile.

My suspicion is aroused when $G-$ scores are accompanied by $F-$ (desurgency) scores, which are indicative of pessimism, and $O+$ (guilt proneness) scores, which are indicative of poor self-esteem and guilt proneness. Also concomitant is a lower score on Factor B (intelligence) than is suggested by the client's educational history, job status, and vocabulary, as well as other sources of information about the client.

Variant 1: Amorality. People who have few moral values obtain extremely low G scores when they truthfully answer the G scale items. Here I am referring to people thought to be *amoral,* that is, without suprapersonal concerns. They are like the pre-moral infants in Kohlberg's second stage of moral development. When one talks to these examinees, it becomes clear that they see goodness as what they want and like.

> *Example:* A man who had been allowed to live rent free in the home of an altruistic couple was told he must leave because he refused to stop smoking in bed, even though on one occasion he had fallen asleep and almost set the mattress afire. He showed his level of moral development when later in a therapy session with me he asserted that this couple had behaved very badly by inconveniencing him.

A careful analysis of the histories of 28 examinees whom I assigned to this variant convinced me that these individuals had made little progress in moving away from the egocentric orientation of early childhood, and had throughout their entire lives formed only weak emotional attachments to others. It follows that, since they did not achieve strong attachments, they were unable to make the social identifications which Bowlby (1946) and others have convincingly demonstrated are necessary for internalizing the values of the culture. When attachment and its successor, identification, do *not* occur at certain critical periods in childhood, it is difficult, if not impossible, for subsequent moral development to occur in later years.

An amoral variant interpretation of $G-$ scores does not necessarily indicate an antisocial personality disorder as currently described in the DSM-III, although certainly lack of moral development enters into this diagnosis. A reading of the DSM-III diagnostic criteria for antisocial personality, as well as that of major studies in this field, e.g., Checkley (1964), will show that the antisocial personality, in addition to failing to acquire adequate moral standards, incorporates other characteristics:

(1) callousness, (2) inability to learn from mistakes, and (3) lack of appropriate fear. Although the first of these attributes is intricately woven with the amoral person's lack of normal social identification, the others are not.

Whether or not the above antisocial characteristics are present determined the subjective experience, social responses, and adjustment difficulties of the G− examinees I assigned to this variant. Examinees who did not have these characteristics, but who had simply failed to acquire moral standards, seemed to suffer most from anxiety. They were anxious, not because they were concerned about their wrongdoing, but because the *results* of their social transgressions had come back to roost on their doorsteps. For these examinees, social transgressions seemed to be ultimately inevitable, even when their profiles showed that their lack of moral development was counterbalanced by other traits like B+ (intellectual ability), F− (cautiousness), or C+ (ability to tolerate frustration), for in the long run there is probably no real substitute for a strong conventional superego for keeping out of trouble. Their tendencies towards being manipulative and dishonest also contributed to their anxiety. Because "it is impossible to fool all the people all the time," they were hypervigilant and guarded.

However, since it is possible to fool many people some of the time, reactions to this variant of G− examinees tended to be mixed, much depending on how well they were able to hide their true motives. If they were intelligent, which was usually discernible from their B score, and if they were socially shrewd and poised, as indicated by N+ scores, they were apt to make good initial impressions by dishonestly ingratiating themselves upon new acquaintances.

In my organizational consulting work, I discovered that, time and time again, these individuals were hired for jobs on the basis of their good self-presentation by interviewers who did not check references. But these initial impressions quickly faded when their actual job performance failed to approach expectations. Frequently tardy and erratic in their work, they came to be resented both by their employers and coworkers. Consequently, it is not surprising to me that one of their outstanding characteristics was the frequency with which they changed jobs.

The histories of amoral G− people showed that, like their jobs, their relationships were short-lived. Friends became disillusioned and drifted away when the opportunism and undependability of these individuals became apparent. I discovered that

one of the most reliable diagnostic signs for deciding if a G−
examinee belonged in this amoral variant was when the person
had completely lost touch with his or her family of origin and
with children from previous marriages.

Nowhere was their lack of commitment more obvious than
in romantic relationships. They reported numerous sexual
liaisons and many had married several times. They had married
for better, never for worse, and were likely to leave a relationship
when their partner faced sickness, financial reverses, or other
difficulties.

Variant 2: Moral Immaturity. This variant, to a greater degree than the amoral variant just discussed, is associated with
anxiety. It is also associated with neuroticism. When viewed in
context of a complete 16PF profile, this association is discernible
by the accompaniment of C− (low ego strength) scores, as well
as one or more other components of the second-order anxiety
pattern: H+ (shyness), L+ (suspicious insecurity), O+ (guilt
proneness), and Q_4+ (nervous tension). An interpretation of
moral immaturity, rather than amorality, is also suggested when
the history of a G− examinee shows that he or she internalized
parental values but later failed to develop them along more mature lines.

The somewhat primitive moral orientations of the 67
examinees I assigned to this variant were similar, possibly identical, to Kohlberg's second and third stages of moral development,
i.e., avoidance of punishment, reciprocity of favors, and equation
of goodness with being either a "good boy" or a "nice girl." In its
most extreme manifestation, their superego contents seemed to
result from the child's uncritical swallowing of parental do's and
don'ts, and continued, even in adult life, to center on outmoded,
childlike concerns.

In some instances, this developmental failure was due to
cognitive impairment, i.e., either low functional intelligence or
brain damage. The former, but not necessarily the latter, condition was discernible by the accompaniment of low B (intelligence)
scores on the 16PF profile. In some, brain damage was detected
through a mental status examination or through psychoneurological testing.

In the other cases in which cognitive impairment was not an
issue, the origin of moral immaturity seemed often to be associated with excessive parental coerciveness during formative

years. Possibly, these persons received so many directives that their development of moral autonomy was stifled. It is also possible that the parents themselves may also have been morally immature, since they overemphasized such values as cleanliness, avoidance of social disapproval, and following correct procedures, to the neglect of the more sophisticated moral concerns.

A striking characteristic of this immature superego structure is that, though inferior in its content, it is often remarkably strong in its action, evoking ardent responses. In clinical sessions, I noticed that clients with these kinds of superegos often revealed that they re-enacted internally the coercion/submission interactions which once occurred between them and their parents. It seemed that having internalized their parents' injunctions and admonitions and taboos, they continued to respond to these now internally generated instructions by vacillating between obedience or anxious rebellion, as they did as children. The peculiar outcome was that they showed as much conscientiousness, persistence, and effort as G+ examinees.

As the clinically experienced reader may have recognized, what is being described here is obsessive-compulsive behavior, especially since it focuses on orderliness, proper conduct, cleanliness, and other forms of behavior which parents often laud as highly desirable.

Finally, the reactions I uncovered to examinees of this variant were usually not flattering. They were seen as being anxious and precise but shallow in their values, and persons who were more morally mature routinely reported that they found them tiring to be around.

Variant 3: Non-Conventional Morality. I encountered G− scores in the profiles of conscientious, socially well-bonded and mature individuals who showed genuine concern for the welfare of others and who experienced appropriate guilt. These individuals differed, not only from those of other G− examinees, but also from high-or-average examinees by having values and following self-appointed rules outside the mainstream culture.

In exploring these examinees' reasoning for endorsing such a G scale item in a way that reflects that they would disobey certain laws, I discovered two quite dissimilar subgroups. One I called the Sherwood group because it was made up of modern-day Robin Hoods. These individuals, whose profiles often showed that they had average or high scores on Factor C (ego strength) and that they were Q_1+ (nonconforming), saw themselves or identified with others whom they saw as economically or politically disenfranchised. Commonly, they belonged to a reference group that has had little or no part in forming the societal rules which they are expected to obey.

Since they were neither amoral nor morally immature, but made morally based choices to go against the existing social code, their $G-$ scores were best seen as having political rather than clinical significance.[5]

The other subgroup of unconventionally moral individuals often comes to the attention of mental health professionals via the legal system. Unlike the Sherwood group, they have failed to endorse conventional moral standards out of naivete rather than political awareness. Failure to grasp how the socioeconomic system actually works seems to be the most prevalent form of naivete.

> *Example:* A 23-year-old female court-referred client, to supplement the income of her aging father, habitually stole and used credit cards. She never used the goods she obtained by this fraud for herself. She told us that she would never incur debts for which the credit card owners were responsible as she felt that would be "terribly unfair." She had no compunction, however, about having the financial organizations sustain the losses, saying, "that way nobody really gets hurt."

Variant 4: Post-Conventional Moral Development. Moral values are not static. And, as Factor G taps one form of values, i.e., conventional morality, it is theoretically possible for the most morally advanced persons to achieve $G-$ scores. The moral development to which I am referring I have called "post-conventional," in keeping with Kohlberg's suggestion that some persons progress beyond the morality of their contemporaries to find higher levels of values and understanding.

History seems to support Kohlberg's suggestion, as Jesus, Buddha, Mohammed, and Moses are all generally recognized as having attained new understandings that transcended the moral development of their times. They abandoned the prevailing morals after perceiving that they did not adequately address urgent

---

[5]The much publicized Soviet view, but one which is now hopefully changing, is to consider any individual whose moral standards differ from the official morality as being mentally ill.

questions regarding human purpose and meaning. Later, their new higher order moral systems put them at odds with the old ones. They were moral revolutionaries, and should they have been tested by a G scale fashioned after the morality of their contemporaries, they would no doubt have negatively endorsed many items as being incompatible with their new understanding, thereby achieving low scores.

To date I have only found, among my sample of 159 examinees, two whom I can confidently assign to this variant. (There have been some other morally evolved examinees who have obtained moderate scores of 4 or 5.) These individuals were unselfish and socially concerned "citizens of the world," who found it difficult to reconcile problems such as overpopulation, nuclear energy, space exploration, and right-to-life issues with existing moral institutions.

Chapter 8

Factor H: Boldness and Timidity in Human Temperament

THE CONSTRUCT
Constitutional Determinants
Differences of Reactions to Fear-Producing Stimuli
Male and Female Differences Throughout the Life Span
Heredity

HIGH SCORES ON FACTOR H
Intrapsychic Data
Interpersonal and Social Data
H+ and Childhood
Clinical Relevance of H+ Scores
Important Correlations Between H+ Scores
and Other 16PF Factor Scores

LOW SCORES ON FACTOR H
Intrapsychic Data
Interpersonal and Social Data
H− and Childhood
Important Correlations Between H− Scores
and Other 16PF Factor Scores
Clinical Relevance of H− Scores

FACTOR H: CHARACTERISTICS OF H+ (PARMIC) AND H− (THRECTIC) EXAMINEES

Left Score H− (THRECTIA)		Right Score H+ (PARMIA)
(Shy, Timid, Restrained, Threat-sensitive)	vs.	**(Adventurous, Thick-skinned, Socially Bold)**
Shy, Withdrawn	vs.	Adventurous, Likes Meeting People
Retiring in Face of Opposite Sex	vs.	Active, Overt Interest in Opposite Sex
Emotionally Cautious	vs.	Responsive, Genial
Apt to Be Embittered	vs.	Friendly
Restrained, Rule-bound	vs.	Impulsive
Restricted Interests	vs.	Emotional and Artistic Interests
Careful, Considerate, Quick to See Dangers	vs.	Carefree, Does Not See Danger Signals

THE CONSTRUCT

Constitutional Determinism

Factor H comes close to being the most constitutionally determined factor in the entire temperament domain, as demonstrated by its physiological associations with EKG patterns and by autonomic responses, such as those that occur in the cold pressor test, which records differences in recovery of pulse rate following shock (Cattell, 1973). At essence, it is thought that this factor measures the reactivity of the nervous system based on an individual's proclivity to be either sympathetic or parasympathetic dominant.

The right pole, H+, is called parmia, which is a neologism for parasympathetic dominance. Persons scoring in this direction underreact to external dangers and stressors and are risk takers and adventurers who enjoy excitement. By contrast, the left or H− pole, threctia, indicates sympathetic dominance. In contrast with their high-scoring opposites, persons who score in this direction overreact to any form of perceived threat. As a result, they prefer to stay with whatever is certain, predictable, and safe.

Differences of Reactions to Fear-Producing Stimuli

In my early days of trying to understand this factor, my understanding was enhanced when I noticed that, in two separate studies, H+ showed a relationship to a dynamic factor measuring fear, in the Motivation Analysis Test. The first of these studies was reported by Cattell in 1957, and the second was reported by Krug in 1980. Although these correlations were only .15 and .12, respectively, and not statistically significant, they were noteworthy because these similarities were *(a)* gleaned from studies performed on very different samples more than two decades apart, and *(b)* consistent with my observation that, contrary to the popular notion, H+ individuals, rather than being fearless, experience fear.

At first I was tempted to interpret this relation between H+ and fear according to a counterphobic hypothesis, i.e., confronting what one fears to conquer the associated feelings. But more sustained observations of H+ examinees, however, showed that, rather than acting counterphobically, they sought out dangerous types of experiences because they *enjoyed* feeling fearful. A motivational principle is involved in this observation: that, in contrast to other innate drives such as, for example, sex, hunger, and territoriality, which seek quietessence, there exists another drive that seeks satisfaction through arousal of disequilibrium. In other words, it can be proposed that humans seem not to want to feel *too* safe. The fact that people enjoy rollercoaster rides, ghost stories, and horror movies testifies to this proposition, as does the history of our species, the progress of which is replete with examples of persons becoming bored with secure and comfortable lifestyles and venturing forth in search of the uncertain and unpredictable.

That pleasurable feelings of excitement are produced by stimulating fears suggests that H+ behavior is based on physiologic underactivity, which in turn results in higher fear-sensation thresholds. The behavior of H+ persons, therefore, can be explained by these individuals needing unusually intense, and often potentially more dangerous, experiences to feel thrilled or exhilarated.

Just as the positive correlation between the fear dynamic on the Motivation Analysis Test and H+ scores run counter to what might be supposed, so does the correlation of low dynamic fear with H− scores. This latter correlation suggests that H− persons experience actually less, rather than more, fear than their H+ counterparts. And, based on my observations of H− examinees, I interpret this correlation as reflecting behavior that avoids normal levels of fear-producing stimuli. The physiological over-reactivity of these individuals made even the average environment too fear producing. Therefore, they learned to avoid risks and to constrict their lives so that they would have less objective cause for fear than most persons.

Male and Female Differences Throughout the Life Span

There is a significant gender difference on Factor H for the general population. The mean score for men is 28.50, and is substantially higher than that for women, which is 25.42. Thus, men are more venturesome than women. By contrast, the standard deviation is almost identical for both sexes, men 9.82, women 9.90, and is the widest among all of the 16PF factors. This spread suggests that persons of both sexes vary greatly on this dimension of human personality.

Heredity

The heritability of Factor H is .37, which, though high, is somewhat less than what Cattell had initially expected, since the genetic endowment is considered to be very strong in most physiologically based traits. Therefore, its substantial environmental component presupposes that early experience must influence the physiology of the nervous system.

Along these lines, there is evidence that some children who have been subjected to protracted, anxiety-producing experiences become "nervous," and do not seem to recover fully neurologically (Zigler & Glick, 1986). Although less frequent, this neurological damage can occur later in life. For example, adults who have contracted post-traumatic stress disorders, after exposure to unusually potent stressors, may not return to their premorbid neurological condition (Jelinek & Williams, 1984). However, change in adults seems to be comparatively rare, since Factor H scores remain unusually stable over time (Cattell, 1973).

HIGH SCORES ON FACTOR H

Intrapsychic Data

Dubbed originally the Errol Flynn factor pole, H+ is also reflected in a more contemporary figure who also demonstrates bold, adventurous, swashbuckling, libidinous qualities—James

Bond. In former times, H+ individuals swelled the ranks of soldiers of fortune and were the "have gun, will travel" figures of the Wild West. Nowadays, I would expect them to be well represented among racing car enthusiasts, astronauts, test pilots, and those who volunteer for dangerous missions. In everyday life, few of us will fail to recognize among our acquaintances at least one of these strong-nerved, confident, somewhat romantic roving souls.

To elaborate on the inner manifestations of H+ people, it is necessary first of all to distinguish between H+ and its close relative, F+ (surgency). Although both H+ and F+ individuals are often outwardly conspicuous as self-displayers and excitement seekers, the feelings that prompt this similar behavior are quite different. F+ individuals have a strong liking for the limelight, and especially like being center stage. They seek attention as an end in itself. By contrast, people who are H+ find that they don't need to exert effort to gain attention, as their colorful personalities naturally invite the limelight. The bigger difference, however, is in the kinds of stimuli each seeks. F+ (surgent) people seek stimuli to be entertained, deriving pleasure from its variety and novelty, whereas H+ persons want to be thrilled. ("Thrill" is defined by Webster as "to cause to experience a sudden sharp feeling of excitement.") H+ people prefer stimuli that involve challenges and risks.

> *Example:* Two colleagues took a vacation together to a certain exotic place in the Himalayas. One colleague I knew to have an H score of 9, but he was only moderately F+ (surgent). The other I knew to be highly F+, but he had only a moderate H score. Much to their surprise, they found that once there—although they both enjoyed the surroundings—they found little to do together. The F+ person preferred to spend his time experiencing the sensual kaleidoscope of sights, sounds, and smells. The H+ person, however, was more interested in trekking off to some poorly marked destination, climbing dangerous slopes, or trying to get to know the natives, though he did not understand their language or know how they would receive him.

As I have already said, H+ persons' physical underactivity provides immunity to physical and social threats that others would find noxious. Rarely did the 97 H+ examinees in my sample seem to experience the sensations most people have in similar situations—a sensation in the pits of their stomachs before an exam, a missed heartbeat when attention is suddenly focused on them, or palpitations, weak knees, and shaking when confronted by dangers. They were, therefore, able to pursue goals from which more ordinary types are apt to retreat in timidity. It is probably for this reason that H+ persons generally suffer from fewer long-term self-imposed frustrations and are better able to get on in the world.

Interpersonal and Social Data

H+ persons are valued in occupations in which their boldness, willingness to take risks, and strong nerves are useful. It is not surprising, therefore, to find they succeed as salespeople, classroom teachers, psychiatric technicians, and psychotherapists (Cattell, 1973). H+ scores also appear in the profiles of firefighters, politicians, airline pilots, flight attendants, life insurance salespersons, managers, administrators, school counselors, mechanics, writers, artists, special education teachers, anaesthesiologists, physicists, accountants, and judges (Rieke & Russell, 1987).

In social gatherings, my H+ examinees were often seen as friendly, since they took the initiative to introduce themselves to others, and led in opening conversations. This behavior, however, was more likely due to lack of social inhibition, rather than to warmth. When their H+ behavior (parmia) was not balanced by other traits like A+ (affectothymia) or I+ (premsia), they were not attuned to the subtlety of others' feelings, so were sometimes seen as thick-skinned. As Cattell (1973) discovered, H+ people may also be seen as ineffective, long-winded speakers who are insensitive to clues that others are becoming bored.

Cattell also noted that, in his ratings, H+ persons were considered "brash" and "pushy." Although I, too, have heard the same unflattering evaluations, I am also cognizant that these attributes account for much of the social and material success of these individuals. It is significant that many of them come from socially and economically disadvantaged backgrounds and are upwardly mobile. Moreover, a cursory observation at most mixed gatherings will show that H+ women tend to command attention while other women are neglected. H+ men have the added advantage of representing the masculine ideal and so are often possibly even more attractive to the opposite sex. These men, however, seem to be becoming less attractive since there is a cultural shift toward valuing gynandromorphy, i.e., incorporating into the behavior of both sexes traits that have been traditionally dichotomised as being masculine or feminine.

In marriage, H+ individuals, though involved in planned role-sharing, meet many of their wants and needs independently of their partners. They frequently also have uninhibited sexual philosophies, according to Barton and Cattell findings (1972a). Similarly, I discovered 11 (about 10%) of the H+ examinees in my sample opted for open marriages, and that, furthermore, these arrangements proved successful in some situations, possibly because both partners had similarly high scores.

Finally, the proclivity of H+ people for putting themselves into dangerous situations can be of grave concern and deeply frustrating to those who care about their health and safety. This point was well illustrated several times in the life of the obviously H+ Beryl Markham.[1]

> *Example:* Beryl Markham made her living, among other ways, as a pilot scouting for elephant in Africa. In her autobiography she speaks of this experience despite its associated health problem as "a legacy of excitement—a release from routine, a passport to adventure." In contrast to her reaction, she quotes an admonishing letter from her friend Tom who wrote, "I am awfully upset to hear that you have been so ill, but trust that by now you have completely recovered. It seems to me that you are rather overdoing it—living on your nerves too much . . . you have got to be capable of accepting non-hazardous, ordinary, sane, dull, everyday work that requires a balanced brain and steady reasoning.
>
> "All this is to tell you that if you had one grain of sense you wouldn't make a regular habit of flying for elephant in elephant country. Financial worry may be eased by one or two safaris but as a steady business it's sheer madness and damnably bloody dangerous." (p. 198)

This example, as well as what I have learned first-hand from conversations with their spouses, parents, lovers, and friends,

---

[1]Excerpted from: *West With the Night,* Copyright © 1942, 1983 by Beryl Markham. Published by North Point Press and reprinted by permission.

indicates that emotional involvement with H+ persons is fitting only for the stouthearted.

H+ and Childhood

Most of what is known from the standpoint of research about the relationship between H+ scores and childhood experience comes from the research of Barton and Cattell (1972b). This research found that H+ adults grew up in environments that were conducive to shaping boldness and vigorous self-confidence. H+ adults generally reported that, as children, they had their early dependency needs adequately met, had received much parental affection and little punishment, and had been subjected to just enough childhood stressors to provide the opportunities for learning coping skills.[2] No hypothesis, however, was presented in this study, nor has one been advanced later, about how this type of environment might have interacted with preexisting physiology so as to strengthen the dominance of the parasympathetic nervous systems.

Cattell (1957) reports that H+ children are rated by their peers as cooperative and friendly, but also as lazy and disorganized, and as tending to choose friends of whom their parents disapproved. My own observation, though less systematically gathered, substantiates these findings. I have also noticed the liking of H+ children for associating with peers who share their fondness for dangerous sports and taking risks. These children are often sexually precocious, which may have provided yet another reason for their parents to take a dim view of their friends.

On the academic front, except for a small positive correlation with mathematics, H+ scores were found to be unrelated to school achievement (Cattell, 1973). This finding also agrees with my observations.

---

[2]The notion that children should be protected as much as possible from unpleasantness has been challenged by Michenbaum (1977). In what he metaphorically calls Innoculation Theory, Michenbaum proposes that early stressful experiences, provided they are not overwhelming, are desirable, as they allow children to acquire psychological strategies that enable them to cope better with the demands in adulthood.

Important Correlations Between H+ Scores and Other 16PF Factor Scores

Table 8.1 reports the important correlations between H+ scores and those of other 16PF factors.

Table 8.1

Important Correlations Between H+ Scores and Other 16PF Factor Scores

Factor Pole	Correlation	Possible Associated Traits Indicated by Correlation
F+ (Surgency)	.45	Happy-go-lucky, Enthusiastic
O− (Untroubled Adequacy)	.43	Self-assured, Placid, Secure, Complacent, Serene
C+ (Ego Strength)	.39	Emotionally Stable, Mature, Faces Reality, Calm
A+ (Affectothymia)	.38	Outgoing, Warmhearted, Easygoing, Participating
Q_4 − (Low Ergic Tension)	.33	Relaxed, Tranquil, Unfrustrated, Composed
Q_2 − (Group Adherence)	.32	Group-dependent, A "Joiner" and Sound Follower
E+ (Dominance)	.31	Aggressive, Stubborn, Competitive

Table 8.1 shows the highest correlation is between H+ and F+ scores. This is a substantial correlation of .45, and explains why one often encounters both H+ and F+ in the same individuals. In other words, H+ people, in addition to being bold and adventuresome, are likely to be exuberant and happy-go-lucky. They are also likely, according to the correlation of .43 with O− (untroubled adequacy) and the correlation of .39 with C+ (ego strength) to be self-assured and to have strong egos. This O−/C+ combination (as it has been mentioned earlier in Chapter 4, and will be elaborated upon later in Chapter 13) is usually an indicator of strong defense mechanisms, which in the present instance is somewhat supported by the lower correlation of .33 with Q_4− (low ergic tension). A low score on Factor Q_4 signifies a lack of what is commonly referred to as nervous or physical

tension, as would be expected in persons who are defended so as to experience little guilt or self-reproach.

Finally, the correlations with A+ (.38), E+ (.31), and Q_2- (.32) convey the kind of social orientation commonly shown by H+ people. Respectively, these correlations say that H+ people are also apt to be sociable, dominant, and inclined to rely more than most people on the support and physical presence of others. The dependency suggested by the correlation of H+ and Q_2- is not a quality that one would anticipate in the kind of dynamic, even overbearing, personality depicted here. Not unexpectedly, therefore, I have discovered that when a profile follows the same pattern of correlations reported in Table 8.1, the examinee is likely to express dependency very covertly.

Clinical Relevance of H+ Scores

When H+ persons come to the clinician's attention, it is frequently because they are actively opposing society's rules. The 16PF Handbook reports extreme H+ scores in the group profiles of persons with a sociopathic diagnosis,[3] a trend which was reflected in my sample. Moreover, in collecting data for a study on the High School Personality Questionnaire, I noticed that H+ scores appeared routinely in adolescents diagnosed as having one of three DSM-III adolescent conduct disorders: Undersocialized, Socialized Aggressive, and Socialized Nonaggressive. H+ scores did not appear in the Undersocialized Nonaggressive group. (These adolescents were more apt to have H− scores, which I interpret as indicating that they were easily led by bolder peers whom they did not have the courage to resist.) Given these findings, my colleagues and I have speculated about how H+ (parmia) may contribute to failure in socialization. The present state of our reasoning is that since H+ (parmia) represents a lack of reactiveness to threats of punishment or even to punishment itself, it provides immunity to the normal pressures that society uses to induce conformity.

On this point, I must mention the work of Farley (1981, 1985), who for over 20 years has amassed an impressive body of knowledge regarding what can only be the extreme poles of Factor H.

---

[3]p. 279.

He refers to H+ as "Type T" (or Big T) and to H− as "Type t" (or "little t") personalities.[4]

Farley draws attention to the fact that H+ persons are risk takers and thrill seekers who seek adventure and challenge. When H+ people can't find opportunities that provide these experiences, they will manufacture them either in socially creative and productive ways (like Hilary who first climbed Everest, or like Watson and Crick,[5] the DNA researchers) or destructively (like the infamous bank robbers Bonnie and Clyde). Farley maintains that, since social circumstances play a key role in determining if these individuals become creators or destroyers, prevention and correction of antisocial behavior could be made easier if society provided opportunities for H+ persons to satisfy their needs for excitement so that they did not resort to more mischievous means. He cites, for example, vocational rehabilitation programs in prisons and other correctional institutions, where he claims H+ individuals abound. These places usually offer preparation only for traditional trades such as carpentry and plumbing, which are rule governed, relatively routinized, and, therefore, unexciting. Since H+ individuals are temperamentally ill-suited for these trades, they are likely to become bored, to drop out, and to revert to the more exciting life of crime. Farley contends that they are more likely to respond favorably to other occupations that provide exposure to higher levels of physical or mental arousal such as rodeo performer, explorer, stunt man, or trouble-shooter.

My own experience with socially delinquent H+ types compellingly supports Farley's proposition. I have found that their participation in programs like Outward Bound, offering outdoor survival experience, altered their antisocial tendencies more effectively than the hundreds of hours of counseling that preceded it.

---

[4]Although it is obvious that Factor H is what Farley is describing, his observations are slightly adulterated by the inclusion of Factor F characteristics. This confusion is inevitable in the absence of the deeper analysis that only factorings of data can provide, since there is a strong correlation between Factors H and F in the general population, so that it is difficult just by observation to separate H+ from F+ characteristics.

[5]*The Double Helix* (Watson, 1969), which describes the events leading up to Crick and his coworkers' discovery of DNA, reads like a thriller. Readers interested in this more intellectually sublimated form of H+ may wish to read this book.

Not every H+ individual without a ready source of excitement resorts to antisocial behavior. Moreover, finding the right kind of environmental fit is not the only consideration involved in the treatment of H+ clients who find themselves at odds with society. Their maladaptive behavior is also due to how other traits combine with their H+ behavior. For example, H+ in concert with low moral conformity (as G− scores may suggest), can be expected to lead to rule-rejecting and thrill-seeking behavior and, in some cases, involvement in criminal activities.

There are three other combinations which, though less obvious, are nevertheless worth mentioning, since they were reliable predictors of certain kinds of behavior.

H+ (parmia) and A− (sizothymia). H+ scores on a profile did not by themselves signify that the examinee has a callous disregard for others. Only when combined with A− (sizothymia) scores of 1, 2, or 3 did they suggest a hard, ruthless nature, much as we would expect to find historically in slavers, for example. In more modern times, I expect that many members of organized crime syndicates would show this H+/A− combination, if tested. The most striking illustration in my sample was a "hit man" who admittedly killed, for profit, five persons against whom he had no personal enmity. Fortunately, this kind of callousness in H+ persons is comparatively rare, since H+ and A− scores are not correlated in the general population.

H+ (parmia) and B− (concrete thinking). Examinees showing this combination of scores were likely to be the "fools that rushed in where angels feared to tread." Their bold inattentiveness to danger signals and the press for excitement, in combination with low intelligence, inevitably resulted in poor and rash judgments. This parsimonious explanation often accounted for the behavior of clients who might otherwise be considered self-destructive.

The proclivity for these clients to take risks doomed to fail was particularly predictable especially if their profiles showed F+ (surgency) scores. These people were also overly optimistic about the probability of success. At the very least, they were apt to be accident-prone. Two in my sample were tragically short-lived.

---

[6]p. 279.

This combination of B− and H+ is often found in prisoners, as is indicated by the profiles taken on prison populations that are reported in the 16PF Handbook.[6]

H+ (parmia) and C− (low ego strength). H+, adventurousness and boldness, in concert with the characteristics of C− (low ego strength), e.g., poor reality testing, low frustration tolerance, and reactivity, revealed itself in behavior similar to that shown by examinees with the H+/B− combination shown above. By contrast, however, the tendencies towards accident proneness of H+/C− examinees turned out to be due, not to inability to recognize their errors, but because they took on dangerous undertakings without realistically assessing the probable consequences.

LOW SCORES ON FACTOR H

Intrapsychic Data

Persons who score at this end of the continuum are what Farley (1985) describes as the Type t (little t) personalities I have alluded to earlier. These people cling to certainty and predictability, and tend to be neither criminal-like nor creative. To understand their subjective experience, Krug (1980) suggests that, in contrast to their H+ counterparts, H− persons have such a low tolerance for fear and arousal that they must protect themselves from situations and stimuli that threaten their delicate internal homeostases. Consequently, he argues, they become avoiders of any experiences that further increase their timidity and shyness.

It was undoubtedly based on observations of H− persons that Kretschmer as early as 1925 described what he called the hyperaesthetic personality:

"... feel all the harsh strong colors and tones of everyday life as shrill, ugly, even to the extent of being psychically painful. Their autism is a painful cramping of the self into itself. They seek as far as possible to avoid and deaden all stimulation from the outside." (pp. 115-116)

In my sample, the subjective lives of H− examinees, to varying degrees, agreed with Kretschmer's description. Commonly, they spoke of themselves as living in a shell.

Example: One client, whose H score was only 1, was without any psychopathology but was extremely shy. She provided us with the following insight into her feelings: In a fantasy exercise she likened herself to a sea creature living on a busy ocean floor, encased in a shell. This shell both protected her and imprisoned her. Camouflaged so as to be almost imperceptible from her physical background, she was scarcely noticed and safe; but as she watched other fish swim by she felt apart, different, and bitter.

This client's metaphor of her shell as both protection and prison illustrates the dilemma I have witnessed in H − individuals. They minimize stress by avoiding risks, competition, and new experiences like travel and encounters with strangers. But they concomitantly close off opportunities for personal gain, friendships, adventure, and much else that ordinarily brings pleasure and joy to life.

H − people also experience considerable animosity from observing other people's pleasures and successes. In other words, they are often jealous, for it is out of shyness and fear, not lack of desire, that they fail to compete. Another frequent outcome of their frustration is that their pent-up desires become excessive, as evidenced by the Walter Mitty compensatory fantasies of personal grandeur that a disproportionate number of H − examinees confide in therapy.

Even beyond their escape into fantasy, it was fairly characteristic for the H − examinees in my sample to not attend sufficiently to what went on around them, but to become absorbed in their internal processes. I discovered from talking to them that their self-absorption, rather than being due to the ambiance affording so little satisfaction, resulted, somewhat paradoxically I thought, from their overconcern about others' reactions about them. Consequently, they were preoccupied with rehearsing their future actions and reexamining old ones. Psychoanalytic writers have suggested that there is a bit of grandiosity about this kind of overconcern, attributing it to a persistent infantile narcissism, in which they, like young children, see themselves as having a more important role in ordinary human events than is actually so. But my findings did not support this proposition, as I found that my H − examinees did not attach undue social importance to themselves per se. Rather, they were excessively afraid of being singled out for attention, especially when it was negative.

Interpersonal and Social Data

In casual observations, it is sometimes difficult to discriminate elements of H − from those of three other traits which were discussed in previous chapters: A− (sizothymia), E− (submissiveness), and F− (desurgency). In the first instance, H− reticence may be mistaken for A− cool indifference, as Tennyson recognized: "Shy she was and I thought her cold." In the second, H− social timidity may be mistaken for E− submissiveness and unassertiveness. And in the third, H− self-consciousness may be mistaken as F− inhibition. Recognizing these differences is essential to understanding one's interactions with H− people.

Not wishing to draw negative attention to themselves, H− individuals try to be well behaved and considerate of others' sensibilities, as Cattell (1957) has noted. But whether their aim succeeds frequently depends on how well they are endowed with a good social facade. (This assessment can be made from their scores on the 16PF Factor N [social shrewdness], as discussed in Chapter 12.) Without this facade, it is sadly ironic that H− people frequently attract the attention they wish to avoid. For instance, their discomfort may be manifested in inappropriate or out-of-context remarks that are made because these people are too preoccupied with rehearsing their own response to be listening to what others are saying. An actual example was overheard in the following exchange between two clients, one of whom had a score of 2 on H, while they waited for group therapy to begin:

> *Example:* Mr. X: "Hi. How are you today?"
> H− Client: "Fine, how's yourself?"
> Mr. X: "To tell you the truth awful. My wife and I got into an auto accident Thursday. They kept her in the hospital because she hurt her back. I hurt all over so I think I should be there, too. Besides, taking care of the kids is hell."
> H− Client: "Glad to hear that."

Typically, H− persons interact most comfortably in routinized kinds of exchanges where responses are predictable and prescribed and where opportunities for saying anything "stupid" or doing the "wrong thing" are minimized. Since they are likely to find even casual conversations extremely stressful, it was hardly surprising that Cattell and Stice (1960) discovered, in their studies of group dynamics, that H− persons frequently concentrate steadily on work or similar activities. This quality is usually much appreciated by employers and supervisors, and even hosts and hostesses. It is a good guess that the person who can be relied upon at parties to pass the canapes or help in the kitchen would have low H scores. But just as they are apt to draw attention to themselves by their out-of-context remarks, they also do so by the fact that they tend to contribute little to conversations, since their silence may be interpreted as rejection or silent criticism. On the other hand, persons who accurately perceive their underlying shyness and timidity may respond by trying to put them at ease. Several couples that I have seen in marital therapy had this kind of beginning to their relationships. Although H− persons usually benefit from having partners who are more socially adventurous, they often become too dependent, as I shall soon explain.

H− and Childhood

Cattell and Barton's research on the early environments and experiences of H+ children has already been cited. Unfortunately, this research provides a less clear picture of the lives of H− children, as it only reveals that their lives lack those characteristics which mark the lives of their H+ counterparts, a finding which indicates differences but not opposites.

H− adults in my sample did not usually recall having had happy childhoods. The most common theme they recalled was acute discomfort when separated from familiar surroundings and routinized schedules. Moving to new neighborhoods, changing schools, and having to recite in class typically stood out in their memories as particularly uncomfortable incidents.

My most vivid direct observations of H− children indicates that they, like their adult counterparts, are difficult to discriminate from F− (desurgent) children. Both appear quiet and restrained and want excessive reassurance—though in F− children this behavior arises out of being subjected to too much social inhibition, rather than from the physiological skittishness that underlies H−. Especially, playmates seemed liable to confuse H− and F− traits, lumping F− (desurgent) and H− (threctic) children together under the rubric of "scaredy cats."

Important Correlations Between H− Scores and Other 16PF Factor Scores

In order of magnitude, the correlations in Table 8.2 indicate that H− persons are often F− (quiet and serious), O− (self-reproaching and apprehensive), C− (have poor ego controls), A− (are reserved and detached), Q_4− (are tense and frustrated), and Q_2+ (rely on themselves rather than seeking support and comfort from others). This picture of H− individuals presents them not only as shy and timid but as extremely ill at ease.

Table 8.2

Important Correlations Between H− Scores and Other 16PF Factor Scores

Factor Pole	Correlation	Possible Associated Traits Indicated by Correlation
F− (Desurgency)	.45	Sober, Taciturn, Serious
O+ (Guilt Proneness)	.43	Apprehensive, Self-reproaching, Insecure, Worrying, Troubled
C− (Low Ego Strength)	.39	Affected by Feelings, Emotionally Less Stable, Easily Upset, Changeable
A− (Sizothymia)	.38	Reserved, Detached, Critical, Aloof, Stiff
Q_4+ (Ergic Tension)	.33	Tense, Frustrated, Driven, Overwrought
Q_2+ (Self-sufficiency)	.32	Self-sufficient, Resourceful, Prefers Own Decisions
E− (Submission)	.31	Humble, Mild, Easily Led, Docile, Accommodating

Certainly, it is not a picture that fits well with the cultural ideal. Consequently, it can be supposed that many H− persons may have difficulty in maintaining socially approved self-images. This assumption is supported to some extent by the fact that the correlation between H− and Q_3− (lower self-sentiment) scores[7] is nearly significant. This cultural bias may be more damaging to men's self-images, since, unlike women, they are rarely forgiven for being "shrinking violets." In fact, in earlier 16PF primary scale correlations calculated separately for males and females, significant positive relation was found between H− and Q_3− scores for men but not for women (Clinical Analysis Questionnaire Manual, 1980).

Clinical Relevance of H− Scores

As Karson and O'Dell (1976) stated, H− scores are of more interest to the clinician than H+ scores, since their appearance

---

[7]The correlation between H− and Q_3− scores is .20 and does not appear in Table 8.2.

in a profile always signifies that the examinee is experiencing some unpleasant affect and, in extreme instances, may mean schizoid withdrawal. The particular type of schizoid withdrawal they may signify is further discernible by the magnitude of the A scores that accompany them. In my experience, examinees who meet the DSM-III diagnostic criteria for having schizoid personality disorders show very low A scores, which convey the lack of social interest basic to this diagnosis. By contrast, higher A scores, of 4 or above, suggest some presence of social interest; these examinees may wish to interact with others, but be held back by fear. This latter combination suggests an avoidant rather than a schizoid personality disorder.

Another clinically interesting combination is the conjunction of H− scores with E− scores, which Krug (1980) insightfully discusses in the following example:

> *Example:* A man convicted of murdering two men claimed that he acted under duress because his accomplice threatened to kill him if he did not commit these murders. Krug argues that this claim has psychological, if not legal, validity, in light of the man's 16PF profile, which showed a score of 1 on both the E and H scales. These scores together suggest that the examinee is a virtual "door mat," adapting to circumstances no matter the cost.

This same passive adaptation to environmental demands, accompanied by a sense of being overwhelmed by external forces, as cited in the example above, has been reported often by my own clients whose profiles showed H− and E− scores, but under less dramatic conditions.

In my sample, H− scores appeared in the profiles of certain kinds of examinees who were either addicted to or who inappropriately used alcohol and drugs. These individuals linked their substance abuse to social anxiety, and it was typical for them to report that they initially used drugs, particularly alcohol, to combat fear or to "steady their nerves," especially in stressful social situations such as attending parties or dating. Because of the profound sense of relief or even "false courage" that these substances provided, the clients proceeded to become habituated to the use of these substances.

A key characteristic of these substance-abusing, H− individuals was their remembering the exhilaration, as a result of the disinhibiting effect of the alcohol, that accompanied their first drinking episode.

> *Example:* A 40-year-old alcoholic male recounted the details of his first drink in an AA group. Here is his more or less verbatim account: "When I was 18 I was a virtual wallflower at parties, blushing when girls spoke to me and hiding out with a couple of good friends I had known since grade school. Finally, at one party someone persuaded me to drink some whiskey. I hated the taste but managed to get it down. A few minutes later, I felt wonderful, confident, relaxed, ready to take on the world. I laughed, danced, sang, and felt more at ease than I had ever felt in my life. I was no longer scared about what people thought of me. I thought I had discovered heaven in a bottle."

It was characteristic, as in the example above, for those who abused alcohol to undergo what appeared to others as dramatic personality changes during their periods of intoxication. These changes were also apt to be towards hostility as well as happy self-confidence, since all the negative and angry feelings that they were too fearful to show while sober were liable to come out when they were drunk. Many readers will recognize this type among their acquaintances: the nice, quiet, and polite person who becomes blatantly hostile after a few drinks.

I saw a disproportionate number of H− clients in marriage therapy. Typically, the therapy was initiated by their spouses, who complained that the couple's joint social life was constricted, sometimes almost nonexistent. They also said that their partner disliked activities that involved meeting new people, and refused to entertain in their homes anyone other than immediate family members or old friends. Resolving this conflict was often delicate, since the most obvious recourse was for the non-H− spouse to develop a separate social life, so that his or her social needs could be satisfied without subjecting the partner to uncomfortable demands. But I noticed that H− individuals felt threatened by such arrangements, usually being quick to see that they might provide opportunities for their spouses to meet potentially more congenial companions; they also knew that their shyness and timidity would make it difficult for them to replace a spouse who had cast them off.

As with several other factor poles, there are no advantages, as far as I can see, for being H−. H− persons are the silent sufferers of their own self-imposed restrictions, whose social adjustment is based on avoidance, substitute gratifications, and personal relinquishments. Moreover, because they fail to draw positive attention to themselves, their potentials and even achievements are apt to go unrecognized under usual circumstances. Of them, it can truly be said that because nothing is risked, nothing is gained.

The good news is that H− scores tend to move towards the opposite pole over time; most H− individuals will become less timid and shy with age. Relief, though, is also often more immediately available through clinical intervention. Desensitization techniques have been particularly helpful in treating H− clients in my own clinical practice. These can help decrease social anxiety and inappropriate fears, thus enabling H− people to live less restricted lives.

Chapter 9

Factor I: Feeling vs. Thinking—Contrasting Modes of Evaluating Experience

THE CONSTRUCT

History of the Construct: James and Jung

The Tendency Towards Thinking or Feeling
in Evaluative Responses

Right and Left Hemispheric Specialization

Male and Female Differences Throughout the Life Span

Heredity

Important Correlations Between I
and Other 16PF Factor Scores

A Golden Mean Factor

HIGH SCORES ON FACTOR I

Intrapsychic Data

Interpersonal and Social Data

I + and Childhood

Clinical Relevance of I + Scores

LOW SCORES ON FACTOR I

Intrapsychic Data

Interpersonal and Social Data

I − and Childhood

Clinical Relevance of I − Scores

FACTOR I: CHARACTERISTICS OF I+ (PREMSIC) AND I- (HARRIC) EXAMINEES

Left Score I - (HARRIA)		Right Score I + (PREMSIA)
(Tough-minded, Rejects Illusions)	vs.	**(Tender-minded, Sensitive, Dependent, Overprotected)**
Unsentimental, Expects Little	vs.	Fidgety, Expecting Affection and Attention
Self-reliant, Taking Responsibility	vs.	Clinging, Insecure, Seeking Help and Sympathy
Hard to Point of Cynicism	vs.	Kindly, Gentle, Indulgent to Self and Others
Few Artistic Responses (but Not Lacking in Taste)	vs.	Artistically Fastidious, Affected, Theatrical
Unaffected by Fancies	vs.	Imaginative in Inner Life and in Conversation
Acts on Practical Logical Evidence	vs.	Acts on Sensitive Intuition
Keeps to Point	vs.	Attention-seeking, Flighty
Doesn't Dwell on Physical Disabilities	vs.	Hypochondriacal, Anxious about Self

THE CONSTRUCT

History of the Construct: James and Jung

The neologisms used to describe the poles of this factor are instructive. The right (I+) pole is called *premsia,* a condensation for "protected emotional sensitivity." By contrast, harria abbreviates hardness and realism at the left (I-) pole. Cattell credits William James for first recognizing, then popularizing, these poles. Dubbing them as "tough-mindedness" and "tender-mindedness," James saw them as being the underlying emotional orientations that shape one's philosophical views, tastes, and preferences. Also, since he realized that he was describing the extremes of a normally distributed trait, he clearly recognized that the majority of persons cannot be strictly classified as exclusively belonging to either one.

In my view, however, more credit should be given to Jung than James for recognizing these polarities, which he did in his descriptions of the "feeling" and "thinking" functions. I will pause here to summarize what he had to say about them in his general theory of psychological types.

According to Jung (1928), there are four operations or, to use his own words, "functions," by which persons respond to their environments: feeling, thinking, sensation, and intuition. Feeling and thinking are evaluative functions, i.e., constrasting ways of arriving at judgments, while sensation and intuition, as the perceptual functions, refer to the two main modes used to process information. Over time, one of each pair of functions comes to be used more frequently than its opposite, to the extent that a habit is established that classifies persons as feeling versus thinking, or sensing versus intuitive types.

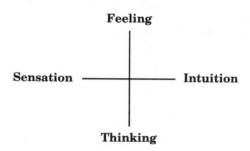

Figure 9.1. The Four Functions in Jung's Theory of Personality Types: Feeling, Thinking, Intuition, and Sensation

In Figure 9.1 above, feeling and thinking are placed in juxtaposition, as are sensation and intuition. This is to illustrate the opposition that exists between these dichotomies, since Jung asserts that it is not possible *simultaneously* to evaluate by feeling and thinking or to perceive by sensing and intuiting.

Jung also asserts that, just as the preferred function in the dichotomy becomes developed by use, the less preferred and hence less used one becomes atrophied. This, since process affects outcome, eventually results in an image of reality that directly contrasts with what would have been formed should the opposite function have been primary—hence, a different personality structure.

Further discussion of Jung's perceiving, i.e., sensing and intuiting functions will be postponed until Chapter 11, where they will be compared to the polarities of Factor M. In this chapter, we are interested only in his feeling and thinking functions. The former appears in I+ scorers as a proclivity for making evaluations based on subjective impressions and emotional reactions.

Consequently, these individuals produce judgments based on personal values, aesthetics, taste, and approach/avoidance tendencies. By contrast, I− individuals tend to be objective, often to the point of discounting or being unaware of what they are feeling. They are more considerate of verificity, probability, and accuracy in arriving at their judgments.

The Tendency Towards Feeling or Thinking in Evaluative Responses

In a nutshell, what Factor I essentially taps is the habitual tendency to respond to events, ideas, and experiences, either with feeling or with thinking. I+ people rely on their empathetic understanding to make evaluations; they are compassionate and sensitive as well as attuned to their own vulnerability. These kinds of feelings gradually fade and are replaced by more objective responses in persons scoring further down the factor continuum, until they are virtually absent in extremely low scorers. I− individuals have few protective illusions and believe that the harsh realities of life should be accepted without much complaint. As a consequence, they are typically unindulgent, towards both themselves and others, and have utilitarian rather than aesthetic values.

To illustrate the personality contrast between I+ and I− scorers to my students, I sometimes refer to Felix and Oscar, the central characters in Neil Simon's play, *The Odd Couple,* on which the popular television series of that name was based.

> Felix and Oscar are caricatures of I+ and I− characteristics. Premsic Felix (who would probably achieve a 16PF I score of 10) is fastidious, tasteful, romantic, artistic, repulsed by whatever appears crude or harsh, brimming over with sympathy and sentimentality. He is indulgent, easily hurt, and expectant that others will have the same acute sensibilities as he does, and that they will, therefore, treat him lovingly and gently. By contrast, the I− Oscar is "rough and ready," unemotional, lacking in empathetic understanding, and not given to self-indulgence or analysis.

Right and Left Hemispheric Specialization

I am often asked if Factor I has any relation to *hemispheric specialization.* Hemispheric specialization refers to a preference for using one side of the brain over the other. There is some evidence that the *right* side of the brain processes information subjectively and emotionally, and is the locus of artistic and "spiritual" kinds of interests, whereas the *left* side has to do with objective, linear, nonemotional modes of processing and operates on the practical and concrete aspects of reality (Sperry, 1968). Although the descriptions of these specializations match closely with $I+$ and $I-$ and the mutually inhibitory relationship between these dichotomies, no formal investigations have yet been performed to confirm whether any connection exists. I am hopeful, however, that investigations along these lines will be performed in the future, for if a connection is established, much psychoneurological information can be harnessed to augment what is presently known about Factor I.

Male and Female Differences Throughout the Life Span

Implicit in $I+$ and $I-$ are the notions of masculinity and femininity. Emotional sensitivity, subjectivity, compassion, and empathy have traditionally been regarded as "feminine" traits, whereas objective thinking, toughness, and repression of feelings is synonymous with what is considered masculine in our culture. This association with gender stereotypes is evidenced by the strong correlations of this factor with the M/F (Masculinity/ Femininity) scale of the MMPI (Karson & O'Dell, 1976).

Other psychometric evidence arises from the large difference in means that exists between the sexes on this factor. The mean score for women is 25.78, which places them towards the $I+$ pole, whereas for males it is only 18.25. Although both sexes score at the $I+$ pole when they are first measured at age six, even at that early age girls score one-and-a-half stens higher than boys (Cattell & Cattell, 1975).

Later, though, girls become even more $I+$, and the gap between boys and girls continues to widen until it reaches two stens by their 10th year, and three stens by their 15th year. As the age curve graph on page 153 of Cattell (1973) shows, this difference in stens is maintained until both sexes reach their 40s, after which it gradually decreases. Then, women become more $I-$ and men more $I+$, reflecting an occurrence in keeping with the folklore that women become tougher with age, and men mellower.

This large difference of means between the sexes is matched only by the difference between men and women on one other factor in the 16PF continuum. The other large difference occurs on Factor E (dominance/submission), and women are generally less assertive than men. As with Factor E, it is probable that these differences will be less marked in future collections of normative data because of the present erosion of sexual stereotypes and their replacement with more androgynous styles of behavior.

Heredity

Apart from the environmental influences, heredity plays a significant role in influencing one's eventual place on the Factor I continuum. The most recent evidence (Cattell, 1982) is that genetics contributes 47% of the variance. Moreover, constitutional associations, such as a correlation between AB blood types and I+ scores, have been discovered (Cattell, R. B., Young, H. B., & Hundleby, J. D., 1964), and further behavior genetics research may, hopefully, reveal more about the nature-nurture interactions of this trait.

Important Correlations Between I
and Other 16PF Factor Scores

The only significant correlation between I scores and other 16PF factor scores is with Factor M, which, as I have already proposed, measures perceptual styles similar to Jung's intuition and sensing functions. Because a more thorough understanding of these styles is fundamental to understanding the relation between I and M scores, I shall wait until Chapter 11, which discusses Factor M, to explore the meaning of this correlation.

A Golden Mean Factor

Persons who score in the middle ranges of Factor I move with versatility between thinking and feeling responses. Since this versatility allows for the incorporation of both subjective and objective reality, it can lead to a more complete understanding than when one is overemphasized to the detriment of the other. For this reason, I consider Factor I as being one of the "golden mean factors," meaning that it is more adaptive to score in the average range of Factor I.

HIGH SCORES ON FACTOR I

Intrapsychic Data

In the early days of listening to the self-reports of I+ examinees, I initially tended to confuse I+ as a trait with A+ (affectothymia) and C− (low ego strength). In the first instance, my confusion resulted from the way in which the kindly responses of I+ individuals were similar to those observed in A+ people. But with further experience, especially in listening to those whose profiles showed I+ scores accompanied by low or moderate A scores, I noticed that their social responses were not mediated by sociability and liking for people, but by empathetic understanding, which allowed them to know through emotional identification just what others were experiencing.[1]

In the second instance, my tendency to confuse I+ (premsia) and C− (low ego strength) resulted from my observation that I+ examinees were apt to be emotional, changeable, and indecisive —all characteristics similar to those which mark the poorly functioning egos of C− scorers. But after listening carefully to the self-reports of these individuals, I discerned that their behavior, unlike that of C− scorers, did not arise from poor frustration tolerance or inability to correctly differentiate their feelings. Rather, these qualities stemmed from strong emotional responses and diminished capacity for objectivity.

Like other observers, I noted that it is often difficult for I+ persons to communicate their impressions to others. This is undoubtedly because feeling, unlike thinking, is not naturally aligned with linear linguistic expressions, denotations, and symbols. Probably it is for this reason that I+ people generally enjoy art and metaphor, since these forms lend themselves better to the language of feelings. It was noteworthy that all of the I+ examinees in my sample showed artistic appreciation or ability, and that I+ scores have been found in the group profiles of artists, musicians, and writers (Rieke & Russell, 1987).

By far the most important modulator of premsia is the second-order extraversion/introversion pattern. Seventy-one examinees

---

[1]The somewhat reclusive but emotionally sensitive Rousseau exemplified my conception of I+ unadulterated by A+.

(about 35 percent of my 204 I+ examinees) were decidedly introverted. I observed that, for the most part, these individuals usually kept their strong emotional responses to themselves. This
was apparent especially in those whose introverted patterns
showed extreme F− (desurgency) or H− (threctia) scores. Being
taciturn, shy, and timid, they were likely to have intense, bottled-
up feelings, since they did not easily confide in others. And because this is undoubtedly painful from a mental-health
standpoint, I have come to prefer to see I+ combined with extraverted tendencies, for it is more likely that these examinees
will dissipate their painful feelings by sharing them.

I discovered that unusually extreme H+, A+, or F+ scores
(which are part of the second-order extraversion pattern) of, say,
9 or 10, are particularly meaningful in conjunction with I+
scores. Extreme H+ scores indicate boldness and adventure-
someness, which, when blended with I+ emotional responsivity,
produces ardent and dynamic natures. Several examinees who
showed this combination were, or had been, civil-rights activists.

The gregariousness and positive human orientation indicated
by A+ (affectothymia) scores in conjunction with I+ scores
convey examinees who are sympathetic, generous, and kind.
Extreme F+ and I+ scores (especially when accompanied by
more moderate scores than usual on the other extraversion
scales) indicate tendencies towards dramatization and self-
centeredness.

I+ clients in group therapy have often astonished me by
arriving at astute insights by discerning hidden motives and
attitudes missed by clients with more moderate scores on Factor
I in the group, and even by the therapist. When asked how they
obtained these insights, they were apt to answer that it somehow
involved their ability to put themselves in another person's place.
They were referring, of course, to their ability to empathetic
understanding, which, I must specifically state, is not intuition.
(Intuition is a way of organizing subliminal perceptions and making associations, as will be explained in the discussion on Factor
M in Chapter 11.)

There are two other core characteristics I have consistently
noted in I+ examinees. First was their romantic attitudes, which
permeated their judgment and orientation. As far as I could tell,
these attitudes resulted from their capacity for disencumbering
themselves of objective facts, thereby allowing them to indulge
their wishful thinking and fantasy.

The second was that they were so finely attuned to their feelings that they were able to experience an unusual "here and now" immediacy and a sense of aliveness. The negative aspect of this was that they were unable to distance themselves from their more painful feelings and therefore suffered more intensely than lower-scoring persons. Nevertheless, it remains a value judgment as to whether it is better to experience emotional peaks and valleys or to maintain a more moderate course. The association of I+ scores with neuroticism might suggest the latter.

Interpersonal and Social Data

In noting how others responded to the I+ examinees in my sample, I discerned that the most important variable was the degree to which the responder was him- or herself oriented by feelings. It followed, therefore, that I− scorers had negative responses towards I+ people, typically finding their proclivity for understanding by empathy, rather than by objective analysis, almost incomprehensible. Their animosity showed itself particularly in work situations.

The most frequent complaints I heard regarding I+ employees was that their emotional sensitivity caused them to agonize over harsh decisions, sometimes creating excessive delays. Consequently, when clients with I+ scores seek vocational guidance, I discourage them from entering occupations that require quick unemotional reactions, such as nursing or police work. Fortunately, I+ people usually are not attracted to these kinds of occupations anyway, for, according to data gathered so far, I+ scores are found much more frequently in other dissimilar groups, such as clergy, psychiatrists, professors, social workers, biologists, educators, and psychiatric technicians, as well as in the more aesthetically inclined occupations mentioned earlier (Rieke & Russell, 1987).

Probably the I+ disposition makes its most significant social contributions through the arts. I+ persons who resisted their natural tendency to recoil in repugnancy from cruel, ugly, or coarse situations, but who make sensitive observations which they then share with their less empathetic fellows, have a special place in history. England's Charles Dickens, who described the brutal effects of poverty on the Victorian lower classes in such novels as *Oliver Twist* and *David Copperfield,* and Harriet Beecher Stowe, who wrote of the atrocities of slavery in America in *Uncle Tom's Cabin,* are, in my opinion, two examples of I+ people of this kind.

The descriptive capsule at the beginning of this chapter indicates that in their interpersonal relations, I+ individuals expect affection, are clinging, and seek help and sympathy. One way to look at these responses is that they are natural, hence more appropriate, in children, and, therefore, I+ in adults could be construed to indicate a form of immaturity.

In addition, I have already suggested that one other way to look at I+ is its consistency with the traditional picture of femininity. Although our culture now considers I+ to be less an embodiment of the ideal female than in former times, strongly I+ women still retain their attractiveness to some macho-inclined men, who prefer to play protective and controlling roles in their gender relationships. But, judging by the number of dissatisfied men married to I+ women seen in my clinical practice, this attractiveness seems short-lived. In the long run, these women seem to prove to be burdensome partners in meeting the demands of contemporary life.

Though they were apt to play maternal roles in meeting their husbands' emotional needs, women married to I+ *men* in my sample expressed more satisfaction than those married to I− men. Many reported having a high level of mutual understanding with their husbands. There is a statistical basis for the frequency of this occurrence. Since women are generally more I+ than men, the chances are higher that the couple has similar tastes and views, which leads to mutual liking (Aronson, 1972). In particular, women seem to have rapport with I+ men generally, valuing them as confidants and friends. Relationships between women and men with artistic and feminine interests are ubiquitous examples of this phenomenon.

I+ and Childhood

Factor I accounts for more variance in the personality of children than it does in adults. It ranks as the fourth largest temperament trait in children, but then fades into eighth place by the time they reach adulthood.

Since all humans start their lives by responding on the basis of feeling rather than thinking, it can only be supposed that the degree to which feeling responses are rewarded or punished has some influence on the frequency with which they continue to be used. In this regard, Cattell (1973) reports that I+ in adults is associated with an overly indulgent and protective childhood.

The HSPQ handbook (Cattell & Cattell, 1975) summarized the research that had been accumulated on I+ children up to the date of its publication, focusing primarily on their relations with their parents. These various researches led to two main findings. First, I+ children had a high incidence of psychosomatic complaints. They became easily tired and complained of headaches, stomach upsets, and other vague symptoms. Second, and more importantly, their parents appeared to overindulge their dependency needs.

> "The central feature of I+ is the emotionally indulgent overprotective home. Though it has cultural associations it would be a mistake to identify it with 'higher' culture or refined ideals, for high I often occurs in homes of quite low cultural status where discipline is neglected, indulgence maintained, the parents side with the child against society, and sensitivity to individual subjectivity is high." (p. 32)

The HSPQ handbook (p. 32) also reported that I+ children display other behavioral characteristics similar to their adult counterparts. They shun rough, adventurous, or strenuous activities, are disinterested in sports, prefer subjects like art and literature, are neat and fastidious but not well organized, are emotionally dependent, and do not respond well in emergencies.

Turning now to my personal observations, I noted that I+ children generally behaved in accord with what is reported in the HSPQ handbook. Moreover, they were what is popularly known as "highly strung," i.e., easily upset and emotional; they needed more than average amounts of reassurance and support. Often they were scornfully regarded by their more self-reliant and stoic peers.

I+ boys, who were referred to as "sissies," were particularly scorned by other boys because of the aversion with which young males typically view any behavior among them that seems feminine or immature. Readers will undoubtedly be able to conjure up some image of a gentle, sensitive, and obviously squeamish little boy from the playgrounds of their own youth who fits this description.

I was relieved to find that I+ youngsters fared much better with their adult acquaintances. This was probably due to their eagerness to please. It was not uncommon for the brighter ones to become the proverbial teacher's pets and for adults generally to act protectively towards them, having the maturity to recognize their tender-heartedness and lack of self-protective callousness.

Clinical Relevance of I+ Scores

Even though I+ scores alone do not necessarily indicate poor adjustment, from the foregoing it might be supposed that there would be a relationship between I+ and C− (low ego strength). But (as it has been said earlier in this chapter), although these traits sometimes manifest themselves similarly, their underlying roots are distinctly different, and the statistical evidence is that they are not usually correlated. Nevertheless, when I+ and C− scores do appear together on the same profile, they indicate that the examinee is an extremely subjective, probably overemotional, individual who does not solve problems well. Since life is usually difficult for persons of this sort, it is hardly surprising that Krug and Sherman (1977) report that stress-related illnesses, particularly of the coronary vascular system, are associated with an I+/C− combination of scores.

I+ scores enter into the neuroticism pattern, which is made up of E− (submissiveness), F− (desurgency), G− (low superego), H− (threctia), O+ (low self-esteem), and Q_4+ (nervous tension), in addition to C− (low ego strength).[2] Given this link, it is helpful for clinicians, when interpreting a profile that shows an elevation on Factor I, to check to see how the I+ score aligns with these other factor scores.

LOW SCORES ON FACTOR I

Intrapsychic Data

By asserting that the mental life of I− individuals operates by logic and reason, Cattell (1973) emphasized the cognitive aspects of I− behavior. More recently, Karson and O'Dell (1976) and, to a lesser extent, Krug (1980) have shown more interest in the emotional meaning of this trait, by noticing that it also indicates

---

[2]*Handbook for the 16PF,* p. 264.

repressed emotion. Similarly, the thorough in-depth mental status examinations my colleagues and I performed on 39 I – clients focused on both their feeling and thinking, and on the relationships between these two processes. If the results of these examinations can be generalized, they show (just as Jung's theory of the thinking function would predict) that I – people form their understanding on the basis of detached objective analysis. They generate far fewer empathetically based judgments than their I + counterparts. Accompanying this way of processing information is an orientation that emphasizes survival and security concerns and places value on whatever is tangible, practical, and possible, rather than on abstractions and aesthetics.

Just as I + is susceptible to being misinterpreted as ego weakness, the stoic mental orientation associated with I – can be confused with C + (ego strength). Not only are these traits unrelated (it has already been explained that Factors I and C are not correlated), but they are based on quite different intrapsychic strategies. Unlike those with strong egos, whose stoic composure comes from setting their internal houses in order and by prioritizing and adjusting their needs to outer realities, I – persons achieve a similar mental state by constricting their range of emotional experience.

I – simulates two additional traits: A – (sizothymia) and H + (parmia). Like A – scorers, the I – examinees in my sample were cool and unsympathetic. But, unlike A – scorers, for whom this attitude was part of their overall social indifference, these same qualities in I – examinees seemed to stem from the same lack of emotional indulgence that they held towards themselves. They rejected their own vulnerable feelings as much as they did those of others. In *The Moon and Sixpence,* Somerset Maugham (1984)[3] illustrates this self-orientation in the character of Strickland, his fictional equivalent of the artist, Gauguin.

When Strickland was being nursed back to health after he had been found sick, alone, and starving, his friend commented:

> I have never known a more difficult patient. It was not that he was exacting and querulous; on the contrary, he never complained; he asked for nothing; he was perfectly silent; but he seemed to resent the care that was taken of him; he received all inquiries about his feelings or his needs with a jibe, a sneer, or an oath. (p. 96)

---

[3]Originally published 1929.

My I− examinees resembled examinees who had H+ (parmic) scores, in that they stayed calm in threatening situations. Here, too, their behavior was attributable to their Spartan-like disregard for their own vulnerability and to harsh self-attitudes. Unlike H+ people, who were thrill seekers and who actually sought out dangers, I− people did not find these situations exciting. Their under-reactivity came from repression of feelings.

Interpersonal and Social Data

The adjectives used in the *Handbook for the 16PF* (p. 93) to describe I− individuals are "tough, masculine, practical, mature, group-solidarity-generating, and realistic." Looking at them in the context of interpersonal relations, they portray the kind of person whom people would want to police their neighborhoods, pilot planes on which they are passengers, or to be at their side when facing a natural disaster. This type, however, is certainly not a desirable companion for accompanying one to a ballet, sharing sentimental moments, or for giving sympathy or comfort. Neither would an I− person, just as Karson and O'Dell (1976) point out, usually be selected for a counselor or therapist, unless one is seeking clear, unemotional directives.

> *Example:* Readers who remember Sergeant Friday, the hardboiled city detective from the old TV series *Dragnet,* will immediately get a sense of the quality of the I− person's interactions. In gathering information from persons who had often seen or had been victims of violent crimes, his standard response to their emotional reactions was to request, "The facts, please. Just the facts."

It is easy to guess that when I− persons experience interpersonal difficulties, it is most likely to be in their intimate relationships. Many joined my sample of examinees when their more I+ spouses became dissatisfied with the I− person's lack of empathetic understanding and poor expression of romantic feelings.

Although I have had several I− women in marital therapy, their lack of emotional sensitivity did not appear to contribute directly to the problems for which the couple sought help. This might be explained by their husbands' happening also to be I− people who appreciated their practicality and down-to-earthness.

"No fuss, no frills" was how one such man responded when asked what he most appreciated about his wife.

In keeping with the plan used throughout this manuscript, I− has been presented so as to appear as if harria alone dominated certain people's personalities and entirely accounted for the quality of their interpersonal relations. However, let me remind the reader again that this is a literary liberty and does not fit with what actually occurs, as each trait is influenced by all other traits in the human psyche.

Of particular importance in revealing how I− examinees will relate to others is their score on Factor A. An I− examinee whose profile shows A− (sizothymic) scores will be cool as well as insensitive, and so will most assuredly have difficulty in making any kind of emotional connection. On the other hand, an I− examinee who shows A+ (affectothymic) scores will have a sociable and outgoing disposition, even though he displays insensitivity to others' feelings.

Naturally, therefore, the emotional dualism displayed by I−/A+ persons can be confusing to those who interact with them. These persons are likely to give practical help to a depressed friend, while at the same time advising them to "shape up." They may bring chicken soup to the invalid, but leave at the first complaints of pain; they may generously donate time and money to solving a social problem, but have a simplistic understanding of the human subtleties involved.

Especially confusing is the lack of comprehension an I−/A+ individual may show regarding the impact of what he or she genuinely intends to be a helpful suggestion.

> *Example:* An I−/A+ man in my sample told his fiancee that he was breaking off their engagement, as he had decided to return to his ex-wife, out of concern for his children of this former marriage. After making this announcement, he reassured his fiancee that he still had loving feelings for her and that he saw no reason why they could not remain friends. He then suggested that they go out to a movie. When his sobbing fiancee told him she was too overwhelmed by his news to see a movie, he responded that it was a good movie and would cheer her up. He was shocked when she accused him of being insensitive.

I− and Childhood

There is virtually nothing in the Cattell literature about the kinds of early environments that influence the development of I−. Although I do not have sufficient first-hand observations to correct this omission, I have accumulated a sufficient number of childhood recollections of I− examinees that tentatively suggest certain possibilities.

Maturation and gender identification themes were strongly and routinely featured in these recollections involving both male and female I− examinees. Frequently, they reported that, as children, they had placed a high value in what are culturally labeled as "masculine characteristics" (e.g., being objective as opposed to subjective, and liking mathematics rather than literature). Many were reared in environments that discouraged expression of vulnerable feelings such as fear, disappointment, and self-pity.

> *Example:* A male client who scored 1 on Factor I told me that he was sent to a British boarding school at age 8. He recalled that he had always known he would go to boarding school because that was the tradition of his upper-middle-class family. He was very homesick, but knew he could not show these feelings if he were to get along with the other boys. The unofficial motto of the school seemed to be, "Don't be a crybaby." He resolved to make himself think about other things whenever he started thinking about his mother. This habit of repressing vulnerable feelings by stopping unwelcome thoughts persisted into adulthood.

My historical data also suggested that birth order may contribute to the developing of an I− temperament. A disproportionate number (about 46%) of I− examinees reported that they had been brought up in large families or had been among the older siblings in their families. They saw themselves as having been pushed prematurely to abandon age-appropriate behavior, so that their parents could better attend to the younger brothers and sisters.

Clinical Relevance of I− Scores

While the appearance of I− scores in a profile do not by themselves indicate psychopathology, they do suggest that the examinee has at least a strong potential for having difficulties in intimate interpersonal relations. Since I have already gone into this matter in an earlier section, I will not elaborate on it here.

Another important clinical indicator of I − scores is that they convey that the examinee is probably out of touch with tender or vulnerable kinds of feelings such as fear, pity, or dependency. If O − (high self-esteem) also appears on the profile, then this range of repressed or disowned feelings is extended to include those to do with self-censure or blame, like guilt or shame.

From the point of view of tolerating stress, there is some benefit in being I −, according to Karson and O'Dell (1976). Even so, there is a dark shadow to this tolerance, since there is a danger that I − scorers will fail to complain until after their endurance has been exhausted. This might prevent them from getting needed and timely help. For example, they may so severely underestimate the severity of illness that others may also discount its significance, as is illustrated in the following example.

> *Example:* The husband of one of my patients died after being sent home from a hospital Emergency Room where he had been taken by friends after they noticed that he was pale and breathing laboredly. A subsequent investigation of the medical records showed that he had so minimized his symptoms that the attending physician was not given enough information to evaluate his condition accurately. Although I had no testing on this man, his wife's description clearly suggested that he would have obtained an I − score if he had been tested by the 16PF.

Finally, although research to date has not linked I − scores with psychosomatic symptoms, they have appeared in the group profiles of asthmatic patients (Rosenthal, Aitken, & Zealley, 1973). This preliminary finding suggests that future investigations into the mind-body relationship, especially in regard to emotional repression, may discover that I − plays more of a role in physical illness than is presently supposed.

Chapter 10

Factor L: Alienation vs. Identification in Social Orientations

THE CONSTRUCT
Factor L as a Measurement of Social Identity

Jealousy

Suspiciousness

Defensive Projection

Male and Female Differences Throughout the Life Span

HIGH SCORES ON FACTOR L
Intrapsychic Data

Interpersonal and Social Data

L+ and Childhood

Important Correlations Between L+ Scores
and Other 16PF Factor Scores

Clinical Relevance of L+ Scores

LOW SCORES ON FACTOR L
Intrapsychic Data

Interpersonal and Social Data

L- and Childhood

Important Correlations Between L- Scores
and Other 16PF Factor Scores

Clinical Relevance of L- Scores

FACTOR L: CHARACTERISTICS OF L+ (PROTENSIVE) AND L− (ALAXIC) EXAMINEES

Left Score L− (ALAXIA)		Right Score L+ (PROTENSION)
(Trusting, Accepting Conditions)	vs.	(Suspecting, Jealous)
Accepts Personal Unimportance	vs.	Jealous
Pliant to Changes	vs.	Dogmatic
Unsuspecting of Hostility	vs.	Suspicious of Interference
Ready to Forget Difficulties	vs.	Dwelling upon Frustrations
Understanding and Permissive, Tolerant	vs.	Tyrannical
Lax over Correcting People	vs.	Demands People Accept Responsibility for Errors
Conciliatory	vs.	Irritable

THE CONSTRUCT

Factor L as a Measurement of Social Identity

As Factor L's highest pole is so closely tied to disturbed interpersonal relationships, I have done more clinical research towards understanding it than on most other 16PF factors. I have now come to interpret Factor L as measuring the degree to which one feels identified with others, not merely immediate kin and close friends, but the human race generally. For L+ scorers this feeling is largely missing, since their sense of personal boundaries are so tightly drawn that they feel separate from most others.

By contrast, the experience of L− scorers is of feeling at one with their fellow humans. They see themselves as being "made out of the same cloth," and as sharing similar characteristics, fates, and struggles.

Possibly because social identification, or lack of it, is implicitly sensed rather than being consciously and explicitly recognized, it has not hitherto been noticed as forming the underlying core of Factor L. Instead, earlier descriptions have focused on the topical but florid manifestations of its absence—jealousy, suspicion, and defensive projection. These traits, which are pronounced in L+ examinees, are less present as the Factor L score decreases. At the left pole of the factor, the antonymic traits "trusting" and "accepting of conditions" dominate.

Even though this material would normally appear in the section that presents the intrapsychic data on L+ examinees, let us pause here to define jealousy, suspiciousness, and defensive projection. A preliminary, in-depth understanding of these three constructs will elucidate further discussion, because *(a)* their presence or absence represents the most important manifestations of L+ and L− traits, and *(b)* they are the source from which minor Factor L traits are derived.

Jealousy

First, let us examine jealousy as a feeling. We recognize it as resentment experienced toward another—or others—who seem superior to us in some attribute or possession, or who seem to receive approval, recognition, or affection that we would like for ourselves. While few have not felt this "green-eyed monster," it is usually fleeting, or is focused on a specific individual. By contrast, this feeling is permanently welded into the characters of L+ individuals, coloring their overall perceptions and spewing bitterness.

Though one of the most tormenting of emotions, it can be argued that jealousy is not without value; it undoubtedly served evolutionary purposes by promoting competition. Even now, when the raw fight for the survival of the fittest is over, jealous feelings are sometimes used to fire competitive and dominant behavior, bringing personal gain and achievement. But it is important to note that this form of jealousy is not of the L+ variant; examinees whose jealous feelings undergo this transformation show E+ (dominance) scores on the 16PF profiles, rather than L+ scores.

Jealousy, as it is measured by L+ scores, as far as I can tell, seems to have no redeeming purpose. Though originally developed as an attempt to restore self-esteem, the significant positive correlation between L+ scores and O+ (low self-esteem) indicates that jealousy, instead, "mocks the flesh it feeds on."[1]

So far I have talked about jealousy as a feeling, which is an epiphenomenon of jealousy as a trait. My understanding of it as a trait owes much to Gaylin (1979), who, in his excellent treatise, dissects jealousy into a series of four psychological components.

---

[1]Othello, Shakespeare.

As these components[2] compare so well with what I have discovered in the psyches of L+ clients, I shall set them forth below, adding my own insights and clinical findings. However, since none of this material, neither Gaylin's nor mine, has been subjected to controlled research methods, they are at this time tentative.

   1. First Component in Jealousy Series: Sense of Deprivation. The essential component of jealousy is an experience of deprivation, a sense that something meaningful to one's happiness (e.g., love, material possessions, personal or physical attractiveness) has been denied. In clinical sessions, it is sometimes possible to get L+ clients to focus just on this component, whereupon they report concomitant feelings of sadness, emptiness, and even anger.

   2. Second Component in Jealousy Series: Unfavorable Comparison Between Self and Others. The second component of jealousy lies somewhere between a sense and a perception. Other persons are perceived, either in actuality or fantasy, as having whatever has been deprived. Even though listed as the second component of the jealousy amalgam, it may sometimes be experienced as the first, since a sense of deprivation (first component) can be *evoked* by viewing the disparity between one's own lot and that of others.

> *Example:* One L+ client reported that she first perceived that she lacked love and attention from her parents after a TV set was installed in her home when she was nine years of age. She compared warm and caring parent-child interactions in shows like "Leave It to Beaver" to her relationship with distant and cold parents.[3]

When my L+ clients were able to focus on only this component of their jealousy, they often reported a self-judgment of inadequacy. Feelings of shame typically accompanied this judgment, as well as a strong wish to right this disparity. Further,

---

[2]Although Gaylin refers to the trait as envy, I prefer "jealousy," which is in keeping with the capsule description, found in the 16PF Handbook, of the L+ pole.

[3]Similarly, television is often cited as a prime cause of unrest among the economically disadvantaged. Via scenes of hitherto-unseen affluence, television shows provide contrasts to many people's own poor material conditions.

they felt bitter, but not yet bitter enough to desire depriving others or seeing others' downfall. (This desire comes later, with the addition of the third component.)

This second component combines with the first to create emotional tensions from which all but the most masochistic individuals try to escape. Some escape into the future, believing that their inequitable position will be righted in eternity after death. Others, with a more temporal orientation, change their existing reality, either by obtaining what has been denied them or by finding a substitute gratification, such as money or alcohol. If these strategies successfully reduce inner tensions, then the psychological progression to the following jealous components will stop here. (The profiles of people who feel only these first two components of jealousy typically do not show L+ scores.)

3. Third Component in Jealousy Series: Impotence to Redress Disparity Between One's Own Condition and That of Others. When attempts to relieve the tensions created by a combination of the previous two components fail, then the development to full-fledged jealousy continues. A demoralizing sense of helplessness and frustration, which are felt as depression and hostility, creep into the existing tensions. This added pressure further weakens the already-wounded self-esteem. To restore self-esteem, it becomes necessary to progress to the fourth component.

4. Fourth Component in Jealousy Series: Defensive Action to Restore Self-Esteem by Attributing the Cause of One's Own Deprivation and Impotency to Others' Bounty and Forces Outside One's Own Control. This final component completes the jealousy amalgam. It is an effort to restore self-esteem by assuring oneself that what is lacking in one's life, and one's inability to redress the deprivation, are not due to personal shortcomings, but rather to other people's unfair, competitive, or controlling practices. Having firmly established that the enemy is without, the individual is vindicated and self-doubt is replaced by depreciation of others. Self-esteem then becomes predicated upon a belief of personal superiority over others. But the individual who fails to accomplish this act of self-vindication will show a pattern of learned helplessness. He or she will, in short, "give up on life," and truly believe that he or she is inferior. This person's 16PF profile will probably not show extreme L+ scores.

My data suggest that jealousy as I have described it appears to be based on early chilhood insecurities, including unresolved sibling rivalry (which I will go into later). However, an artifact of jealousy may also elevate L scores. This artifact, found most conspicuously in members of socially underprivileged groups, may be found in an entire nation as well as in a cultural minority. It is what Gaylin (1979) calls "class-action feeling." This feeling differs from jealousy in that "class-action feeling" is based on *actual* rather than imaginary inequities, and is usually accompanied by a lack of power to redress these wrongs. Given these facts, interpretation of L+ scores in the profiles of Black or Hispanic examinees, for example, should be made carefully, recognizing that the root may not be a defensive strategy, but an artifact of one.

Suspiciousness

I have described how L+ persons reconstruct the internal threat as an outside enemy. This externalization requires that they become, not only hypervigilant, but that they must also be able to find reassuring clues that danger exists. Thus, suspiciousness must inevitably become the other main artery from which Factor L draws its sustenance. Suspiciousness and jealousy, merged, form defensive projection.

The suspiciousness of people who score high on Factor L means that they are biased observers who search for confirmatory evidence.

> *Example:* In my consultations with a business, I noticed that one employee, whose L score was 9, frequently used the expression, "It figures," whenever he saw what could be construed as a fault or shortcoming in one of his coworkers, or when he read of some misdeed in the newspaper. The satisfaction, and even triumph, with which he made this utterance made it obvious that he was confirming a cherished belief about human fallibility.

Defensive Projection

I must immediately distinguish my definition of projection used as a defense from the popular notion of projection. Often, projection is thought of as an unconscious process whereby wishes, motives, ideas, and feelings that are threatening to self-esteem are disowned, and are then perceived as being present in others. I reject this simplistic definition on empirical grounds, as I, like other experienced clinicians, have rarely found a direct one-to-one correspondence between what people repudiate in themselves and what they perceive in others. Instead, it is more usual for projection to undergo one more final turn before manifesting itself. For example, a person's projected belief of being poisoned rarely turns out to be his or her own wish to poison the suspect. On this matter, I quote Shapiro (1965), ". . . it is more generally true that the internal tension achieves external form, first by transformation into defensive tension and then by projective reconstruction. The projective content will, therefore, be generally determined by the content of the defensive tension."[4]

It should be stressed that defensive projection is a necessary, though not sufficient, condition for a paranoid diagnosis. Indeed, Krug (1980) reports that, although L+ scores do correlate positively with the paranoia scale of the CAQ, this correlation does not reach statistical significance (p. 22). Moreover, the criteria listed for paranoid mental disorders listed in DSM-III show that these conditions involve more than defensive projection, or, for that matter, the full spectrum of L+ traits. Two of them (*paranoia* and *schizophrenia, paranoid type*) require, as a diagnostic criterion, the existence of delusionary ideas. This is an advanced and complicated form of defensive projection, well beyond what is tapped by L+ scores.

Although delusionary ideas are not a criterion for the third DSM-III mental disorder (*paranoid personality disorder*), a person fitting this diagnosis must demonstrate signs and symptoms drawn from three separate sets of criteria: (1) pervasive suspiciousness, (2) hypersensitivity, and (3) restricted affect. Although L+ defensive projection relates strongly to the first two of these criteria, it (like other L+ traits) does not account for the third.

Differences Throughout the Life Span

Scores for both sexes share similar standard deviations (women, 5.33 and men, 5.06) and means (women, 14.05 and men, 14.78) and follow much the same course in the life-span data collected so far. A decline in scores follows the mid-teens and continues until the 40th year, after which scores gradually rise, moving again toward the L+ pole. For reasons that cannot yet even be tentatively explained, in the 60th year men's and women's scores start showing different trends. Men's scores return to the level

---

[4]Originally, defensive projecting was considered to be synonymous with Factor L (Cattell & Wenig, 1952). Hence, the factor was named protension, which is a neologism for projection of tension. Later studies, however, revealed that, although projection is undoubtedly measured by the factor, it is only part of a wider trait.

close to that of the mid-teens, while women's scores lag behind men's scores by almost one full sten.

HIGH SCORES ON FACTOR L

Intrapsychic Data

In the previous discussion on jealousy, suspicion, and defensive projection, I described the core elements that appeared to color the subjective lives of the 201 L+ examinees I interviewed. Although these elements remained constant, it became increasingly clear as the data accumulated that they assumed two quite different variants, which turned out to be similar to those advanced as "paranoid styles" by Shapiro (1965).

The two variants were distinguishable in 16PF profiles, according to whether the L+ scores combined with O+ (guilt proneness) or O− (untroubled adequacy) scores. One form, which Shapiro describes as furtive, constricted, and apprehensive, I consistently found in L+ examinees whose 16PF profiles showed O+ scores. This L+/O+ combination, which was by far the most usual, indicates the failure to restore self-worth and confidence.

The other, and smaller, variant I encountered is characterized by arrogance and grandiosity. I noticed this style in L+ examinees whose 16PF profiles show O− (untroubled adequacy, or low guilt proneness) scores. This atypical combination indicates that projection has been successful. Examinees see themselves in a positive light and experience little self-doubt. My clinical investigations confirm that, unlike their L+/O+ counterparts, they feel threatened from without and rarely from within.

In interviews, L+ examinees of both variants did not readily admit their protensive attributes. Perhaps this was because they were self-deceived, or perhaps they recognized that it is socially reprehensible, for example, to take joy in another's downfall. An exception is that they admitted to suspicious thinking. In some cases, they were even quite proud of their perspicacity in discerning that people are "no damned good" (an expression undoubtedly invented by an L+ person) and considered it highly desirable to be on guard against trickery and deceit. One jesting examinee in truth informed us, "I believe nothing I hear and only half of what I see."

Thus, they prided themselves on being critical observers. Ironically, though they made diligent and systematic searches and amassed many facts, their observations were gathered to support pre-existing biases; other facts that appeared to be in contradiction were often disregarded.

Biases also prompted them to look for hidden meaning. Whenever an ulterior motive existed, they were likely to find it. But, more significantly, they were just as likely to find one where none existed. Worse yet, they sometimes perceived a negative motive in gestures, such as compliments, that were prompted by good will and that were genuine. Thus, they rejected the very stuff that would nourish their self-esteem, transforming positive feedback into poisons that further increased their alienation.

> *Example:* A therapist trainee reasoned that her L+ client (who was among my sample of examinees) would become less protensive if his self-esteem could be increased. She thereupon introduced positive verbal reinforcement into the treatment sessions, making it a practice to give the client liberal but honest praise. The therapeutic relationship deteriorated, and the client terminated therapy prematurely. In a routine clinic follow-up, the client complained that the trainee thought him unintelligent and was manipulating him into giving her a good evaluation.

This example may also illustrate that L+ people react adversely when presented with surprises, even pleasant ones. This reaction, which is also characteristic of paranoid clients, occurs, as Shapiro (1965) points out, because any new material is a potential threat, as it may be discordant with current defensive biases.

Before leaving this section, I must acknowledge that my colleagues and I have encountered a few instances where the subjective experiences of L+ examinees did not fit the patterns described above. These examinees form a distinct subgroup that was first recognized by Cattell (1957). Additionally, I have found them to have distinctive 16PF profiles that combine L+ scores with A− (sizothymia) and B+ (high intelligence) scores, with a low or moderate O (untroubled adequacy) score as well. As associated traits, these scores indicate indifference towards people, high intelligence, and strong self-esteem. Examinees who were in this subgroup were elitists who generally did not have sufficient interest in their fellow humans to get involved with them, even negatively. Their jealousy and suspiciousness were directed toward abstract nonhuman phenomena, and were transmitted into critical and skeptical intellectual analyses. These examinees were all creative, scientific researchers.

Interpersonal and Social Data

Karson and O'Dell (1976) have noted that the following characteristics are routinely observed in L+ scorers: insisting on getting their point across, feeling people are talking about them behind their backs, being unable to endure human frailties, being oppositional, being likely to fight and antagonistic, and quick to take offense. Obviously, therefore, L+ people are recognizable in daily life as the "fault finders" and "injustice collectors," and as having a "chip on their shoulder."

It is hardly surprising that almost all of the L+ examinees in my sample showed disturbances in their interpersonal relations. Their reality distortions and jaundiced views became self-fulfilling prophecies that invited retaliation. In many instances, persons, particularly those who were the target of their projections, came to eventually act toward them in ways that supported their preconceptions. As it turned out, for example, my examinees were often actually correct in assuming that people talked about them behind their backs. What they failed to see, however, was how they themselves invited these responses. Instead, on discovering this underhandedness, they pounced on it as evidence to support their negative positions.

I noticed that, generally, people felt threatened or challenged by my L+ examinees. Whether they stayed to fight with them or fled depended on the nature of their role relationship, their particular temperament, and how they interpreted the L+ person's behavior. For example, H− (timid) persons were likely to stay, whereas H+ (bold) persons were more likely to look for more congenial companions. Others, like their minor children, had, of course, little choice but to stay.

A phenomenon I frequently observed was that people who do not understand the difference between defensive projection and naive projection remain enmeshed with L+ people. This is because, rather than recognizing that the L+ person's distortions are essential to preserving self-esteem, they assume that he or she would gladly correct these distortions if simply supplied with new and accurate facts. As this does not turn out to be the case, the outcome is inevitably a series of never-ending arguments about the nature of reality.

Not surprisingly, persons I interviewed who were romantically involved with my L+ examinees frequently complained about their partner's "suspicious jealousy," to use Gaylin's (1979) term. While it is common to experience mixtures of suspiciousness and jealousy when in love, the feelings of more-moderate-scoring individuals come, not from preexisting self-esteem problems, but from comparing themselves with the inflated and idealized image of the beloved, against which they can only judge themselves as being inadequate or one-down. By contrast, the feelings of L+ individuals have a very different origin, being rooted in their low self-esteem and inability to trust.

Although I have emphasized the oppositional quality of their relationship, many L+ examinees showed that they were capable of forming close identifications. But a closer look revealed that the individuals to whom they related had to become narcissistic extensions of the L+ person. Like Echo in the Narcissus myth, the partner must faithfully repeat the L+ person's reality, in words, beliefs, and actions. Moreover, since L+ people generally see themselves as having some external enemy, it was necesary for those who entered into relationships with them to share a "them against us" stance.

Persons who chose to enter into these kinds of extensional relationships with my L+ examinees, since this meant interpersonal harmony rested upon sharing their biases and projections, were usually dependent. It can only be supposed that their deep need for affiliation had overcome their skepticism, and that they were gratified by one of the closest bondings of all—rallying against a common enemy. If the L+ examinee was of the grandiose and arrogant type, and had ideas that were along good versus evil lines (a person like Hitler, for example), these relationships sometimes took on cultist or crusading overtones.

In observing their interpersonal responses, it was sometimes difficult to distinguish between L+ and E+ (dominant) people in my sample; they resembled each other in showing controlling, dogmatic, and aggressive behavior. Upon closer examination, however, I usually discerned that E+ scorers' perceptions were less jaundiced than L+ scorers' perceptions. Another, but slightly more subtle difference was that the E+ scorer's interest was typically directed towards social *position*, whereas the L+ scorer's was more apt to be directed towards what others *had*.

More specifically, E+ scorers monitored the rank aspects of their position, so that they could maintain control and avoid subjugation. L+ scorers, on the other hand, focused their awareness of their position with covetous interest, searching to see if they were somehow being deprived of what was rightfully theirs, or if anyone had received an advantage over them. These differences are exemplified below.

> *Example:* Group therapy sessions in which the same set of clients met over a six-month period provided me with the opportunity to compare behavior between an E+ client and an L+ client. The E+ client got into power struggles with the therapist and tried to assume a leadership position by attempting to become recognized as the group spokesperson. The L+ client did not attempt a leadership role but was always quick to challenge anything that he perceived as giving another person an advantage over him, as when the therapist focused on a new client in the group.

L+ and Childhood

The majority of the L+ examinees I have interviewed so far tended to recollect a common theme of childhood alienation, explaining the sense of deprivation that underlies this pole. To use their own words, they felt that they "did not belong," were "not wanted," or "were second class," either in relation to the community or within their own family circles.

The L+ scorers who felt alienated from their communities but not from their families were raised in families not integrated into the wider community. Often, on closer inspection, these L+ scores were an artifact, as they did not reflect a defensive projection. Examinees whose L scores could be classified this way were usually members of socially disadvantaged groups, and their suspiciousness and hypervigilance were appropriate and realistic responses to an environment that was often inhospitable in their adult lives, as it had been in their childhood.

A variant of this condition, also resulting in artifactual L+ scores, was found in examinees whose family's alienation was not due to social ostracism but to its own elitism. Members believed themselves to be racially, culturally, or religiously superior. Cattell (1973) was probably referring to this subvariant of L+ examinees when he summarized the research to that date with the following statement, ". . . father and mother of the protensive person were given to discussion and argument. As a child, he had high confidence in himself, found school unpleasant but felt superior and experienced mutual admiration and support within the family." (p. 169)

L+ examinees who were truly, rather than artifactually, protensive (i.e., those who were defensively projecting their inner tensions), were more likely to recollect the strict and demanding homelife that Krug (1980) reports as being linked with L+ scores. These examinees also recalled experiences of alienation within their families. They perceived that they had been rejected and unfairly treated, or that they were temperamentally unlike other family members. I do not know if these recollections had a factual basis. It does not really matter, as to paraphrase Big Chief in *One Flew Over the Cuckoo's Nest* (Kesey, 1975), "It was true even if it never really happened."

> *Example:* A refined, artistic L+ woman brought up in a fairly typical blue collar family told us that because her interests, values, and tastes were so different from most of her other family members, she reasoned she must have been adopted. During most of her childhood and through her adolescence, she waited for her parents to confess this to her. Since she was not adopted, the years passed and it did not happen. Finally, on the eve of her departure to college, she astonished her parents by telling them that they need not keep her adoption a secret any longer.

Important Correlations Between L+ Scores and Other 16PF Factor Scores

The five correlations that occur between L+ scores and other 16PF factor scores appear in Table 10.1 below.

In testimony of their reflection of psychological discomfort, all of these scores, with the exception of E+, enter with L+ scores into the second-order anxiety pattern. If they are all present, they indicate tendencies towards Q_4+ (physical tension), $O-$ (low self-esteem), Q_3- (identity problems), and $C-$ (ego weakness). I see these correlations as adding support to my concept of protension as a defense mechanism that has failed in its intended purpose—maintaining a positive self-orientation.

Table 10.1

**Important Correlations Between L+ Scores
and Other 16PF Factor Scores**

Factor Pole	Correlation	Possible Associated Traits Indicated by Correlation
C − (Low Ego Strength)	.38	Affected by Feelings, Emotionally Less Stable, Easily Upset
Q_4 + (Ergic Tension)	.38	Tense, Frustrated, Driven Overwrought
O + (Guilt Proneness)	.33	Apprehensive, Self-reproaching, Insecure, Worrying, Troubled
Q_3 − (Low Self-sentiment)	.28	Undisciplined Self-conflict, Lax, Follows Own Urges, Careless of Social Rules
E + (Dominance)	.24	Assertive, Aggressive, Stubborn, Competitive

Clinical Relevance of L+ Scores

From a medical point of view, L+ scores are important indicators of proneness to stress, which shows most conspicuously by physical illness (Sherman & Krug, 1977). For example, a study performed by Calsyn (1979) found a significant correlation between L+ scores and the number of clinic visits for low back pain. Also, Krug (1980) reported evidence of a consistent relationship between the incidence of L+ scores and coronary heart disease, as well as general illness. It is not surprising, therefore, that many L+ people are seen by mental health clinicians through physician referrals. Another common way they come to the attention of a mental health clinician is as individuals contributing significantly to the problems of already-identified patients.

Only those with low self-esteem, i.e., those with O+ (guilt proneness) scores, are likely to be self-referred. (The L+/O− types, i.e., arrogant and grandiose, are more successful in projecting their tensions outwards, and thus do not tend to seek treatment for themselves.) Having low self-esteem, they are apt to initiate treatment to relieve their discomfort. This is a fairly favorable prognostic sign. Nevertheless, clinicians spotting this

$L+/O+$ combination on the profile must be prepared to render long-term treatment, as what lies ahead is the delicate task of dismantling the client's projective defenses, whilst building his or her self-esteem. The clinician should first focus more on the $O+$ qualities of guilt proneness, self-doubt, and unworthiness, rather than the $L+$ aspects of the client's personality. Specifically, this means challenging only those projections that are not essential to the client's sense of self-worth and competency. Moreover, as illustrated in the earlier example, building self-esteem is made difficult by the distrust and defensiveness that inclines these clients to distort their therapist's expressions of positive regard.

When treatment is progressing well with $L+/O+$ clients, repeated 16PF measures will show, *first,* a downward movement in O (guilt proneness) scores, as they move toward the self-esteem pole. A gradual reduction in $L+$ scores follows. An initial reduction in $L+$ scores but not $O+$ scores is an ominous signal, possibly foreshadowing the onset of severe depression, since the client's defense against feelings of inadequacy and worthlessness is being eroded.

LOW SCORES ON FACTOR L

Intrapsychic Data

The inner experience, as outlined in the description of $L-$ traits at the beginning of this chapter, implies a trusting and tolerant orientation toward others, and a freedom from the frustrations that accompany social ambition.

I can add little to what is already understood about the subjective life of $L-$ persons. One reason for this is that, although I interviewed 75 examinees whose L scores were three stens or below, I was rarely able to perform in-depth mental examinations, as only 17 were clinical clients. These persons as a rule were comfortable with both themselves and others, so they infrequently entered treatment, either for themselves or as contributors to the problems of identified clients. Thus, there has been little opportunity for me to study them. What information I have managed to glean has come mostly from my work in occupational settings, which provides fewer opportunities for intensive analyses of introspective material.

Nevertheless, it was through observing these examinees that I arrived at my recognition of what forms the basis of Factor L. I came to recognize that L— scorers conspicuously lack jealousy, suspiciousness, self-aggrandizement, and competitiveness. Since these feelings cannot coexist with strong social identification, I concluded that the L— person's lacking these feelings arose from an underlying sense of identity with their fellow humans. Take jealousy, as an example: to feel jealous of the object of one's identification would be to feel jealous toward oneself, a condition that is without psychological validity. Jealousy, it follows, can only occur in the presence of alienation.

I commonly found that the experience of many examinees with extremely low scores on Factor L at times bordered on the mystical feeling of oneness reported by religionists of all faiths (James, 1958). In the poetic imagery of Alan Watts (1972), these examinees had overcome the illusion of being individual, skin-encapsulated egos, seeing themselves instead as part of the whole human organism. Psychologically, this experience, though it implies coextensiveness with others, does not reflect the clinical syndrome called "weak ego boundaries," i.e., weakly developed self-identities. Rather than showing a developmental failure to individuate, these L— scorers did not have dependency problems. Rather, they tended to support the general view that L— scores should be interpreted as an indicator of good mental health and well being.

This notion, however, applies only when the L— scores reflect the person's true position on Factor L, rather than being based on the examinee's self-misperception. Answers that reflect self-misperception are *unintentionally* distorted (as opposed to deliberate faking). This type of responding occurs when the examinee's beliefs about him- or herself are in actuality false. Ironically enough, L+ scorers are particularly prone to this error. They are self-deceptive, and need to see themselves in a favorable light. This naturally leads them to believe that they are very different from what they are, so that ultimately they endorse factor items in the L— rather than the L+ direction.

My way of discerning the validity of L— scores is by examining their fit with other scales in the profile. The most questionable combinations are departures from the usual C+ (ego strength), E— (submissiveness), O— (untroubled adequacy), Q_3+ (self-sentiment), and Q_4- (low ergic tension) pattern that appears in Table 10.2.

The appearance of an E+ (dominance) score with an L− score suggests potentially incompatible behavior. This combination makes one wonder how traits like aggression (E+) can coexist with self-effacement and cooperativeness (L−). One possibility is that examinees showing this combination may have a distorted self-image, causing them to incorrectly report about a certain set of behaviors on one scale and another set of behaviors on the other.

Special attention should also be accorded to the presence of L− and H− (threctia) scores in the same profile. The H− score means that the examinee is reporting that he or she is feeling socially threatened—a feeling that is inconsistent with the strong sense of identification that an L− score implies. This combination is unlikely to arise out of the examinee's self-misperception, but is usually an indication that he or she behaves in an L− way out of fear. The occasional exceptions are examinees whose L− scores are accurate, even though the person is also demonstrably H− (threctic). These individuals, though truly L− in their accepting and identifying with others, are lacking in self-security.

Social Data

I only need to refer to the typical qualities of L− people to show why my L− examinees were generally well liked. Lacking in jealousy, they were able to share wholeheartedly in the joys and sorrows of others. Their trustfulness made them expect human nature to be praiseworthy and good, rather than reprehensible. Above all, they were easy to get along with. Uninterested in competition and status, they were generous and cooperative.

When asked, people usually reported that they "felt accepted" by my L− examinees. As this impression was so frequently reported, I learned that, whenever I heard several people use this term in reference to a particular individual, it was almost invariable that they were referring to someone who was L−. Thus, for me, this phrase turned out to be an excellent predictor of L− scores.

Less positively, because of their trustful orientation, which makes them disinclined to search for complex motives, L− persons are the natural prey for "con artists" and others with unscrupulous intentions. They are the proverbial used-car dealers' natural delight! People were often perplexed when they saw L−

examinees exploited and tricked more often than their peers of comparable intelligence, education, and life experience. Especially when they repeated the same errors in judgment with the same people, it was often wrongfully concluded (not only by persons knowledgeable of popular psychology, but also by clinicians) that they were masochistically "setting themselves up." These observers did not realize that their behavior resulted from their trusting and forgiving natures and belief in giving others "the benefit of the doubt."

Consequently, rather than searching for a more complex motive to explain a person's behavior when that behavior seems to invite betrayal or disappointment, it is useful to know something of his or her L score, as illustrated below.

> *Example:* A parole officer was threatened by dismissal after accepting too many excuses from a parolee for not finding a job, although gainful employment was a condition of continued parole. The parolee's records clearly showed that he had a proclivity for lying and avoiding work. The parole officer's supervisor confided to me that after giving the matter much thought he had arrived at three alternate hypotheses that might explain his subordinate's behavior. These were: (1) he was acting out passively some aggression towards the criminal justice system, (2) was stupid, or (3) for some obscure, unconscious reason wanted to lose his job.
>
> Psychological testing did not support any of the supervisor's alternatives. The 16PF showed the parole officer had average scores on Factor E (dominance), indicating that he was able to assert himself adequately and so would have no need to resort to passive-aggressive behavior. He also had a B (intelligence) score of 8, showing he was far from stupid. The Motivation Analysis Test, which was also administered to assess unconscious motives, showed that, rather than work-related conflict, which would have been in keeping with a hypothesis of wanting to lose his job, he actually was strongly interested in his career. Having ruled out these hypotheses, his L score of 2 pointed toward the real cause of the problem.

Based on the above example, it is fortunate that L− persons do not often seem to be attracted to careers in the criminal justice system, or similar occupations that require hyperalertness to the wrongdoings of others. Career profiles collected so far indicate that L− scorers are attracted to a wide assortment of occupations, including special education teachers, university administrators, social workers, pilots, airline attendants, dental assistants, kitchen workers, Lutheran clergy, biologists, and physicists (Rieke & Russell, 1987).

L− and Childhood

The literature contains no information on the early backgrounds of L− persons. One reason for this is that L− behavior is not directly observable in children and adolescents, as Factor L does not clearly become discernible until early adulthood.

As with several other factor poles, I had to rely solely on retrospective reports to get some notion of its childhood origins. Given the recollections of early alienation that showed up so systematically in the reports of L+ examinees, I had expected that their L− counterparts would recall the opposite kinds of experiences. In other words, I expected that alienation themes would be entirely absent from their childhood histories, and instead reveal that they had felt well integrated into early social environments that nurtured their self-esteem and fostered positive bondings. My expectations were not realized. Although this type of experience was reported by some examinees, others were just as likely to report having had childhoods similar to those reported by L+ examinees.

These confusing findings have led me to speculate that L−, like L+, may, at least in some cases, originally serve defensive purposes. Is it possible, having not been able to beat the enemy, they joined it? This mechanism of identifying with the feared person as a means of defusing fear and hostility, is convincingly discussed by Sandler and Freud (1985).

Important Correlations Between L− Scores and Other 16PF Factor Scores

Table 10.2 below shows a correlation between L− scores and Q_4- (low ergic tension), C+ (ego strength), O+ (untroubled adequacy), Q_3+ (high self-sentiment), and E− (submissiveness) scores. Together, they portray the typical L− person as someone who, in addition to being trusting and accepting, may also be relaxed, self-satisfied, emotionally mature and controlled, and not aggressively self-assertive. Since the E− score appears in a context of well being, concerns about dysfunctional behavior might be put aside in examinees showing this overall pattern.

Table 10.2

**Important Correlations Between L− Scores
and Other 16PF Factor Scores**

Factor Pole	Correlation	Possible Associated Traits Indicated by Correlation
C + (Ego Strength)	.38	Emotionally Stable, Mature, Faces Reality
Q₄ − (Low Ergic Tension)	.38	Relaxed, Tranquil, Unfrustrated, Composed
O − (Untroubled Adequacy)	.33	Self-assured, Placid, Secure, Complacent, Serene
Q₃ + (High Self-sentiment)	.28	Controlled, Exacting Will Power, Socially Precise, Compulsive
E − (Submissiveness)	.24	Humble, Mild, Easily Led

Clinical Relevance of L− Scores

To restate what has already been said, I have so far seen no instances where L− scores (providing, of course, they were valid and not artifacts) pointed to psychological disturbances. Rather, my observations are in accord with those reported by other observers, who conclude that L− scores can usually be taken as indicators of emotional well being.

Because L− behavior promotes good human relations and team spirit, I expect I will continue to hold this position even if future research on a larger sample supports my conjecture that it is traceable to an early defense born out of the darker side of human emotions. Unlike L + (protension), L− behavior achieves its defensive aim, benefiting both the L− individual and others, generally. I am content, therefore, to take the poet's advice: "Where the apple reddens never pry."

Chapter 11

Factor M: Intuiting and Sensing as Contrasting Perceptual Modes

THE CONSTRUCT
Two Modes of Perceiving
Jung's Sensation and Intuition Functions
Right and Left Hemispheric Specialization
Male and Female Differences Throughout the Life Span
Heredity

HIGH SCORES ON FACTOR M
Intrapsychic Data
Interpersonal and Social Data
Important Correlations Between M+ Scores
and Other 16PF Factor Scores
Clinical Relevance of M+ Scores

LOW SCORES ON FACTOR M
Intrapsychic Data
Interpersonal and Social Data
Important Correlations Between M− Scores
and Other 16PF Factor Scores
Clinical Relevance of M− Scores

FACTOR M: CHARACTERISTICS OF M+ (AUTIOUS) AND M− (PRAXERNIC) EXAMINEES

Left Score M− (PRAXERNIA)		Right Score M+ (AUTIA)
(Practical, Has "Down-to-Earth Concerns)	vs.	**(Imaginative, Bohemian,** Absent-minded)
Conventional, Alert to Practical Needs	vs.	Unconventional, Absorbed in Ideas
Concerned with Immediate Interests and Issues	vs.	Interested in Art, Theory, Basic Beliefs
Prosaic, Avoids Anything Far-fetched	vs.	Imaginatively Enthralled by Inner Creations
Guided by Objective Realities, Dependable in Practical Judgment	vs.	Fanciful, Easily Seduced from Practical Judgment
Earnest, Concerned or Worried but Steady	vs.	Generally Enthused, Occasional Hysterical Swing of "Giving Up"

THE CONSTRUCT

Two Modes of Perceiving

Human beings have two modes of perceiving and, as individuals, tend to favor one over the other. One mode relies more on immediate sensory experience, deriving awareness from the direct contact of the five senses with the environment. The other relies less on the immediacy of the senses, being more focused on how information about the environment becomes organized with an inner scheme of connecting thoughts, speculations, and subliminal connections. In Cattell's words, these two contrasting modes are a "temperamental proclivity to give either sensory data or ideational contents more immediate intensity" (Cattell, 1957). The sensate proclivity is measured by Factor M's left or minus pole, and is called praxernia, a neologism for practical concern. Conversely, the neologism that contracts internally autonomous processing, autia, measures the ideational proclivity at the right or plus pole. Unlike the majority of people (i.e., the 64% whose M scores are between 4 and 7 and who, therefore, to varying degrees, mesh both of these perceptual forms), the minorities who score at the extremities of Factor M habitually come to rely on one mode, and neglect the other. Their bias may prove helpful or hurtful, depending on their life goals and upon how the bias combines with other aspects of their personalities.

Readers conversant with the history of philosophy will recognize in the M−/M+ dichotomy the two major competing epistemological systems—the correspondence and coherence theories of truth. Correspondence theory was initially propounded by the naturalist Aristotle, who was probably praxernic, i.e., an M− type. Aristotle asserted that knowledge of the objective order of things can only be arrived at sensually, i.e., through seeing, hearing, smelling, or touching. This view was challenged by the coherence theory developed by the autious (M+) Plato and his followers, who argued that sense perceptions are by nature hallucinatory and, therefore, that reality can most confidently be verified on the basis of how well sensory information harmonizes with an existing system of established truths.

Jung's Sensation and Intuition Functions

As we have already mentioned in the chapter on Factor I, Factor M bears strong resemblance to one of the bipolar dimensions in Jung's type theory of human temperament. The reader may wish to review Diagram 9.1 in Chapter 9. In that chapter, I noted that Jung had proposed that there are two dichotomous modes of feeling and thinking for evaluating experiences. He also proposed that perception is also divisible into what he called intuition and sensation processes, and that a preference for using one over the other will result in different constructs of reality, leading in turn to different personality styles.

When I describe Jung's sensate function, most students readily recognize it as consistent with M− (praxernia) but see a less clear link between his intuitive function and M+ (autia). This difficulty seems to arise out of the semantic confusion surrounding the term "intuition." In popular speech, intuition appears to mean "hunch," and to describe the subjective experience of suddenly perceiving a hitherto unrecognized relationship, or having a solution to a problem appear "out of the blue," or without conscious mental effort. Jung's use of the term *intuition* has a much broader meaning. This is apparent from interpreters of his type theory. Wheelright (1964) and Myers (1962), for example, explain it to be a habitual tendency to focus on a higher ratio of ideas, associations, and other internal mental processes, rather than to focus on external stimuli. This tendency is, of course, entirely consistent with M+ (autia).

My position with the Factor M polarities in regard to Jung's typology is very similar to what I have adopted for those of Factor

I. Having recognized the similarity between M+ and M− and the intuition and sensation functions has allowed me to draw on observation amassed by Jungians, to aid in my understanding of M+ and M− examinees.

Right and Left Hemispheric Specialization

Just as with Factor I, I am frequently asked about the relationship of Factor M to hemispheric specialization. According to this theory, persons who show a strong tendency to favor the use of the right side of their brains tend to respond emotionally and subjectively (like I+ scorers, as I said earlier). M+ scorers' perceptions are diffuse and draw heavily on subliminal information, and these qualities, too, seem right-brained.

Conversely, left-hemisphere-favoring persons resemble M− scorers, as they have perceptions that are more sharply focused and closely connected to immediate physical stimuli. Again, I can only say that this appears to be a likely connection which has not yet been systematically investigated, but hopefully will be in the near future.

Male and Female Differences Throughout the Life Span

The group mean scores for men is 24.54, and for women is 25.86. Both sexes have a similar, moderate standard deviation of scores. Age curves for Factor M are similar for both sexes, with males and females moving toward the M+ pole starting in their mid-teens and declining in their mid-30s.

When measured in their 60th year, scores for both groups show decreases reverting to the same level achieved in their mid-teens. The psychological interpretation I derive from this data is that persons in their earlier and later years rely more on direct sensory input than they do in their middle years.

Heredity

The heritability quotient for Factor M has not presently been established. Moreover, it has not yet been possible to investigate the early conditions contributing to its environmental component. This problem seems to result from Factor M's not appearing as a distinct factor, either in the self-reports or ratings measurements of children. Further, retrospective reports of M+ and M− scorers fail to show reliable connections with childhood histories.

Consequently, this chapter, unlike most others, contains no sections referring to childhood antecedents.

HIGH SCORES ON FACTOR M

Intrapsychic Data

Signifying, as it does, an intense inner life relative to the reality and demands of the outer world, Krug (1980) proposes that M+ (autia) is personified by the caricature of the absent-minded professor, who wanders across campus absorbed in thought and is inattentive, even oblivious, to his surroundings. The majority of my 196 M+ examinees usually readily identified with this image. They reported that they are forgetful, misplace things, lose track of time, and do not notice what is obvious to others.

Since M+ persons typically find it difficult to pay attention to anything other than what they currently happen to be concentrating on, it is possible for them to obtain deep levels of comprehension. Probably it is partially for this reason that they are often highly creative. They are also apt to be radical in their thinking. Indeed, I discovered that the examinees in my sample were apt to have such precocious ideas they were often ahead of their time and dismissed as being "too far out." It would have been desirable for them, therefore, to have public relations advocates to make their ideas more generally understandable.

A positive but often overlooked aspect of autia is that it affords an inner refuge from unpleasant surroundings. Take, for example, the following literary description of the subjective life of Frank Harte, a young laborer in the Yorkshire mills of England. Frank lived under drab and harsh physical circumstances.

> "This morning he seemed forlorn in his gray work shirt and baggy trousers, hand-me-downs from Winston (his older brother) and his legs in their carefully darned gray socks, dangling over the edge of the chair looking pathetic and far too weak to lift the great boots, which were too large and ugly and had also once belonged to Winston. But in reality, and in spite of his appearance, there was nothing forlorn about Frank Harte, for he occupied an inner world so filled with beautiful images and soaring dreams and expectations, it made his day-to-day existence seem totally inconsequential. And this

perfect world protected him from the harshness of their poverty stricken life, nourished him so completely he was, for the most part, quite oblivious to the deprivation and spartan conditions in which they lived." (p. 102)[1]

On the negative side, I discovered that my M+ examinees tended to be so preoccupied with their thoughts that they were often oblivious to physical dangers in their surroundings. This tendency can be generalized beyond my sample, since M+ scores have been found to be correlated with accident proneness of all kinds.

Another characteristic shown by my M+ examinees was that they did not do well at detailed work. They tended to ascribe this to having difficulty in "keeping their minds on what was going on" about them. Upon further investigation, this proved to be due to their tendency to attend to internal associations in the form of memories, ideas, and thoughts evoked by external stimuli, rather than on the external stimuli itself. This, of course, is essentially what M+ (autia) is. Resisting this natural tendency for directing their attention inwards required considerable effort. Whether or not they were willing to engage in this effort was discernible from their other 16PF scores, specifically C+ (ego strength), G+ (superego strength), and Q_3+ (self-sentiment). C+ scores would indicate that they were concerned about consequences, G+ scores that they were conscientious, and Q_3+ scores that they wished to maintain a socially approved self-concept. Any one of these traits provides the motivation for attending to the details that M+ persons otherwise naturally overlook.

Other traits can also strongly affect M+ scores, either by compensating for the M+ person's inner-directedness or by modulating it in some other way. Chief among these is the second-order extraversion/introversion pattern. I found that introverted M+ examinees had perceptions that were insightful, penetrating, and highly original, which they seemed to enjoy as ends in themselves. They were, in short, introspective thinkers. Unfortunately, though, it was not common for them to share their ideas.

On the other hand, extraverted M+ examinees were *doers*, who were not content unless they could eventually turn the fruits of their imaginations outwards. They were especially insightful

---

[1]Bradford, B. T. *A woman of substance.* New York: Avon Books, 1979.

toward people and could use their perceptions to be persuasive and charming. Also, on the positive side, they were more alert to their environments than their M + counterparts who got low or moderate extraversion scores; therefore, M + extraverts were less prone to accidents.

Factor I's premsia-harria extremities were only slightly less important as a modulator. Due to M + and I + scores' being positively correlated in the general population, more M + /I + people are encountered than M + /I − people. Examinees who showed M + /I + score combinations had rich inner lives, but often lacked objectivity, even when highly intelligent.

The few examinees (approximately 18%) whose profiles showed M + and I − scores of 3 and below demonstrated remarkably innovative thinking. Their good imaginations, combined with their I − respect for bare, unadorned facts, led them to see all kinds of possibilities from an objective and unemotional point of view. Those whose profiles also showed B + (intelligence) scores, especially if they were also somewhat introverted, often had distinguished careers in the physical sciences. Other intelligent M + /I − examinees who were more extraverted, showed more interest in social innovations, engineering, and architecture.

I have already mentioned that strong egos, superegos, or self-sentiment can modulate M + tendencies in a positive direction. Conversely, when these agencies of self-control are weak, they can exacerbate M + tendencies by reinforcing the inattentiveness to the environment. M + scores in combination with C − (low ego strength) scores convey that, either the examinee's contemplative style is not being counterbalanced by a concern for thinking through of environmental consequences, or that the examinee is withdrawing from a stressful environment.

Cattell's early formulations that link M + with a Bohemian lifestyle must have been based upon M + people with weak superegos. Examinees whose profiles showed this M + /G − combination were apt to have unorthodox ideas about sex, religion, and politics, as well as having imaginations that were unrestrained and uninhibited by conventional moral standards. If they were also extraverted, they were apt to act out their fantasies.

Finally, M + scores accompanied by Q_3 − (low self-sentiment) scores convey a lack of concern for maintaining a socially approved self-concept. Although they, too, may reflect a somewhat

Bohemian lack of social orthodoxy, they were more likely, in my experience, to indicate that the examinee had either withdrawn inwardly following an unsuccessful identity struggle, or that the examinee was too preoccupied to notice his or her impact on others. When one notices someone with mismatched socks, for example, it is a good guess that he or she is M+ and Q_3−.

Interpersonal and Social Data

In observing the reactions of others, my most cogent impression is that M+ people are liable to be depreciated. These reactions result, not merely from negative judgments about their characteristically M+ inattentiveness to their surroundings and obvious inner preoccupation, but from misattributing the cause of these behaviors to other traits. The most common confusion about my M+ examinees was that they were considered unintelligent (B−), lacked conscientiousness (G−), or were cold and aloof (A−). Because these mistakes played such an important role in coloring how others perceive M+ behavior, I will direct much of the latter part of this section to understanding how each can so easily occur and its specific consequences.

1) *M+ misinterpreted as A− (sizia).* As I have already stressed, unless they are extraverted, M+ scorers are inattentive to their social environments. As a result, they often fail to notice people. They forget names, and they behave in other ways that are seen as indicating coldness and social indifference. It is understandable, therefore, that they are often seen as A− (sizic).

But, although their superficial behavior may resemble that of A− scorers, the absence of correlation between A and M scores shows that M+ persons are not necessarily lacking in warmth towards people. The following example shows how this warmth can be obfuscated by their inner preoccupation.

> *Example:* An M+ colleague took time out from her busy schedule to buy a Christmas gift for the parking lot attendant in the building in which she worked. On attempting to deliver the gift she found that he no longer worked there, having died four months earlier. She had been so internally absorbed in her own mental processes that she had failed to notice that someone she obviously liked and appreciated was missing from such a conspicuous spot as the entrance to the parking lot that she passed by twice every working day.

2) *M+ misinterpreted as B− (lower intelligence).* Probably the most common error that others make about M+ persons is to underestimate their intelligence. It is easy to see how easily this mistake can occur, given the M+ propensity for forgetting important information, for failing either to make quite ordinary observations or to retain recently relayed instructions, and for losing track of what they are doing.

To avoid being seen as intellectually duller than they are, it is helpful for M+ individuals to have at least above-average intelligence and the credentials to prove it. Parenthetically, I might say here that, for those unfortunate enough to actually be below average in intelligence, the negative aspects of their M+ are seriously compounded because they find it difficult to make accurate observations and to perform the simple tasks necessary for dealing adequately with their environments. It is particularly difficult for them to get and hold jobs, since most jobs suitable for M+ persons' contemplative and dreamy style require them to have at least average intellelctual ability. The lives of examinees whose profiles showed M+ and B− score combinations were consistently beset by crises, both big and small.

3) *M+ misinterpreted as G− (superego weakness).* The behavior of M+ people is often misinterpreted as being due to a poorly developed superego. But, on closer examination, it often turns out that their offbeat styles are due to their lack of attentiveness to social clues and to their proclivity for making naive projections.[2] That is, they assume that others share their values, motives, and ideas, which is why they are "often careless about things like punctuality and formality" (Cattell, 1957, p. 149).

Given this, it is understandable that many of my M+ examinees reported below-average job satisfaction, received fewer job promotions, were less accepted by their coworkers, and found that their suggestions, though often acknowledged to be creative, were eventually rejected as being too idealistic or impractical. (This finding agrees with what is reported in the *Handbook for the 16PF.*)

M+ examinees also had difficulty finding jobs for which they were temperamentally suitable, since many fields (e.g., factory

---

[2]Naive projection differs from L+ projection, described in the previous chapter (Chapter 10) in that naive projection does not entail externalization of a conflict.

production, teaching, nursing, clerical work, law enforcement, and sales) call for attention to detail, alertness, and good memories, all qualities in which M+ people are usually lacking. Based on the occupational groups tested so far, the results indicate that M+ people are most suited for creative work in the arts and sciences, certain kinds of editorial planning, and top-level editorial jobs. These jobs, which require above-average intellectual ability and training, are also fewer in number.

In their personal lives, M+ examinees in my sample were apt to receive some of the same reactions that plagued them in the occupational front. These individuals heard a different drummer. It takes an unusually understanding marriage partner, friend, or other associate to recognize this and not feel rejected by their frequent retreats into their own worlds. It was not surprising, therefore, to find that these examinees' M+ behavior often resulted in marital discord, particularly when it involved failure to pay attention and forgetting anniversaries, important appointments, and promises to fill certain commitments. Maybe it is for this reason that Cattell discovered that M+ is often connected with many unhappy love affairs (Cattell, 1973).

Important Correlations Between M+ Scores and Other 16PF Factor Scores

Table 11.1

Important Correlations Between M+ Scores and Other 16PF Factor Scores

Factor Pole	Correlation	Possible Associated Traits Indicated by Correlation
Q_1 + (Radicalism)	.33	Imaginative, Bohemian, Absent-minded
I + (Premsia)	.26	Tender, Sensitive, Clinging, Over-protective

I+ (premsia) scores, which refer to a fundamental proclivity for making evaluations that are based on feelings and subjective responses rather than on logical reasoning, have already been discussed in Chapter 9. Q_1 + (radicalism) scores, which will be discussed in detail later in Chapter 13, are interpretable just as their name implies—a progressive orientation, coupled, at least intellectually, with a willingness to depart from tradition.

The weak but significant correlations of M + scores with I + and Q_1 + scores are .26 and .33, respectively. These correlations suggest that M + people may often be found to combine their inner preoccupation with a rich emotional life and an openness to unconventional ideas. Examinees whose 16PF profiles show this pattern may be overly creative. They need to have some grounding traits, like ego strength (C +); otherwise, they may be too fanciful to meet the ordinary demands of life.

Clinical Relevance of M + Scores

What has been described above is the meaning of M + scores in the normal population. High M scores are present in the group norms of three major clinical syndromes: substance abuse, schizophrenia, and major depressions. In each of these, the M + score may refer to somewhat different psychological conditions. Substance-abusing clients usually prefer to derive pleasure from directly changing internal states, rather than by thoroughly reacting to outside stimuli. In schizophrenic clients, poor social attachment and preoccupation with ideas often leads to only tangential connections with their environments. With depressed clients, withdrawal and, in severe cases, retreats into psychosis may be suspected, especially if Factor M scores increase on repeated administrations of the 16PF.

In addition to these clinical connections, knowledge of a client's Factor M score provides useful information for occupational counseling. The scores have helped me to guide clients towards choosing careers that took into account the nature, assets, and limitations of their M + temperaments. (They have also helped me to assist organizations in making appropriate personnel selections.)

In my clinical practice, many M + individuals have presented themselves for treatment, naming job dissatisfaction as a primary complaint. Some found that they functioned inefficiently and were chagrined to receive poor performance ratings. Others experienced strain and effort in performing tasks that so obviously went against their natural grain.

It was common for all these individuals to have poor understanding of how their M + style produced the kinds of difficulties they experienced at work. Some attributed their difficulties to the quality of the work, which they considered to be boring, monotonous, or disinteresting. Others blamed some defect in their characters, or psychological functioning, for their failures. As an example of the latter attribution, it was not unusual for more sophisticated M+ clients to suspect they suffered from some peculiar neurological problem.

> *Example:* An intelligent, conscientious, newly graduated nurse requested psycho-neurological testing because she was concerned about the adequacy of her performance in a busy surgical ward. Specifically, she had difficulty keeping track of the demands that simultaneously demanded her attention. After discovering her psycho-neurological testing to be essentially normal, I administered the 16PF. Her score on Factor M was 9. Her story ends happily. After receiving feedback about her test results, along with my explanation that M+ persons tend to do better at jobs that require their introspection and contemplation than at those requiring close monitoring of the environment, she left her job and found work as a psychiatric nurse counselor. This position allowed her to use her excellent imagination and intuitive processes. Her superior performance later won her a scholarship to further her education in psychiatric nursing. Today, she teaches in the nursing school of a prestigious university where her penetrating analysis of psychiatric problems is fascinating, even if slightly disorganized in their presentation.

LOW SCORES ON FACTOR M

People who have low scores on Factor M value the concrete and sensately obvious. They disdain abstractions or complicated conceptual inferences. When I summon up a picture of the typical M− examinee in my sample, it is of someone who proudly proclaims that he or she believes in "calling a spade a spade."

Given that it is fundamental to M− to focus attention on outer rather than inner stimuli, I discovered, as I anticipated, that the M− examinees in my sample were not inclined to introspect. Therefore, they reported so little about their subjective lives that I had to rely more than usual upon my own inferences in this matter. What I have inferred is essentially in agreement with what has been reported in the *Administrator's Manual for the 16PF* (1986):

> "Low scorers on Factor M tend to be anxious to do the right things, attentive to practical matters, and subject to the dictation of what is obviously possible. They are concerned over detail, able to keep their heads in emergencies, but are sometimes unimaginative. In short, they are responsive to the outer, rather than the inner, world." (p. 28)

Despite their differences in focus, M − examinees showed a rigidity of perceptions that was similar to their M + counterparts. The attention of M − examinees was as firmly bound to external stimuli as the attention of M + examinees was to inner stimuli. In their own way, both groups found it difficult to flexibly shift back and forth between observations of the environment and inner reflection. As a result of being captivated by their immediate physical environments, it was almost impossible for M − examinees to disassociate or distance themselves from their immediate surroundings. No problem arose when all was well with their surroundings, but when it was not, their inability to transcend caused them to suffer. To recapitulate to the example of Frank Harte, if he had been M − instead of M +, he would have been keenly aware of the poor conditions under which he lived. M − people characteristically lack imagination and so do not conjure up the kinds of images and possibilities that high-scoring and even moderate-scoring individuals create. Moreover, their well-documented capacity for maintaining composure in emergencies can probably be credited to their poor imaginations.

I discerned three other characteristics coloring the subjective lives of the M − examinees in my sample. First, they strongly preferred the familiar and predictable. They felt most comfortable in situations which had minimal imponderables and that required little innovation, allowing them to act in standard, reliable ways. Second, they often had phenomenal memories; they seemed to notice and remember even irrelevant details. (Undoubtedly, their memories owed much to the intense sense impressions with which they made their original observations.) Third, they had difficulty in organizing information into meaningful frameworks or forming theories, despite their perceptual acuity; that is, they tended to "see the trees and miss the forest." This difficulty, as far as I can tell, was largely attributable to their disinclination to reflect on or use other internally focused operations needed to relate facts to a broader body of understanding.[3] In many situations, this turned out to be a serious limitation since, as Kant has noted, "precepts (sensations) without concepts are blind."

The most influential scores modulating the subjective lives of my M − examinees were *(a)* on the second-order extraversion-introversion factor and *(b)* on Factor I. Extraverted M − examinees were strongly oriented towards their social environments. They used their keen interest in people to remember all kinds of facts about them and rarely forgot names.

> *Example:* A personal relative who fit this M − extraverted description was an excellent resource for collecting family genealogy, amazing everyone by her recall of the full names of long-deceased family members, as well as the accurate dates of their births, marriages, and deaths.

Introverted M − examinees, on the other hand, were less interested in persons and more concerned about how to manipulate objects and the practical use of facts. They were often unusually skillful at operating machinery. Good at figuring out *how* things worked, they rarely were interested in discovering *why*. Although their observations were factually correct, they did not readily check their interpretation with others. So it was hardly surprising that they drew idiosyncratic conclusions or had "peculiar ideas" about the facts they observed, especially if they involved human behavior.

The second most important set of modulating traits were the Factor I polarities: I − (harria) and I + (premsia). M − examinees whose profiles showed I − scores (and most did) were unemotional and logical individuals, the so-called "super realists." By contrast, the small minority who showed I + scores were emotional, kind, and sensitive individuals, but not sufficiently introspective to have much self-understanding. Doers rather than thinkers, they were intensely practical. In their good works they were the Marthas rather than the Marys of the world.[4] Several

---

[3]This characteristic is in direct contrast to what I observed in M + individuals, who were able to make well-organized theories based on few facts and sometimes false premises gleaned from inadequate observations.

[4]Martha and Mary are referred to in the Bible as two sisters who showed their devotion to Christ in different ways. Mary basked worshipfully in Christ's presence, whereas Martha busied herself in the practical details of providing food and comfort for him and his disciples.

of these examinees showed artistic interests. Sometimes they were musical, but mostly they liked useful art forms like quilt, rug, or pottery making, or gardening. Typically, they were neat and orderly housekeepers.

Social Data

M– scores have been found in the group profiles of engineers, pilots, flight attendants, miners, geologists, and police, all of which can be considered concrete, nonsubjective occupations. Moreover, they should do well in many other kinds of jobs since, as we have already observed, the majority of occupations favor M– persons because they are practical and alert to the environment, they adapt easily to routine, they are able to see whatever is immediately necessary, and they have good memories for exact facts.

Despite having these useful qualities, I noticed that one problem kept appearing in the work-related experience of my M– examinees. Although they did well at maintaining and running operations, especially when procedures and policies were clearly delineated, they were not good innovators. Thus, although they were appreciated by supervisors and coworkers alike for their dependability, they were often passed over for promotion for positions requiring progressive and creative thinking. Consequently, it was not uncommon to discover that even the most intelligent among them were stuck in mid-management positions. Once, when a colleague and I were invited to sit in on a board meeting for selecting a new department head, we observed how this happened first hand.

> *Example:* The obvious choice seemed to be "good old reliable John," who knew the company thoroughly, was punctual and organized, and could always be depended upon to get the facts straight. After extolling all of John's virtues, one committee member pointed out that the new position required "vision," whereupon by tacit agreement John was dropped from further consideration.

The same qualities which made them valued in work-related relationships make M– individuals appreciated in their more intimate and social relations. Eventually, however, their predictable and practical natures may sometimes come to be regarded as rather boring. I often heard this complaint in marital therapy, from spouses who found them dull and monotonous company.

Probably the most frequent general complaint I heard about my M− examinees was that they could be unusually frustrating when engaged in arguments. While able to overpower their opponents with a recitation of correct details, they tended to fail to organize the content of those facts and grasp their meaning. I have also noticed this failure in therapy sessions and have come to appreciate how sometimes "Facts are the enemy of truth," speculating that it was a conclusion reached in exasperation by someone who had tried to get an M− person to see the latent meaning of occurrences.

Important Correlations Between M− Scores and Other 16PF Factor Scores

Table 11.2 shows a correlation of .33 with both Q_1− (conservatism) and .26 with I− (harria), indicating that there is a tendency among M− persons to prefer familiar and traditional ways, and to give higher credibility to judgments based upon logical reasoning rather than upon emotional insights. These traits in combination with M− empiricism and down-to-earthness suggest the practical, conservative, unemotional New England farmers described in Robert Frost's poems. The negative side of this triad of traits, however, is that they depict someone who may be slow to make even desirable changes.

Table 11.2

Important Correlations Between M− Scores and Other 16PF Factor Scores

Factor Pole	Correlation	Possible Associated Traits Indicated by Correlation
Q_1 − (Conservatism of Temperament)	.33	Conservative, Respecting of Traditional Ideas
I − (Harria)	.26	Tough-minded, Self-reliant, Realistic

Clinical Relevance of M− Scores

Even though, according to the 16PF Handbook (p. 259), they are not clinically important, M− scores in a profile alert us to two valuable pieces of information. First of all, when they appear with F − (desurgency) scores, the examinee is likely to be a careful, unimaginative person who focuses on concrete and practical facts. As these M − and F − characteristics are mutually reinforcing, they can create a narrowly tunnelled perception of life. Discovery of this combination in a prospective client is the harbinger of hard and tedious psychological treatment, as it is certain that he or she will find it difficult to introspect and will be skeptical about interpretations that are not face valid.

The second piece of information that M − scores signal is the possibility that the client may have some obsessive-compulsive qualities. This is, he or she cannot obtain enough distance from discreet, often trivial, details to grasp "the big picture." This characteristic is listed in the DSM-III as one of the criteria for an obsessive-compulsive personality disorder. Consequently, should the profile show, in addition to M − scores, an elevation in the second-order anxiety score, this diagnosis should be seriously considered.

Chapter 12

Factor N: Self-Presentations in Social Situations

THE CONSTRUCT
The Social Mask
Heredity
Male and Female Differences Throughout the Life Span

HIGH SCORES ON FACTOR N
Intrapsychic Data
Social Data
N+ and Childhood
Important Correlations Between N+ Scores
and Other 16PF Factor Scores
Clinical Relevance of N+ Scores

LOW SCORES ON FACTOR N
Intrapsychic Data
Social Data
N− and Childhood
Important Correlations Between N− Scores
and Other 16PF Factor Scores
Clinical Relevance of N− Scores

FACTOR N: CHARACTERISTICS OF N+ (SHREWD) AND N- (NAIVE) EXAMINEES

Left Score N− (ARTLESSNESS)		Right Score N+ (SHREWDNESS)
(Forthright, Unpretentious)	vs.	(Astute, Worldly)
Genuine, But Socially Clumsy	vs.	Polished, Socially Aware
Has Vague and Injudicious Mind	vs.	Has Exact, Calculating Mind
Gregarious, Gets Warmly Emotionally Involved	vs.	Emotionally Detached and Disciplined
Spontaneous, Natural	vs.	Artful
Has Simple Tastes	vs.	Esthetically Fastidious
Lacking Self-insight	vs,	Insightful Regarding Self
Unskilled in Analyzing Motives	vs.	Insightful Regarding Others
Content with What Comes	vs.	Ambitious, Possibly Insecure
Has Blind Trust in Human Nature	vs.	Smart, "Cuts Corners"

THE CONSTRUCT

The Social Mask

Factor N represents the social mask, which people don in order to cover whatever about themselves they wish to hide, and to present, instead, an image designed to invoke the kind of responses they desire from others. Readers may recognize this trait in themselves whenever they tell a white lie, laugh at an unfunny joke, exaggerate expressions of sympathy or interest, or act in other ways not congruent with their true feelings or motives, in order to avoid embarrassment, avoid hurting feelings, or win positive responses.

Persons who regularly behave this way would score at the high pole of Factor N, hence its name *shrewdness*. They keep their social masks firmly in place with most people and in most situations. Some use this mask manipulatively while others do not, remaining instead astute observers who are careful to disclose about themselves only what they wish others to know.

By contrast, those who would score at the low (N−) pole make little effort to hide their reactions; theirs is the "transparent self." This pole Cattell at one time called *naivete,* to denote the kind of naive projection these individuals show. This projection is similar to that which I have frequently observed in M+ scorers, i.e., they expect that others will react and feel as they do. I, however, am not completely satisfied with this or its present label, *artlessness,* for I discovered it is not sufficiently comprehensive to include the 20 aggressively abrupt "I've got to be me" types of N− examinees in my sample. These types, rather than being naive, were clearly aware of the unfavorable social impact they created, but still insisted on candidly presenting their raw reactions. Subscribing to the "letting it all hang out" ethic, they disdained what conventionally goes for good manners, tact, and etiquette. The hippy movement in the 1960s and early 1970s probably best exemplified a collective example of this attitude.

Analytically, Factor N has proved elusive to pin down. Possibly this difficulty is not only due to its higher pole measuring a trait that is covert by definition, but to the tendency of people to collude in not acknowledging what they know about each other, as in the Emperor's clothes story when an entire populace "made believe" that the Emperor was beautifully dressed in new robes when in actuality he was wearing nothing at all. In Eastern culture this phenomenon is finely developed. It is called "saving face," and its rules are clearly delineated and understood.

Heredity

Although there is no research on the genetic basis for Factor N, it can be inferred that its heritability is probably low, since it varies substantially across cultural groups. Any trait that shows strong variations of this sort is considered to result more from socialization.[1]

Male and Female Differences Throughout the Life Span

For men, the mean score is 19.76, and women, 21.44. While this difference is fairly large and statistically significant, the standard deviation of scores is almost identical for both sexes. Women's scores, as age curve data show, run about one sten higher than males' scores, through the majority of their lives. Scores for both sexes follow a parallel course between their 10th and 40th years. However, between the ages of 40 and 50, women's scores increase slightly, remaining on an even plateau until measurements taken at their 60th year. Men's scores, for some as yet unexplained reason, take a sharp upward swing between

---

[1]British women score higher on Factor N than American women. (Personal communication from R. B. Cattell.).

their 48th and 55th year, at which time they equal women's. They then continue to climb, and at 60 have bypassed women's by one sten.

HIGH SCORES ON FACTOR N

Intrapsychic Data

Although all of my 185 N+ examinees studiously avoided making a negative impact on others, their underlying motivation divided them into two distinct types. Examinees of one sort prized interpersonal diplomacy as an end in itself. By contrast, other examinees regarded tact and politeness in human relations as less intrinsically valuable. Rather, they tended to use these qualities to ingratiate themselves upon people in order to serve other ends. I labeled the first type *second-natured shrewdness,* and the second, *second-thoughted shrewdness.* These labels are in keeping with the dissimilar subjective experiences each entails.

Second-Natured Shrewdness. N+ examinees whose shrewdness was second natured accounted for 20% of my N+ sample. They were sophisticated and urbane and, like their second-thoughted counterparts, they were mindful of etiquette and careful not to give offense. But, unlike the latter, their good manners were so ingrained (usually by early and exacting training) that they were "second nature" for these examinees. In other words, their behavior was habitual, i.e., autonomous and independent of the rewards and punishments that originally shaped it.

Elizabeth Gaskell and other novelists of that Victorian vintage have provided charming accounts of this kind of second-natured shrewdness, as this was considered the ideal of the times in which they lived.

> *Example:* "When Mrs. Forrester gave a party and the little maid disturbed the ladies on the sofa by a request that she might get the tea tray out from underneath, everyone took this novel proceeding as the most natural thing in the world, and talked on about household forms and ceremonies as if all believed that our hostess had a regular servants' hall, second table, with housekeeper and steward, instead of the one little charity-school maid whose short ruddy arms could never have been strong enough to carry the tray upstairs, if she had not been assisted in private by her mistress, who now sat

in state, pretending not to know what cakes were sent up, though she knew, and we knew, and she knew that we knew, and we knew that she knew we knew, she had been busy all the morning making tea bread and sponge cakes." (*Cranford,* p. 41)[2]

Today this behavior is far less idealized and practiced, due to the increasing preference for open and informal communication. Consequently, only 35 of my N+ examinees were assignable to this second-natured variant. Nevertheless, although rare, its existence is important to remember when interpreting N+ scores.

Second-Thoughted Shrewdness. I named this variant second-thoughted shrewdness by coining the quotation that Cattell (1957) used when he described persons who achieve N+ scores as ". . . second-thoughted courtiers and diplomats." Unlike their second-natured counterparts, the examinees in my sample whom I assigned to this variant used their social skills strategically and with purpose. Not only were they usually socially successful, but they were also often adept manipulators. Even though some could properly be classified as "con men" and "social climbers," others used their manipulativeness in ways that were not self-serving or exploitive, but that instead were for diplomatic and humanitarian purposes. As Cattell (1973) noted, successful clinicians and psychodiagnosticians are often N+ scorers of this kind.

> *Example:* A therapist with a reputation for getting the most resistant clients to talk about themselves shared her secret. She told us that she pretends to appear less intelligent or knowledgeable than these clients. By using this strategy, she claims she protects clients' self-esteem, gives them a sense of being in control and helps stimulate their desire to be helpful, thereby leading them to be more informative than they might be if they perceived the therapist to be their superior or even equal.

Examinees of this second type differed in their self-judgments regarding their shrewdness. When I gave them feedback about their scores, I used my own shrewd capacities, as I often proposed that, among other things, they would make excellent poker players and then observed their reactions to this proposition,

---

[2]Gaskell, E. *Cranford.* Hammondsworth, England: Penguin Books, Ltd., 1984.

which ranged from satisfaction to discomfort. When I went on to inquire about the reasons "they played their cards so close to the chest," so to speak, it often became apparent that many lacked confidence in themselves as likable human beings and that, to be accepted by others, they thought they needed to present a facade.

In this respect, therefore, N+ people resembled L+ (suspicious) individuals, for by acting in ways that compensated for their social insecurity, they had become astute social observers. They differed in style, however, from L+ people. Instead of attempting to confirm pre-existing suspicions, which then led to reality distortions, N+ people performed wily social analyses that allowed them to obtain accurate and insightful perceptions.

To a lesser extent, they also resembled Q_3+ (strong self-sentiment) examinees since both Q_3+ and N+ people are preoccupied with their social images. The difference, however, between these two groups (as will become clearer later in the chapter on Factor Q_3 scores) is that the latter's concern for maintaining a correct social image arises out of a wish to act in accord with their ideal selves, rather than out of the desire to ingratiate themselves into the good graces of others.

Social Data

As I have stated earlier, it is inherent in the nature of shrewdness for it *not* to be readily recognized, and when it is, it is not usually frankly acknowledged by the casual observer, who tends to see the N+ person as "nice." But this is not always the case, and how people react after recognizing what is, after all, a form of duplicity is determined primarily by the degree of congruence they perceive between the projected appearance and actual self.

Thus, N+ examinees who used their social skills as a light cosmetic, intended only to highlight their more positive qualities and to deemphasize their negative ones, were in most instances easily forgiven, even if regarded as somewhat "phony." But, by contrast, those who were suspected of being substantially insincere, that is, more than a little incongruent with the facade they projected, especially if they were also suspected of hiding some reprehensible trait, drew strong negative reactions. Other negative responses were also strongly mediated by (1) the degree to which the N+ person's behavior was manipulative, and (2) whether the N+ person was caught being so.

Notwithstanding these unfavorable reactions, N+ persons generally are often socially successful in their formal kinds of interactions with colleagues and acquaintances. For example, they are seen as being valuable small-group members, who can lead in analytical, goal-oriented discussion and in providing constructive group solutions (Cattell & Stice, 1960).

But these same qualities that bring them success in more impersonal associations work against them in their more intimate ones, according to Cattell (1972) and Krug (1980). I have observed first-hand how this occurs in marital therapy. Often, the N+ partner seems unable to take off his or her social mask, seriously impeding the development of intimacy. Because these N+ people were unable to be spontaneous and share their feelings, their spouses routinely complained of "not knowing" them, or that they were "not real."

Shrewdness and Childhood

Cattell and Cattell (1975) speculate that shrewdness may be molded by a *sauve qui peute* (everyone for himself) childhood environment. With the exception of my second-natured examinees, whose habits of politeness and propriety were usually clearly traceable to rigorous early training experiences, there was some support (though not conclusive) for Cattell's speculation, in the recollections of many N+ examinees. These examinees indicated that a competitive atmosphere had permeated their childhoods. They commonly reported that they had to compete for limited resources, for such things as parental attention, grades, and peer group status. Paradoxically, however, *direct* forms of competition for these resources had either resulted in failure or had been discouraged. I might suppose this dilemma made it necessary for them to resort to more indirect, even devious, methods for meeting their wants and needs; this presumably led to their present social demeanor.

It is somewhat puzzling to me that Factor N has not shown up in analysis of children's temperament data, as it is so clearly observable in the behavior of the "sneaky" child. Frequently this child is detested by peers and adults alike, because insincerity, which is just as unlovable in children as it is in adults, is more obvious in children, for they lack the experience in subtlety for successful cover-ups.

Important Correlations Between N+ Scores and Other 16PF Scores

The two correlations in Table 12.1 are more reflective of traits that might be expected to be encountered in second-thoughted rather than second-natured N+ scorers. E− (submissiveness) scores suggest a reticence about being directly self-assertive. F− (desurgency) scores suggest a cautious life orientation which usually leads to guarded interpersonal relations. Though weak, these correlations fit nicely with what has so far been discerned about the N+ examinees in my sample who could be classified as second-thoughted. That is, they believe that if they were to behave openly and naturally, others would neither regard them favorably nor willingly acquiesce to their wishes.

Table 12.1

Important Correlations Between N+ Scores and Other 16PF Factor Scores

Factor Pole	Correlation	Possible Associated Traits Indicated by Correlation
E − (Submissiveness)	.22	Humble, Mild, Easily Led, Docile, Accommodating
F − (Desurgency)	.22	Sober, Taciturn, Serious

Clinical Relevance of N+ Scores

So far, N+ scores have not been associated with any psychiatric diagnosis, either in the research literature or in my own more informal clinical findings. Probably their greatest relevance from a clinical point of view is that their presence in a profile alerts clinicians that the client may be difficult "to read" in face-to-face interactions. Even though these clients may be presenting an agreeable front, they may be hiding traits like dominance or hostility. Particularly when N+ scores are accompanied by B+ and L+ scores, signifying intelligence, jealousy, and suspiciousness, it is highly possible that some venomous feelings are cleverly hidden under pleasant and disarming facades.

N+ scores may also alert clinicians to the need to consider the possibility that they are being manipulated. For this reason, I tend to be extra careful in acquiescing to requests by N+ clients for such things as interceding with their employer or signing legal forms for them.

LOW SCORES ON FACTOR N

Intrapsychic Data

Earlier, I noted that I am not entirely satisfied with the term "artlessness" as a designation for the N− pole, as it is not sufficiently comprehensive to include those aggressively abrupt N− examinees mentioned earlier. But these individuals were only 20 in number, and for the remaining 73 N− examinees in my sample, artlessness was a suitable designation.

In keeping with the correlations to be laid out later in this chapter, it was not surprising to find that N− examinees tended to be somewhat dominant in their interpersonal relations. This tendency was interwoven with a straightforward childlikeness which pervaded their awareness, expectations, and general viewpoints. They usually knew what they wanted and asked for it directly. Their social orientations were simplistic and were derived, *not* from a set of explicit, thought-out assumptions, but from a failure to pay much heed to the workings of the human psyche and its complexity. In sharp contrast to their "second-thoughted" polar opposites, these individuals were not even *first-thoughted* in their dealings with people.

Their lack of social ambition, and their failure to give ordinary consideration for the benefits they could derive from "putting their best foot forward" or by impressing others, impacted on how they expressed other traits. So, for example, those who were A+ (affectothymic) showed their warmth like affectionate spaniels while, conversely, A− (sizothymic) ones seemed not to attempt to conceal their coolness and indifference.

Recognizing that nature does not tolerate vacuums, and theorizing, therefore, that N− behavior can be construed as reflecting the relative absence of what are usually central human concerns and preoccupations, I was curious about what other matters and interests filled its place. In this regard, I found that most of my N− examinees showed an unusually strong liking and interest in natural, somewhat sensate kinds of phenomena, such as animals, plants, and young children.

Another characteristic of my N− examinees, and a fortunate one given that their openness made them so vulnerable, was their tendency to recover quickly from disappointment. Not only did they forgive, but they seemed also to forget. It was not unusual for them to be repeatedly taken advantage of, sometimes by the same persons. Similarly, they generally were able to "shrug off" extreme rudeness and criticism others would find intolerable, trusting that "others deep down mean well."

> *Example:* The orientation of N− individuals is probably best exemplified by the "flower children" of the 60s. A 40-year-old woman who described herself as "still a flower child," invited me into her home. Her home was small and simply furnished and, though clean, contained a dog, cat, two birds, and a rabbit, and was extremely shabby. Her simple tastes were also reflected by the selection of unsophisticated books displayed on her bookshelf.
>
> Upon talking to her, I found that, although she was college educated, she was unambitious. She had a low-paying job at a nursery and had no hesitation in telling me her hourly wage. It did not seem to occur to her to try to impress me or any other person. Impressed by her "persona-less" quality, I wondered how she would score on Factor N and asked her to be one of my examinees, to which she agreed. I discovered, on interpreting her test, that her score was 2 on Factor N.

Social Data

I discovered that people's reactions to the N− examinees in my sample were sharply divided into two camps. In one camp were those who reacted favorably, describing them as "open, sincere, genuine, unassuming, up front, not putting on airs, honest, natural, and direct." In the other camp were those who reacted less complimentarily, as they described N− people as being "socially inept, easily fooled, awkward, unsophisticated, thoughtless about others' feelings, tactless, and poorly mannered."

Sometimes, the behavior of N− examinees was misinterpreted as rudeness. Poor at the art of the "white lie," their frankness could be particularly upsetting to people who found it difficult to accept the unvarnished truth. These individuals may be well advised not to ask N− persons a question if not prepared to hear an honest answer.

Alternatively, other people who can accept unpleasant truths can often benefit from an N− person's honest feedback.

Example: An acquaintance, noted for dressing well, confided the reason she believed she was able to choose tasteful and well-fitting clothes. When buying clothes, she took with her a certain friend who could be relied upon to express frank and uncensored opinions about the imperfections of her figure, and which clothes looked inappropriate for her age.

On the whole, however, I discovered that most people reacted favorably rather than unfavorably towards my N− examinees (providing they were not of the aggressively abrupt type), appreciating that what they communicated could be taken at face value and that they were not likely to deceive or manipulate. It is possible that it is these qualities that make N− persons do well as classroom teachers, for students can establish a trusting relationship with them.

Besides teachers, other occupational groups that show an association with N− scores are nuns, missionary priests, nurses, and psychiatric technicians—all people who are usually considered trustworthy. I would not expect N− persons to be attracted to those occupations that require slyness and stealth, such as police work, or that require discreetness and tact, as in public relations or sales.

N− behavior has not been a feature problem in the marital relationships of couples I have seen in therapy, except in those instances where one partner has low N scores and the other has high N scores, especially when the latter was given to making good impressions or social climbing. It was then that the other's lack of sophistication made him or her a poor social ally. Unions between these opposites are sufficiently common for it to be the butt of numerous amusing anecdotes and cartoons, like, for example, the bored, tuxedoed man at the opera embarrassing his socially ambitious wife. I have found that the best solution for decreasing friction between these socially incompatible couples is to have each partner arrange, as much as possible, to move in separate social circles.

N− and Childhood

Artlessness is the kind of simplistic social orientation with which all persons undoubtedly begin their lives. Shrewdness, I have hypothesized, develops later, when it is found that natural and spontaneous behavior does not work. Given this reasoning, one way of looking at N− behavior is as a form of arrested social development, but one which is not usually dysfunctional.

Finally, although it makes intuitive sense that N− individuals were exposed to early childhood conditions that made discretion and manipulativeness unnecessary because their natural selves were accepted, it is at this time only speculative, since there are no data that reliably link retrospections of N− adults with their early social experiences. Moreover, since Factor N scores do not appear in analysis of children's and adolescents' temperament data, it has not been yet possible to draw on direct observations to cast light on this relationship.

Important Correlations Between N− Scores and Other 16PF Factor Scores

Table 12.2 below shows the correlations between N− scores and the scores of two other 16PF factors.

Table 12.2

Important Correlations Between N− Scores and Other 16PF Factor Scores

Factor Pole	Correlation	Possible Associated Traits Indicated by Correlation
E+ (Dominance)	.22	Assertive, Aggressive, Stubborn, Competitive
F+ (Surgency)	.22	Happy-go-lucky, Enthusiastic

The correlations in Table 12.2 suggest dominant (E+) and happy-go-lucky, exuberant (F+) characteristics. Just as what was presented in Table 12.1 is consistent with typical N+ (shrewdness), these correlations suggest just the kind of traits which one might expect to encounter in open, forthright, N− personalities.

Clinical Relevance of N− Scores

Even though the statistical evidence is that N− scores usually are healthy, Cattell, Eber, and Tatsuoka (1970) report there is some slight association between N− scores and psychopathology.

My colleagues and I have occasionally discovered N− scores in regressed or immature clients, who showed childlike behavior as part of hypomanic, schizophrenic, or neurotic disorders.

Other than these findings, my experience is that N− scores have the most clinical relevance as indicators that the examinee is lacking in a normal level of social sophistication and skepticism, and has limited insight into others' reactions. In this regard, the clinician may consider which other 16PF traits are being expressed without due regard to their social impact, thereby compounding their potentially negative effects. I have discovered the following three combinations of scores to be meaningful in making this evaluation.

N−(Artlessness) and B− (Lower Intelligence) Scores. N− (artlessness) added to B− (low intelligence) creates the Simple Simon types, fabled in everyday life as well as in nursery rhymes. Unlike unintelligent but more shrewd examinees, who compensated for what they lack in intelligence by being cunning or "streetwise," examinees with this N−/B− combination were gullible, made many errors in judgment, and had difficulty in doing almost anything correctly. Possibly, it is individuals such as these who account for the surprising findings regarding the frequency with which N− scores were encountered in prison populations,[3] thus giving credence to the popular idea that it is the foolish, rather than the clever, criminal who gets caught.

N− (Artlessness) and I+ (Premsia) Scores. People who are I+ (premsic) use their feeling, rather than thinking, responses to make evaluations. They are also inclined towards having sentimental and romantic expectations. When these qualities are combined with a naive social attitude, such persons become particularly vulnerable to exploitation. I have had examinees of both sexes whose profiles showed this combination, and who had been targeted by gigolos. No fewer than 10 had been cheated out of significant amounts of money by lovers and so-called friends. But, although they were sorrier from these experiences, I can assume that they did not usually become wiser, since their N scores failed to rise following insight therapy.

N− (Artlessness) and M+ (Autia) Scores. The N+ qualities of second-thoughtedness, good manners, and insight into others

---

[3]Personal communication from R. B. Cattell.

can offset the M+ persons' proclivity for being absentminded and inattentive to what goes on around them. For example, I have observed many instances when M+ examinees were rescued, by their shrewdness, from a potentially embarrassing situation, such as when they have forgotten a name while making introductions.

By contrast, a combination of N− and M+ characteristics has, as far as I can tell, nothing to commend it, since N− and M+ together compound each other's disadvantages. Examinees in whom I have observed this combination have had difficulty in dealing with social reality and in responding appropriately to interpersonal cues. People were apt to see them as decidedly odd, since they are liable to make the most extreme kinds of social mistakes, and yet were unaware or nonplussed at the reactions they evoked.

> *Example:* An N−/M+ academic of my acquaintance was doing research on human sexuality. Speculating on the meaning of his statistical findings, he entertained various hypotheses, which, though creative, were somewhat startling. He asked various people about their opinions of his hypotheses. One was a female janitor, who was completely unknown to him, but who happened to be assigned to clean his office that day. She reported him to the Department Head, understandably, I thought, believing that he was making obscene remarks to her.

Chapter 13

Factor O: Guilt Proneness and Untroubled Adequacy

THE CONSTRUCT
Difficulty in Naming Factor O

Beyond Guilt Proneness: Factor O
as a Measurement of Self-Esteem

Heredity

Male and Female Differences Throughout the Life Span

HIGH SCORES ON FACTOR O
Intrapsychic Data

Social Data

O+ and Childhood

Important Correlations Between O+ Scores
and Other 16PF Factor Scores

Clinical Relevance of O+ Scores

LOW SCORES ON FACTOR O
Intrapsychic Data

Social Data

Important Correlations Between O− Scores
and Other 16PF Factor Scores

Clinical Relevance of O− Scores

FACTOR O: CHARACTERISTICS OF O+ (GUILT-PRONE) AND O− (UNTROUBLED, ADEQUATE) EXAMINEES

Left Score O − (UNTROUBLED ADEQUACY)		Right Score O + (GUILT PRONENESS)
(Self-assured, Placid, Secure, Complacent, Good Self-esteem)	vs.	(Apprehensive, Self-reproaching, Insecure, Worrying, Troubled)
Self-confident	vs.	Worrying, Anxious
Cheerful, Resilient	vs.	Depressed, Cries Easily
Impenitent, Placid	vs.	Easily Touched, Overcome by Moods
Expedient, Insensitive to People's Approval or Disapproval	vs.	Strong Sense of Obligation, Sensitive to People's Approval or Disapproval
Does Not Care	vs.	Scrupulous, Fussy
Rudely Vigorous	vs.	Hypochondriacal and Inadequate
No Fears	vs.	Phobic Symptoms
Given to Simple Action	vs.	Lonely, Brooding

THE CONSTRUCT

Difficulty in Naming Factor O

Factor O measures feelings that people have about themselves in regard to their self-worth. Sometimes these feelings arise out of current self-judgments; but they can also hark back to earlier, even preverbal times. Named for its high pole, O+, this factor has proven to be the most difficult to define in the entire 16PF contingent. Various labels have been applied to it (depressive tendency, self-depreciation, moodiness, and neuroticism) and then dropped. As in the story of the seven blind men who each attempted to describe an entire elephant according to that part of its anatomy they were touching, each of these labels caught only one dimension of this factor. Although Cattell (1973) finally settled on "guilt proneness" as most approximating the meaning of the factor, he was even here concerned about the topicality of this label. He warned that what Factor O measures *"is* not liability to particular pangs of guilt as much as a global sense of inadequacy, loneliness, and tears" (p. 172). In other words, Cattell emphasized that the essence of this factor is not actual guilt feelings, which are only its subjective manifestations, but an underlying emotional self-attitude.

In my opinion, there are two reasons why guilt proneness shares the errors of all past labels, i.e., that of too narrowly, and therefore misleadingly, defining the factor. First, Factor O's correlation with Factor G (the superego factor, which is usually believed to represent the internal stimulus for guilt), is trivial. Factor O has much stronger correlations with other factors, particularly Factor C (ego strength) and Factor Q_4 (tension). Second, my investigations into the subjective lives of O+ examinees revealed that guilt was in reality only one feeling among a host of others, including shame and self-doubt, to which they were prone.

Factor O as Measurement of Self-Esteem

The feelings experienced by the O+ examinees in my sample overwhelmingly revolved around the absence of self-worth. Therefore, I concluded that the basic core measured by the high factor pole is an absence of basic, healthy narcissism (more popularly called "self-esteem"). Conversely, I conclude that the low pole (O−), which was manifested on my O− examinees as confidence and self-complacency, measures high self-esteem. However, as I shall explain later, the basis of their self-esteem was not well grounded in reality and was actually "pseudo" self-esteem.

Heredity

The genetic contribution to Factor O is moderate (.34). Thus, persons have a constitutional tendency to evaluate themselves positively or negatively in addition to reacting to their life experiences.

Male and Female Differences Throughout the Life Span

The mean group score for men is 17.60 and for women, 23.18. Even though women are significantly more guilt prone than men, both sexes show a similar, moderate standard deviation. Their scores also follow a similar life course, indicating that both sexes show an increase in self-esteem in mid-adolescence and a decrease after middle age.

HIGH SCORES ON FACTOR O

Intrapsychic Data

Suffering dominates the inner life of O+ persons. By their endorsement of O scale items, they are saying that they stay awake at night worrying, become dejected when criticized, act in a self-depreciating way, and are self-reproaching. In clinical interviews, my O+ examinees tended to summarize their feelings about themselves with such phrases as, "I don't like myself." The root of these feelings, as I have already proposed, is a lack of a reasonable sense of self-worth. It is not necessarily the self-hate described by Menninger (1938) in *Man Against Himself,* where—using another descriptive system—the pugnacity/sadism drive[1] is supposedly turned inward against the self.

O+ scores, I must stress, do not always indicate a chronic condition or, in other words, a trait. They may also reflect a transitory response or state. I was able to make this distinction clearly in about 200 of my 276 O− examinees. I found it useful, when making this distinction, to interpret the meaning of O+ scores on a given profile according to the old reactive/characterological dichotomy. Here, something needs to be known about the examinee's present situation or recent past. I asked if he or she had recently experienced failure, illness, reduced status, bereavement, or other loss. The self-esteem of reactive examinees was usually restored to its previous level once their lives returned to normal or their grief processes completed, and was reflected as decreases in O scores in repeated 16PF testing.

Characterological low self-esteem is a different matter. Rather than rising and falling with changing circumstances, it is built into the fabric of the personality. Consequently, the O+ scores of persons who have characterological self-esteem will persist at more or less the same level over a long period of time, which is exactly what I found in 32 O+ examinees who were tested over a three-year period.

A series of test scores upon which to make this reactive vs. characterological distinction is rarely available, however, since in most circumstances it is possible to obtain only a single set of scores. Moreover, although it might seem simple, given what I said two paragraphs ago about the useful role of psycho-social histories in discerning reactive low self-esteem, a complication arises in that I discovered that my characterologically low self-esteemed examinees often believed that they were reacting to recent major losses or difficulties. This phenomenon can probably best be explained by "attribution theory" (Kelly, 1967) research

---

[1]A measurement of the pugnacity/sadism drive is included in the Motivation Analysis Test (MAT.) See Appendix B.

which demonstrates that human beings do not allow their feelings to remain free-floating for long, but tend to attribute them to all kinds of passing occurrences. The technique I employed for uncovering chronic feelings of low self-esteem was to ask O+ examinees what, if anything, they felt this way about last year and the year before that, and so on. This line of questioning usually distinguished the characterological sufferers of low self-esteem from reactive ones, by showing how far-reaching their feelings are.

Parenthetically, it is crucial that clinicians make this characterological/reactive distinction when first presented with O+ scores in a new client's profile, for it often determines whether a person-centered (i.e., emphasis on personality structure) or a problem-centered (i.e., emphasis on the problem) approach is most appropriate. The latter strategy is the treatment of choice for clients who are merely reacting to situational disturbances, but is contraindicated in individuals whose low self-esteem is characterological and who need to focus on changing deeply ingrained self-attitudes.

Despite its subjective discomfort, low self-esteem, even of the characterological variety, may not be without social value. Persons who possess this trait, often by wishing to ward off its associated feelings of guilt, contrition, shame, and self-doubt, act in ways that facilitate the survival and well-being of society. Paradoxically, therefore, it can provide a powerful counterforce against selfishness, greed, cruelty, and irresponsibility. I observed this phenomenon in many of my O+ examinees, who were justly lauded as good, humane, and virtuous by those who knew them.

It is not surprising, therefore, that the 16PF profiles of priests tend to show O+ scores and that there is generally some association between high scores and spiritual yearnings. Cattell believes that truly religious persons, if tested, would show strong tendencies toward low self-esteem. This belief was also shared by William James, who, in his *Varieties of Religious Experience* (1958), proposed that a fragile sense of self-worth and tendency to self-denigration which he called a "sickness of the soul," was a requisite for spiritual awakening. This "sickness" encompasses, not only a sense of sin regarding one's own personal transgressions, but also the belief in the Christian notion of original sin, the evil inherent in human nature.

Social Data

The social reactions elicited by my O+ examinees depended, not only on how they viewed themselves, but on which of two orientations they held toward others: some examinees regarded other people as being more worthy than themselves, while others saw other people as being equally as unworthy as themselves. Socially useful low self-esteem, as I described it in the previous section, occurred only with the first of these attitudes.

Examinees in my sample who saw others as more worthy than themselves typically attempted to mitigate their negative self-evaluations by making personal sacrifices, working hard, and being strongly committed. But even though others reaped rewards from their efforts, unless these O+ people had the capacity to hide their inner turmoil—a quality discernible from their N+ (shrewdness) scores—they had a poor self-presence, and their discomfort was apparent in face-to-face situations. Possibly, it is for this reason that my own data, as well as that of Cattell and Stice (1960), show that O+ persons are rarely selected as leaders, and are seldom promoted.

The annoying habit of some O+ people to act as if they are to blame for negative situations over which they have no control, and, moreover, to see the inappropriateness of this behavior even when it is pointed out to them, is illustrated in the following anecdote.

> *Example:* A college student felt dejected after his girl friend suddenly blew up and broke off their relationship. She told him she was tired of his apologizing, as this required that she reassure him constantly. In discussing what had happened with a guidance counselor, he was clearly confused about his former girl friend's reaction. "All I said," he recounted, "was 'I apologize for the rain this evening.'" He wondered if he should transfer to another college (in Arizona, maybe) where there was less rain.

I noted that vulnerability to feelings of worthlessness and inadequacy made many of my O+ examinees susceptible to manipulation and exploitation. It was easy to "put a guilt trip on them," to use a popular expression, since others' simply pointing to some shortcoming mobilized O+ examinees' deepest fears. Their involvement in relationships with E+ (dominant) persons showed this mechanism most clearly. Relationships between these two types seemed often sadomasochistic, since O+ people's willingness to accept blame and their belief that they deserved punishment made them natural complements for the extrapunitiveness of their E+ partners.

The other O+ examinees, those whose social attitudes were oriented toward seeing others in the same negative light in which they viewed themselves, were cynical about humankind generally. Their 16PF profiles were apt to reflect this view by showing very high (9 or 10) scores on Factor L (protension). My data suggest they may even be at high risk for committing suicide or homicide, possibly because they are despairing of finding much meaning in life, for they expect little that is good and altruistic, in themselves or others. I also discovered a disproportionate number of these individuals in prisons, serving long sentences.

O+ and Childhood

I have wondered if the dichotomies indicated by Factor O are at least in some part what Erickson (1968) proposes as the basic life orientations of trust vs. distrust. According to Erickson, these orientations are derived from interactions with caregivers in the first year of life, who shaped, not only attitudes toward people, but who also shaped the more fundamental trust or distrust in oneself as being worthy of love and caring.

The correspondence between these orientations and Factor O is, in my opinion, sufficiently promising to merit future investigation, especially, as Cattell (1973) is inclined to believe, the notion that there is a relationship between high O scores and disturbed early attachments. In fact, the post-infancy study of school-age children by Barton, Dielman, and Cattell (1972) suggested that persons with O+ scores had memories of later childhood experiences of unsatisfactory parenting. Specifically, these people reported receiving physical punishment and little guidance, particularly from their mothers. Because this taps such an early period of life, my O+ examinees did not have sufficient memories to add to or substantiate this finding.

Since my investigations did not remedy the virtual absence of data concerning the relation between low scores and early childhood experience, I will omit the usual childhood section when I discuss O− examinees.

Important Correlations Between O+ Scores
and Other 16PF Factor Scores

Table 13.1 shows that C− (lower ego strength) and Q_4+ (ergic tension) scores correlate .61 with O+ (guilt proneness) scores. These are among the largest intercorrelations between 16PF factors. Less substantial, but still significant, are the correlations with H− (threctia), $Q_3−$ (low self-sentiment), and L+ (protension) scores. This set of correlations suggests that, in addition to having self-esteem problems, O+ people are somewhat apt to manifest the full spectrum of anxiety symptoms, since C−, H−, L+, O+, $Q_3−$, and Q_4+ scores form the second-order high anxiety pattern. This pattern will be discussed later, in Chapter 18.

Table 13.1

**Important Correlations Between O+ Scores
and Other 16PF Factor Scores**

Factor Pole	Correlation	Possible Associated Traits Indicated by Correlation
C− (Lower Ego Strength)	.61	Affected by Feelings, Emotionally Less Stable, Easily Upset, Changeable
Q_4+ (Ergic Tension)	.61	Tense, Frustrated, Driven, Overwrought
H− (Threctia)	.43	Shy, Timid, Threat-sensitive
$Q_3−$ (Low Self-sentiment)	.28	Undisciplined Self-conflict, Lax, Follows Own Urges, Careless of Social Rules
L+ (Protension)	.33	Suspicious, Hard to Fool

Clinical Relevance of O+ Scores

The presence of an O+ score in a profile is one of the major indicators of psychological pain. The feelings these scores signify are what Karson and O'Dell (1976) call the "bread and butter" of psychotherapists. These feelings form the "emotional" core of depression as well as anxiety.

In addition to contributing to the second-order anxiety factor, O+ scores combine with several other 16PF factor scores in clinically revealing ways. Those that, in my experience, have reliably proven to have the most clinical significance are set out below. I strongly suspect that the O+ scores in these combinations, with the possible exception of the O+/E− (submissiveness) combination, are derived from the dysfunctional nature in other traits. For this reason, my clinical interventions in clients who show these combinations focus on influencing these other traits. Successful treatment results in some changes in their measurements in subsequent 16PF testing, which are finally followed by a lowering of O scores.

O+/G+: Low Self-esteem Combined with High Conventional Morality. From Chapter 8, it will be recalled that G+ scores indicate a strong endorsement of conventional moral standards. When they are combined with O+ scores, they signal that guilt is the most dominant feeling in the low self-esteem complex. Examinees showing this combination typically attributed their guilt to some wrongdoing on their part. Typically, this guilt was often quite inappropriate, for it sprang from the dictates of an overly rigid and unreasonable moral code, often built on childhood misperceptions. Some examinees recognized that they were inappropriately harsh with themselves, but felt helpless to stop the habit of negative self-censure, as in the case of those who grew up with strong religious taboos in which they no longer believed. The majority, however, intellectually and emotionally endorsed these moral codes, and were not fully cognizant of their logical inappropriateness.

The reader may recognize that what is being described here is the phenomenon of neurotic guilt, a long-time focus of psychoanalysts. Taking the lead from psychoanalysis, my treatment of those clients whose low self-esteem results from self-defeating moral codes has been to loosen the superego's grip by demystifying the originators of its content (usually the parents). When successful, a new guide for their behavior was provided by the ego's reality-testing role, so that these clients come to evaluate their actions on the basis of *consequences,* rather than by their conformity to archaic or inappropriate good/bad categories. This was reflected in their subsequent 16PF profiles, which showed *decreases* in both Factor G and Factor O scores and an *increase* in Factor C (ego strength) scores.

O+/G−: Low Self-esteem Combined with Low Moral Conformity. In contradistinction to what was just described above, this combination involves guilt about *not* endorsing conventional moral standards. Karson and O'Dell (1976) have found this combination to be particularly prevalent among adolescents. These authors suggest that the most successful intervention for these adolescents, as well as their adult counterparts, is to help them be more socially conforming so that they will have less to feel guilty about.

Early in my investigation, I noted that Q_3- (low self-sentiment) scores and Q_1+ (radicalness) scores also frequently appeared on profiles showing $O+$ and $G-$ combinations, leading me to hypothesize that identity problems were involved in examinees who had low self-esteem and who were not morally conforming. Further observations have supported this hypothesis, for it became obvious that a disproportionate number of them were clearly rejecting conventional values out of rebelliousness. This, in my experience, inevitably turned out to be an attempt to gain a better sense of selfhood through personal autonomy. For these individuals to increase their self-esteem, it was necessary for them to develop their personal identities by endorsing self-chosen functional values, which may or may not be aligned with conventional morality.

> *Example:* A 24-year-old male client whose initial score on Factor G was 2 and score on Factor O was 9, concluded treatment with both factor scores in mid range. He explained his transformation by saying, "Now I'm free to vote and pay taxes even if my parents and all other parents of the world like it."

$O+/Q_3+$: *Low Self-esteem Combined with High Self-sentiment.* This combination is manifested in behavior similar to that shown by persons who have $O+/G+$ (low self-esteem/high moral conformity) scores. However, in this combination, the unreasonable self-imposed standards do not come from the superego but from the desired self, i.e., their wished-for self-images (to be detailed later in the Factor Q_3 chapter). Examinees with this combination felt not guilt but inadequacy and shame, because they fell short of their personal and social ideals. These ideals invariably were unrealistic or humanly impossible to achieve. To increase their self-esteem, it was necessary for them to bring the images they wished to attain for themselves more into accord with reality. When this occurred, their profiles showed decreases in Factor O scores, and corresponding decreases in Factor Q_3 scores.

$O+/E-$: *Low Self-esteem Combined with Submissiveness.* Unlike the three other variants described above, where low self-esteem appears to be substantially derived from other traits (namely, the superego and the self-sentiment) and can be increased when these other traits are worked upon, this principle does not universally hold here. It holds for E − people who dislike themselves because they behave unassertively, but *not* for those who think of themselves as too unworthy to assert themselves.

In my sample, examinees who said they disliked themselves for the way they behaved (that is, for giving in, not saying no, or in some other way failing to assert their rights) tended to respond well to assertiveness training. This treatment modality often resulted in dramatic increases in their Factor E scores and a lowering of Factor O scores.

By contrast, those examinees who did not feel sufficiently worthy to be assertive did not benefit from assertiveness training; in fact, assertiveness training was often detrimental to them, possibly because it was one more thing for them to feel undeserving about. It would have been better delayed, therefore, until their self-esteem was increased.

O + /F − : Low Self-esteem Combined with Desurgency. Whenever an O + score in a 16PF profile appears when the other anxiety-related factors are not extreme (i.e., the person does not show C − , H − , L + , or Q_4 + , but does show O +), the possibility should be considered that the examinee is depressed. When F − (desurgency) scores appear along with O + scores, suspicion of a depression diagnosis is merited even further, according to Karson and O'Dell (1976). These authors point out that an overly serious, desurgent attitude, in conjunction with low self-esteem, indicates that the examinee, at the very least, is in an anhedonic state.

LOW SCORES ON FACTOR O

Intrapsychic Data

The low pole of Factor O has been less studied than its opposite. According to Cattell (1957), persons scoring at this pole are self-confident, resilient, cheerful, impenitent, uncaring, relaxed, vigorous, fearless, and given to simple action. I observed these qualities in my sample of O − examinees. Further, these qualities seemed founded upon the positive judgments these people have about themselves: they feel worthwhile and competent, and they think they deserve to be loved, respected, nurtured, and to get their needs met. These are, of course, the essential qualities of self-esteem.

However, the rub is that self-esteem, as a steady, unwavering state, falls under suspicion as not being based on realistic self-appraisal. Consequently, extreme O − scores should *not* be taken as indicators of emotional health, even though they reflect a subjectively desirable condition. Self-esteem serves its most useful purpose when it is sensitive to ever-changing aspects of one's behavior and being, and when it fluctuates accordingly.

Let me illustrate this point with an analogy between self-esteem feelings and body senses. The physical parallel to unshakably high self-esteem is the condition/state wherein pain and other sensory receptors of the brain are inoperative. Our bodies use sensory signals to convey information about what we need to do to maintain health: an aching back tells us to correct our posture; fatigue tells us to rest; muscle tension tells us to exercise. So it is with our self-esteem feelings. Twinges of shame, guilt, and doubt are vital feedback signals that something is not well with our behavior. These twinges call for some modification of our way of relating to ourselves or to the world, so that we can maintain or restore a positive self-concept.

Therefore, when O − scores of 1, 2, or 3 appear on a profile, it is wise for the interpreter to consider closely the basis of the examinee's self-esteem. Karson and O'Dell (1976), Krug (1980), and others advise that these low scores may reflect sociopathic tendencies. This is a reasonable inference, in view of the fact that O − examinees are reporting that they rarely accept blame or experience remorse. I give careful consideration to the question of sociopathy whenever an examinee's Factor O score is embedded in a profile that shows second-order extraversion, together with G − (low moral conformity) and N + (shrewdness) scores.

Rather than sociopathy, I discovered that an O − score was more likely to mean that the examinee was excessively blocking, denying, distorting, or repressing from awareness, negative aspects of himself or herself, in order to maintain positive self-regard. I am, of course, speaking of those perceptual and cognitive operations known as *defense mechanisms*. Defense mechanisms are normal and necessary to ordinary functioning. Denying noxious aspects of themselves can have a beneficial effect on psychological functioning. Otherwise, these negatives could cause depression and anxiety (Anna Freud, 1946; Monat &

Lazarus, 1979). However, in O — individuals, unlike more moderate scorers, these defense mechanisms are excessively strong and rigid.

Let us consider again the anatomy of defense mechanisms generally by enlarging on what has already been said, in the chapter on Factor C, about the relationship between Factor O and Factors C (ego strength) and Q_3 (self-sentiment). Here, in considering how these three factors interact and in anticipating the discussion in the chapter on Factor Q_3, the reader may wish to look ahead to Figure 1 in Chapter 16. This figure shows that the self-sentiment is composed of a *wished-for self-image* and a *perceived self-image,* with an evaluator assessing the congruence between them. When the evaluator judges that there is either existing or potential incongruence between the wished-for and the perceived self-images, low self-esteem feelings, or the threat of low self-esteem feelings, follow. To relieve or avoid these painful feelings, people bring their behavior more in line with the standards of the wished-for self-image. However, when for some reason the evaluator does not want to acknowledge incongruences between the wished-for and the perceived self-images, in order to preserve self-esteem, it foregoes its usual reality-testing functions, and instead distorts or suspends awareness.

Without exception, my finding was that O — scores indicated that the examinees' self-esteem was based on some reality distortion and was, therefore, substantially lacking in self-awareness. In addition to their excessive use of defense mechanisms, I also discovered that my O — examinees were likely to employ other behavioral strategies in order to preserve their self-esteem. One of these strategies was to avoid situations that cast doubt on their adequacy or that caused them to fail. Several of them, for example, did not go to college or develop intimate relationships or have children for this reason. Another strategy was to derive reassurance from preoccupation with a valued personal attribute, such as physical attractiveness or intelligence, or from some external association like wealth or status.

Social Data

My best observations of the O — examinees' social behavior came from observing them in clinical settings. Not feeling the emotional pain that typically brings other people for psychological treatment, O — individuals were frequently towed into my office by dissatisfied spouses who complained that their relationship suffered from a lack of emotional contact. Often, these spouses were extremely confused about the nature of the emotional difficulty, especially when the O − persons were A + (affectothymic) and so were warmly involved with their partner. (This was not at all unusual, since there is only a small, negative correlation between scores on Factors A and O.) Not unexpectedly, it turned out that the O − partners lacked empathetic understanding of certain subjective experiences, since empathy, by definition, is the ability to particpate in the emotional experiences of others by matching the others' feelings against a similar repertoire of one's own. These O − examinees were unlike I − scorers, who are also lacking in overall empathetic understanding and who show general insensitivity, in that the emotional omissions of O − scorers were more specific: for the most part, their feeling repertoire excluded doubt, shame, and guilt. Therefore, they were not able to be empathic when, for example, their spouses complained of feeling remorseful about past mistakes. Further, they could not honestly make the simple but psychologically meaningful statement, "I know how you feel."

Intimacy involves exchanging these kinds of empathetic, meaningful responses, and in the marriages of O − persons, intimacy is what is lacking. If their spouses do not feel deprived by this lack or are able to accept that their partners are not *deliberately* withholding empathetic communication, no serious difficulty arises. But, more often, at least in my clinical experience, it leads to frustration and bitterness, further widening the gulf between the couple.

But probably nowhere, judging from my examinees, is the O − scorer's disadvantageous lack of emotional reactivity more apparent than in situations involving their culpability. Although they may be willing to accept blame and even make amends to those they have wittingly or unwittingly injured, they lack a contrite heart. This can be particularly dissatisfying to others, for it seems to be a peculiarity of human nature to disdain the acceptance of a *painless* pound of flesh. We want people not only to accept blame but to *feel* sorry for their wrongdoings. In Christianity, this is called repentance; in psychology, an appeasement response. Consequently, I observed that my O − examinees' failure to make appeasement responses made it difficult for others to stop punishing them.

In my sample, nagging spouses, especially those that repetitiously brought up a litany of past transgressions, often turned out to have O— partners. After observing the regularity of this pattern, I have decided that it is helpful, in maintaining domestic peace, for O— individuals to have high Factor N (shrewdness) scores, so that they can display guilt and remorse even if it is not felt.

> *Example:* Following a series of short affairs in the early years of their marriage, a husband decided to remain faithful to his wife, and thereafter became, in this and other ways, an exemplary husband. Nineteen years later the wife sought therapy because she wanted to relinquish the hurt and anger she still experienced in regard to these affairs. When I asked why she believed she had not been able to relinquish these feelings after so many years, and especially in view of his reformation, she replied: "Because he never really seemed sorry for what he did."

Important Correlations Between O— Scores and Other 16PF Factor Scores

The five correlations between O— scores and other 16PF factor scores are listed in Table 13.2 below.

Table 13.2

Important Correlations Between O— Scores and Other 16PF Factor Scores

Factor Pole	Correlation	Possible Associated Traits Indicated by Correlation
C+ (High Ego Strength)	.61	Emotionally Stable, Mature, Faces Reality, Calm
Q_4 – (Low Ergic Tension)	.61	Relaxed, Tranquil, Unfrustrated, Composed
H+ (Parmia)	.43	Venturesome, Uninhibited, Socially Bold
Q_3 + (Stronger Self-sentiment)	.37	Controlled, Exacting Will Power, Socially Precise, Competitive
L– (Alaxia)	.33	Trusting, Accepting Conditions

According to Table 13.2, O — scorers are typically far removed from the kinds of psychological discomfort that their opposites experience. Those individuals are more likely to be relaxed (Q_4 —), emotionally controlled (C +), adventurous and bold (H +), open and trusting (L —), and be invested in maintaining a socially approved self-image (Q_3 +). These are exactly the kinds of characteristics one would ordinarily associate with persons with the positive self-orientations that O — scores indicate.

Clinical Relevance of O — Scores

Earlier in this chapter, I acknowledged that the strong ego defenses indicated by O — scores can be either advantages or disadvantages, according to the context of the examinee's life situation. Clinicians are repeatedly confronted with the need to make this discrimination, by having to determine whether the benefit a given client derives from denying or distorting reality outweighs other considerations. This determination must be made case by case. It may be that the information being guarded against is useful, even vital, to the client's and other peoples' immediate and long-term well-being, as, for instance, when a child-abusing parent does not realize that he or she is venting frustration, but believes instead that the punishment is serving the child's best interest. It may also be that the self-perceptions that are being guarded against are themselves built on some unfounded ideas about what constitutes personal unworthiness and incompetence, the reexamination of which would show that they need no longer threaten self-esteem.

Nevertheless, in working with O — clients, I find that it is necessary to proceed with caution in dismantling their defenses, remembering that there must have been a powerful impetus for their creation initially, and that their removal may still require confrontation with painful truths. I have observed one or two unfortunate incidents where inexperienced clinicians have bulldozed through these clients' defenses. Subsequent testing with the 16PF showed that, bereft of their protective illusions, their O scores had moved to 8, 9, or 10, reflecting that they were overcome by apprehension, worry, or self-depreciatory ideas.

Chapter 14

Factor Q_1: Orientations Towards Change

THE CONSTRUCT
Psychological Orientation Towards Change
Forward- and Backward-Looking Orientations
Heredity
Male and Female Differences Throughout the Life Span

HIGH SCORES ON FACTOR Q_1
Q_1+ and Childhood
Intrapsychic Data
Social Data
Important Correlations Between Q_1+ Scores
and Other 16PF Factor Scores
Clinical Relevance of Q_1+ Scores

LOW SCORES ON FACTOR Q_1
Q_1- and Childhood
Intrapsychic Data
Social Data
Important Correlations Between Q_1- Scores
and Other 16PF Factor Scores
Clinical Relevance of Q_1- Scores

FACTOR Q_1: CHARACTERISTICS OF Q_1+ (RADICAL) AND Q_1- (CONSERVATIVE) EXAMINEES

Left Score Q_1- (CONSERVATISM OF TEMPERAMENT)		Right Score Q_1+ (RADICALISM)
(Conservative, Respecting Established Ideas, Tolerant of Traditional Difficulties)	vs.	(Experimenting, Liberal, Analytical, Free-thinking)

THE CONSTRUCT

Psychological Orientation Towards Change

Cattell credits Thurstone and Chavel for originally discovering this factor, as it appeared in test questionnaire data, as far back as 1929. Since then, it has been found as a similar pattern, by Guilford and Eysenck as well as by Cattell and his colleagues, in more than eight separate data analyses.

As with the other three Q-labeled primary 16PF factors (Q_2, Q_3, and Q_4), Q_1 appears only in questionnaire data (the Q stands for questionnaire) and not in the ratings of observers. The failure of this factor to be clearly discernible as an observable trait is probably due to the deeper nature of the basic attitude from which it springs. This attitude, according to Cattell, Eber, and Tatsuoka (1970), at essence involves a psychological orientation towards change. Since items that measure it tap social, political, and religious attitudes, they catch only its epiphenomena.

Change, as I refer to it throughout this chapter, is defined as a perceptual readjustment, towards a corresponding temporal phenomenon, that is mediated by emotions and motives on the part of the organism. The research on perception has not yet revealed much about the inner workings of these organic processes. Therefore, psychotherapists and counselors, whose fundamental task, of course, is to facilitate change, are forced to draw their practical understanding from inferences based on the regularities they observe in persons in transition. These observations indicate that change rests on the cusp of two main processes: (1) *decathexis,* i.e., an ending or letting go of present attachments, and (2) *recathexis,* a new beginning, or reattachments to other sources of satisfactions that replace those that are left behind. Undoubtedly, what is involved here is the hedonistic principle that organisms seek pleasure and avoid pain, which is acknowledged by all psychological theorists to be one of the main organizers of behavior. This means that the *less* pleasurable or rewarding one finds a current relationship, situation, life stage, etc., the easier it will be to give it up. Likewise, the *more* pleasurable or rewarding one expects the future to be, the easier to move toward it. Similarly, pleasurable and rewarding experiences will be hard to give up, especially when there is little anticipation of future compensations.

Forward- and Backward-Looking Orientations

Although it became clear to me that an orientation towards change lies at the heart of Factor Q_1, its further elucidation, probably more than with other factors, rested on observing the differences between those who score at the extremes of each pole. The contrast between my two groups of $Q_1 +$ and $Q_1 -$ examinees impressed me as being comparable, on the metaphorical level, to passengers in old-fashioned railway carriages. Compartmentalized into small rooms, these carriages had two parallel rows of seats, one facing the engine and the other facing away from it. From the seats facing the engine, the new horizons continuously flashed into view as the present rushed to meet it, requiring passengers to continuously adjust their perceptions to assimilate and accommodate new information. By contrast, the backward-turned seats did not provide a view of what lay ahead, presenting instead the lingering present as it merged with the past, and demanding few perceptual adjustments. Just like the majority of individuals who score in the middle of the Factor Q_1 continuum, most passengers were versatile in their preferences for forward or backward views, choosing a forward-looking seat, perhaps, when eagerly returning to a favorite spot and a backward-looking one when reluctantly leaving it. But rationalizations of motion sickness aside, others showed preferences for one side over the other.

It seems to me that my extreme-scoring examinees correspond to these travelers on life's journey. Those with $Q_1 -$ scores showed their reluctance to leave their present and past attachments behind, preferring to stay with the familiar, and showing little interest in future innovations. This orientation showed itself, not only in social, religious, and political preferences, but in a liking for tradition and a general nostalgia, which was evident in such things as their preferences for historical novels, antiques, and memorabilia rather than, say, science fiction novels.

On the other hand, my future-oriented Q_1+ examinees were interested in the new and unfamiliar. It was fairly common for them to be less emotionally attached to their pasts than most people would be. Some referred to their past detachedly, or with denigration. It was also common for them to describe themselves as being in some way "liberated" (sexually, politically, etc.). This term, by definition, implies a negative evaluation of the past.

Without recognition that it is an orientation toward change that is at the crux of this factor, it is extremely difficult to predict what a person's score might be when it is based on such topical issues as political party affiliation, especially since the social radicalism of one decade can be the conservatism of the next. Moreover, sometimes what initially seems to be a regressive trend, such as, for example, a back-to-nature movement, may upon closer analysis turn out to be progressive, and vice versa. These considerations have created difficulties in keeping Factor Q_1 *items* valid over time, making it desirable to change them, as Burdsal and Cattell (1974) have detailed, with each generation.

Heredity

Although the heredity quotient has not been established for Factor Q_1, preliminary data suggest it is probably trivial. Thus, what predisposes people to assume radical, conservative, or middle-of-the-road orientations towards change must be presumed to result from their early experiences.

Male and Female Differences Throughout the Life Span

Even though there is insufficient age-curve data available to show how Q_1 scores typically fluctuate over the course of the normal life span, there are some research findings indicating that, contrary to popular opinion, 20-year-olds as a group do not have higher (more radical) scores than 60-year-olds. This finding led Cattell (1973) to propose, by logical extension, that the proclivity to be radical or conservative has little to do with age, except in early childhood. Young children, he points out, are very conservative; they strongly prefer familiar routines, and they tend to resist change. Scores on Factor Q_1, however, do have a strong relation to gender. Women are apt to be much more conservative than men (mean score for women = 16.24, men = 18.20), a difference significant at the .001 level.

HIGH SCORES ON FACTOR Q_1

$Q_1 +$ and Childhood

In this chapter, I will reverse my usual format, by considering the possible childhood antecedents involved in this factor before I deal with the subjective and relationship sections. In so doing, I am paralleling my own lines of inquiry, which I undertook out of regard for the popular proposition that the radical orientations of $Q_1 +$ individuals may have originated in their childhoods. If this were so, I reasoned that an historical perspective might provide a deeper understanding of their subjective and interpersonal experiences.

I was not surprised to discover, therefore, given that a positive orientation to change depends upon a higher ratio of future to present satisfactions, that a disproportionate number (i.e., 120 of the 154 $Q_1 +$ examinees in my sample) recalled being extremely dissatisfied children who were eager to grow up. These children believed that their lives could be most successfully improved by changing, rather than conforming to, their environments. Their willingness to pit themselves against existing conditions is what distinguished them as true, rather than pseudo, radicals. (By pseudo radicals, I mean persons whose ideas, though progressive, had been adopted by default, usually by uncritically assuming the views of their radically thinking parents. These extreme $Q_1 +$ scores are artifacts, as they are not reflective of an active orientation towards change.)

Children, in addition to being naturally conservative, usually also deeply desire their parents' approval. $Q_1 +$ people, in their childhoods, must have felt strongly about resisting conformity, if they were willing to accept the consequences. It may also be supposed that they had to suffer parental disapproval, and, in extreme cases, rejection. Neither the developmentally based research on Factor Q_1 nor my own direct investigations has specifically answered the questions about what contributed to this early behavior. However, some oblique light can be cast on it from another source. Social psychologists have investigated social conformity issues extensively and, according to Aronson (1976), have reached the consensus that persons are most likely to resist conforming to prevailing standards when the following triad of conditions exist: (1) they feel insecure about their place in the reference group to which they are asked to conform, (2) they wish to establish a separate identity, and (3) they possess self-confidence.

Though not specifically connected, these social research findings can be interpreted as being consistent with, and in fact quite similar to, the psychological dynamics that Karson and O'Dell (1976) propose underlie the orientation of Q_1+ persons. Noting the association of radicalness as a trait with pugnacity towards authority, these writers have dubbed the Q_1+ pole *"rebelliousness,"* believing it to be a manifestation of unresolved Oedipal feelings towards the father. In a nutshell, they propose that underneath the resistance to conformity is a generalization of early resentment towards parental control, which has now come to be projected onto present authority figures. Krug (1980) has indicated that there is also some psychometric support for this proposal, since Q_1+ scores correlate positively with scales from other tests, such as the Edwards Personal Preference Scale (EPPS), which measures hostility, anger, and reactivity.

Although I do not accept the mainstream psychoanalytic Oedipal concept as a universal and invariant principle of human development, I am empirically compelled to acknowledge that the anger toward authority shown by at least 60% of the male Q_1+ clients in my sample was frequently poorly grounded in present reality. Many continued to feel angry towards parents whom they believed had treated them unjustly or had been overly controlling. Although I found less evidence of unresolved parent-related animosity in female Q_1+ clients, they, too, on the whole, reported having experienced more than ordinary amounts of turbulence in their early relationships with their parents.

Yet another fairly typical characteristic that I noted in my Q_1+ clients of both sexes, and which I hypothesize may have childhood origins, was a marked dislike for waiting. Their impatience was not due to low frustration tolerance, as occurs in my $C-$ (low ego strength) clients, but came from their eager anticipation of the future. I suspect also that the genesis of this tendency may go back to times when they felt captive in environments which they were once too young and helpless to change.

Intrapsychic Data

Above all, Q_1+ adult examinees in my sample showed a strong tendency to reject tradition and its inevitable offspring, convention, as valid sources of guidance. This rejection, as I have stated, may represent the persistence of childhood attitudes that are preserved and projected onto present day authority figures and institutions. Although they were chronically angry at whatever they perceived as obstructive, unfair, or oppressive, the positive side effect of this reactivity was that they were able to leave situations that were unsatisfactory, like a frustrating job, more easily than most people.

They also had hopeful attitudes. A common danger, however, was for their hopefulness to degenerate into wishful and uncritical enthusiasm for whatever provided a radical alternative to old ways. Nevertheless, theirs was not a welcoming of change like the flighty, random, variety-seeking sort, sometimes shown by $F+$ (surgent) examinees, who enjoyed novelty and excitement just for its own sake. Instead, these Q_1+ people were rebels with a cause, and they sought purposeful change. Moreover, since they were characteristically well informed in their search for directions, most rejected faith as a criterion for truth, insisting instead upon logic and reason. It was characteristic of them, for example, as others have noted about radicals generally, to show a preference for science over religious interests.

Though they appeared similar to $E+$ (dominant) scorers in their sensitivity to power issues, they were unlike them in not wanting to subjugate others, unless they were of the opinion that the best defense in a given situation was attack. They were more keenly focused on their own fear of being controlled, in their interpersonal relationships as well as by social institutions. They were also less self-centered than $E+$ scorers in my sample typically were, because they were likely to be just as offended by instances of unfairness or injustice which did not directly affect them.

Social Data

A series of studies by Byrne and his coworkers (Byrne, 1969) established the principle that persons tend to like one another to the degree that their opinions match. In illustration of this point, Aronson (1980) provides the following example.

> *Example:* Sam goes to a cocktail party and is introduced to Marty. While they chat for a few moments, it turns out that they agree completely on several issues, including the inequity of the tax structure, the status of Douglas MacArthur in world history and the superiority of Beefeater gin. Upon returning home, Sam announces to his wife that he considers Marty a wonderful and intelligent person. (p. 255)

Given the principle just delineated, it follows that, since Q_1+ people tend to hold avant-garde opinions (i.e., opinions contrary to those held by the majority of the population), they are not broadly liked. This fact is also supported by other research evidence which shows, for example, that in small-group discussions (in which they are typically active and make their position known), they are generally rated negatively, even though their ideas are acknowledged as being creative (Cattell, 1973). The reactions they evoke, of course, can be considerably softened when they express themselves tactfully. Those in my sample who were tactful (as reflected in $N+$ scores), and especially those who were also $A+$ (warm), could be and often were extremely persuasive, sometimes even charismatic, trail blazers who inspired others.

Knowing the link between similarity and liking, I discovered that I could quite reliably predict people's scores on Factor Q_1 by their reactions to radicals. Usually those with Q_1- scores found radicals "far out," even dangerous; moderate scorers found them interesting or stimulating, but impractical; and Q_1+ scorers, since they were evaluating mirror images of themselves, found them progressive, "with it," or "wonderful and intelligent," in the words of Sam in the example above.

The Q_1+ examinees I observed in the workplace were often negatively regarded by their superiors. The same observation was made by Karson and O'Dell (1976), who proposed that this was to be expected, since these individuals are generally disruptive in any situation that requires them to submit to authority: "It should be apparent that a Q_1+ person is probably not going to make a very staunch subordinate in a work setting. One can assume that such a person may get into difficulty when he interacts with authority figures. Furthermore, you can be pretty sure that he is going to look for a scrap." (p. 67)

Because of their tendency to rock the proverbial boat, not only with their supervisors, but with their coworkers also, I noted that Q_1+ examinees were liable to be labeled as "troublemakers." They differed from a second group of trouble-making employees whose profiles showed $E+$ (dominant) and $L+$ (protensive) scores. These latter were troublemakers of a different kind; they were belligerent, fault finding, controlling, and suspiciously protective of their status in the organizational pecking order. In distinction, as I have noted already in passing, Q_1+ scorers are often quite unselfish and are frequently champions of the under-dog. It was rare, for example, to find a union steward who did *not* have $Q_1 +$ scores. Moreover, the established methods to which they drew critical attention often contained real problems that had been overlooked or ignored by their more complacent peers. Also, positively, many were innovative thinkers whose ability to break with traditional modes of thinking allowed them to find better ways to perform their work. Consequently, they are well represented in such occupations as artists, writers, professors, engineers, and employment counselors, all jobs offering opportunities for innovation.

Control and authority issues commonly surface as sources of interpersonal conflict, in marital as well as work-related relationships, but for different reasons. Harmonious marital relationships are contingent on partners' agreeing on such important matters as child-rearing practices, sex roles, money management, religious views, and so on. Therefore, since the opinions of $Q_1 +$ scorers diverge from those held by the majority of people, it is fortunate that they tend to marry each other. In instances when they marry lower scoring persons, discord is likely to erupt, especially since $Q_1 +$ people also find it unusually difficult to compromise. With time, however, because of the experiences marriage typically entails, it may happen that their own opinions become less radical and more conservative. This occurrence has been described for the past few decades as "selling out to the establishment."

Because they usually do not endorse traditional views about sex roles, $Q_1 +$ males are likely to be less dominating husbands, which may at least partially explain why they as a group are more stably married than their female counterparts, whom I and others have noted have high divorce rates. Observing this tendency towards unstable marriage in female $Q_1 +$ examinees has led me to hypothesize that it results from *(a)* their ability to initiate and adapt to change and new situations, which allows them to leave unsatisfactory marriages more promptly than conservative women; and *(b)* their eschewing of traditional women's roles, which thereby provides them with a wider range of lifestyle options with which to experiment as an alternative to marriage. Moreover, although I have not personally observed this, Karson and O'Dell (1976) suggest that they seem not to tolerate the foibles of their husbands lightly. These authors have noticed that $Q_1 +$ women, whose profiles also show $B +$ (above-average intelligence) and $H +$ (boldness) scores are likely to develop highly critical attitudes toward their husbands. Along these same lines, Karson and Haupt (1968) found that, even without intelligence and boldness, radical women are likely to become extremely discontented with men who are H− (shy and timid).

Important Correlations Between $Q_1 +$ Scores and Other 16PF Factor Scores

In all, there are three important correlations between $Q_1 +$ scores and other 16PF factor pole scores. Though only moderate, the possible associated traits that these correlations convey reveal the typical $Q_1 +$ individual as a fairly recognizable type.

Table 14.1

Important Correlations Between $Q_1 +$ Scores and Other 16PF Factor Scores

Factor Pole	Correlation	Possible Associated Traits Indicated by Correlation
M+ (Autia)	.33	Imaginative, Absent-minded
E+ (Dominance)	.29	Assertive, Aggressive, Competitive, Stubborn
G− (Lower Superego Strength)	.27	Disregards Rules, Expedient

In addition to their core $Q_1 +$ characteristics of being forward-looking, nontraditional, and open to change, the correlations set out in Table 14.1 suggest that some $Q_1 +$ scorers are more guided by their inner schemes of ideas and possibilities rather than by objective facts (M+); they do not espouse conventional moral values (G−) and, because they are also inclined to be assertive (E+), probably do not hold back on sharing their opinions.

It is noteworthy that H+ (parmia) scores do not enter into this pattern of associated traits. Considering that H+ qualities are associated with physical valor, this omission suggests that $Q_1 +$ scorers are not particularly inclined to take physical risks, and therefore are more likely to be *thinking* radicals who manufacture the ideational bullets for others to shoot, rather than being *physical* activists. This type is epitomized by George Bernard Shaw, the iconoclast whose plays satirized traditional English values. $Q_1 +$ scorers who were *physical* activists in my sample showed H scores of 6 or higher on their profiles.

Also noteworthy is that Q_1+ scores are not significantly associated with Factor C, the ego strength factor. One tends to think that good adjustment is best served by flexibility and sensitivity to discrimination cues. However, the Q_1+ tendency to routinely opt for changing situations, even though it would be wiser to conform, may not be a flexible, sensitive stance. Q_1- people who rigidly conform in situations that could be changed for the better are also inflexible. However, there is no correlation between Factor Q_1 and Factor C. Hence, I can only assume that each extreme group must have ways to compensate for their rigid responses.

Clinical Relevance of Q_1+ Scores

From the foregoing, it is obvious that Q_1+ persons are likely to be perennially in conflict with established authority. Furthermore, they often get themselves into trouble, since the balance of power is inevitably at times held by their opponents who also have the means to forcefully retaliate. For example, many of my Q_1+ examinees had been dismissed from their jobs for insubordination. Incidentally, it is often after this or similar occurrences that they seek treatment from mental health professionals.

Insight therapy, which is most successfully conducted by having clients see connections between present difficulties and unresolved childhood conflicts, proceeds with difficulty with Q_1+ clients, since they are typically adamantly convinced that their grievances are entirely justified. Those who are not able to reason abstractly (which may be discernible from their $B-$ scores) have, of course, the most extreme difficulty, and are likely to continue to find themselves involved in altercations with authority throughout their lives.

Q_1+ examinees who are also $C-$ (low ego strength) and $F+$ (surgent) may be extremely flighty and impulsive people who act on poorly thought-out ideas. This creates havoc, not only for themselves, but in the lives of others. This trait combination is well illustrated in Ann Tyler's fictional portrait of Alicia Leary, a giddy young widow and mother of four children.

> Sometimes Alicia's enthusiasm turned to her children —an unsettling experience. She took them all to the circus and bought them cotton candy that none of them enjoyed. (They liked to keep themselves tidy.) She

yanked them out of school and enrolled them briefly in an experimental learning community where no one wore clothes. The four of them, chilled and miserable, sat huddled in a row in the common room with their hands pressed flat between their bare knees.

Then she turned to something else, and something else, and something else. She believed in change as if it were a religion. Feeling sad? Find a new man. Creditors after you, rent due, children running fevers? Move to a new apartment! During one year, they moved so often Macon had to stand deliberating a while before setting out for home. (p. 64)[1]

LOW SCORES ON FACTOR Q_1

Q_1 − and Childhood

The developmental research reported by Cattell (1972) reveals a connection between Q_1 − scores and the following trends: *(a)* birth order, i.e., being the oldest or only child in the family, *(b)* having strong family ties that persist throughout childhood and beyond, and *(c)* continuing to live at home after achieving adulthood. While these research findings suggest that Q_1 − scorers have been strongly socialized into their families, my clinical case histories often cast doubt on the healthiness of this socialization. Specifically, I have found that the family bonds of roughly 50% of my Q_1 − examinees were based on dependency rather than affection. Many lacked the initiative or trust to extend themselves beyond their immediate kin, even though those relationships were not particularly satisfying. To a lesser extent, others were bound to their families by some shameful childhood secret, such as having been incest victims or having grown up with alcoholic parents. Finally, the conservative temperaments of a lesser number of examinees in my sample appeared to be in some part a reaction to lack of early stability and overexposure to progressive ideas. But because these data are based largely on my clinical sample, I do not know how far they can be generalized to the general population.

---

[1]Tyler, A. *The Accidental Tourist*. New York: Berkley Books, 1986.

Intrapsychic Data

Earlier I proposed that the ease with which people change is chiefly facilitated by their anticipation of a higher ratio of future satisfaction to what they are presently experiencing. This proposition, however, falls short in explaining the resistance to change experienced by Q_1- examinees in my sample, who had extreme scores on Factor Q_1 (stens of 1, 2, or 3). These examinees were not the kind of conservatives referred to by the 19th-century writer Joseph Addison when he wrote, "When men are easy in their circumstances they are naturally enemies of innovation."[2] Actually, this quote describes people who usually turn out to have moderate Q_1- scores (stens of 4 or 5) and not the extreme scores that I am now discussing.

Instead, it was fairly usual for my Q_1- examinees to be resigned to difficult conditions. Cattell (1973) observed this when he noted the presence of Q_1- scores in the profiles of persons who tolerated routine, frustrating jobs. Whenever I encounter persons stuck in unrewarding life situations from which they could, but do not, attempt to extricate themselves, the probability is high that their 16PF profiles will show Q_1- scores.

I have explored with Q_1- examinees their own insights into why they seem to find it harder than most others, not only to initiate change, but to keep pace with life's normal transitions. As far as I have so far been able to discern, their difficulty focuses mostly on the interval between letting go of present attachments and embracing new ones (decathexis and recathexis described earlier in this chapter). At this point there is a crisis, either small or large, in which uncertainty, unfamiliarity, confusion, ambiguity, or even a temporary loss of identity occurs. The self-reports of Q_1- examinees suggest that they found these experiences particularly difficult to tolerate. I cannot explain this response, however, because their ability to put up with difficult situations shows that they are able to bear many other kinds of feelings that are disturbing and unpleasant.

The *Administrator's Manual for the 16PF* (1986) provides a succinct description of some other aspects of the Q_1- individual's personality. Since most of the examinees in my sample readily agreed that this description portrayed themselves fairly accurately, it is presented below in its entirety:

---

[2]Evans, B. (1968). *Dictionary of Quotations Collected and Arranged.* New York: Delacorte Press, p. 94.

Low scorers on Factor Q_1 are confident in what they have been taught to believe, and accept the "tried and true," even when something else might be better. They are cautious and compromising in regard to new ideas. Thus, they tend to oppose and postpone change, are inclined to go along with tradition, are more conservative in religion and politics, and tend not to be interested in analytical "intellectual" thought. (p. 30)

Given what I noted earlier about the difficulty my Q_1 − examinees showed in tolerating the uncertainty that bridges cathexis and decathexis, it was not surprising that in mental status examinations they were apt to agree with some variant of the Latin proverb: "Keep what you have; the known evil is best."[3] Those who did not agree, and who, moreover, on a more personal level acknowledged that the probability was high that their lives could be changed for the better, were more than averagely hesitant to take necessary steps towards bringing about this improvement. It was because many of these examinees were not lacking in self-confidence that I was led to conclude that passivity played a role in Q_1 − (conservative) behavior.

Social Data

Unlike Q_1 + people, who were often vivacious and colorful, the tendency for most of the 167 Q_1 − examinees in my sample was to wear their conservatism like a suit of quiet clothes. Because they lacked imaginative flair, it was not unusual for them to be generally seen as insipid or uninteresting.

In their demeanor, my Q_1 − examinees resembled H − scorers. But, unlike these H − scorers, whose shyness leads them to purposefully avoid being noticed, Q_1 − inconspicuousness was unintentional. Rather, it resulted from lack of originality and failure to keep pace with ordinary innovations.

Sometimes, however, these tendencies had the opposite effect, making them stand out as "old fashioned."

Example: "Who was the first to?" "Remember when?" and "Whatever happened to?" are predictable conversational themes at class reunions. One client reported

---

[3]This sentiment seems to have universal expression. It is expressed by the Irish by the saying, "The devil you have is better than the devil you may get," and by the English as "Don't jump out of the frying pan into the fire."

that at a reunion, after these themes had been exhausted, the discussion turned to speculating about "Who was the last to . . . leave home, start his own business, grow his hair longer, modernize his lifestyle, reduce his cholesterol intake, buy a smaller car . . . ." He was somewhat chagrined to be elected the winner of the "last to" category. This client's Factor Q_1 score was 2.

Though most $Q_1 -$ scorers in my sample preferred to associate with other conservatives, I was intrigued to find many instances of their being strongly attracted to persons very different from themselves. Since this phenomenon has been presented so often in drama and novels, e.g., the quiet businessman and the wild femme fatale, it is fairly widespread and popularly recognized. Commonly in my sample, this attraction took the form of extramarital affairs, about which the $Q_1 -$ individual felt extreme conflicts because his behavior was inconsistent with traditional mores. He or she was very much in conflict in regard to the other person, frequently alternating between fascination for and disapproval of the very traits they were attracted to.

Although often disparaged for their lack of progressiveness and originality, my $Q_1 -$ examinees were also appreciated for their staunchness. Rarely fickle in their relationships, they maintained long-lasting friendships and acquaintances. Once having formed an emotional tie or befriended someone, they were likely to keep in touch with that person for years. In reviewing my records, I discovered that the clients I treated in the far distant past who continue to send annual Christmas cards usually turn out to be $Q_1 -$.

$Q_1 -$ persons are usually loyal employees, provided their conservatism is not complicated by some other trait (like, for example, poor moral development). They can be relied upon to give long and faithful service—a fact that is usually noted in employee ratings, offsetting less laudable comments such as their difficulties in adjusting to change or coping with unexpected demands. In consulting with organizations and agencies, I recommend hiring $Q_1 -$ applicants for jobs requiring steady adherence to the status quo and respect for established methods and ways of doing things. $Q_1 -$ scores appear in the group profiles of occupational groups that rely on following clearly defined policies and procedures such as police, priests, and military cadets (Cattell, 1973).

They also appear in the profiles of athletes, farmers, mechanics, musicians, cooks, and domestics. The relationship between the latter group of occupations and conservatism is less clear to me.

Finally, except for those who develop unexpected attractions to their opposites, $Q_1 -$ persons can usually be counted on to be stable, faithful partners in love and marriage. They have traditional values and are firmly attached to home and children. However, like strongly conventionally moral $(G+)$ persons, it is difficult for them to accept the changes that normally occur when their offspring reach adolescence and become drawn into the more liberal ways of their peers. Their difficulty in adapting to the changes required by this period of their lives often causes them to become depressed or anxious, leading to the adjustment disorders I will describe shortly.

Important Correlations Between $Q_1 -$ Scores and Other 16PF Factor Scores

Table 14.2

Important Correlations Between $Q_1 -$ Scores and Other 16PF Factor Scores

Factor Pole	Correlation	Possible Associated Traits Indicated by Correlation
M – (Praxernia)	.33	Practical, "Down-to-Earth" Concerns
E – (Submissiveness)	.29	Humble, Easily Led, Docile
G + (Higher Superego Strength)	.27	Conscientious, Persistent, Moralistic, Staid

Table 14.2 portrays $Q_1 -$ scorers as a type no less recognizable than their $Q_1 +$ counterparts. All of the correlated traits indicate personality trends that strongly reinforce conservatism. The correlation with M – (praxernia) scores, which is just marginally higher than the others, suggests a "here-and-now" practical orientation, a tendency to be interested in facts as they presently exist, rather than the possibilities and potentials to which they point. The correlation with E – scores indicates compliance and submissiveness. Finally, the correlation with stronger superego scores $(G+)$ indicates alignment with conventional moral values.

Clinical Relevance of Q_1 – Scores

A Q_1 – score can provide clinicians with important information because its appearance in a profile signals that the client is likely to find it difficult to change. It warns that treatment will progress slowly, but that this is not necessarily due to the client's being resistive to therapy or counseling. Rather, it seems to result from his or her characteristic style.

Q_1 – individuals are likely to seek psychological treatment when they foresee some future alteration in their lives, rather than waiting until it has already occurred. Just the anticipation of change may fill them with dread. Even when they recognize that they are likely to benefit from these changes, they may still feel uncomfortable about making the necessary readjustments that are entailed. Along these lines, I have noted the frequency of Q_1 – scores in the 16PF profiles of women who stay with abusive husbands. These scores tell me that these women are not finding some perverse gratification in their suffering, as some perplexed onlookers might suppose, but have unusual difficulty in making transitions.

Cattell (1973) reported finding Q_1 – scores in the profiles of persons with conversion hysteria, psychosomatic disorders, and obsessive-compulsive disorders. These associations make excellent sense when one reflects upon the avoidance motive behind the symptomology manifested in these disorders.

> *Example:* A Q_1 – female client left my office after resolving to sever her relationship with a man who, after a six-year relationship, was not willing to commit to marrying her. She telephoned the man to tell him her decision but found she could not speak. Her family, thinking she had had a stroke, rushed her to a nearby hospital, where it was discovered there was no physical basis for her aphasia.

In my experience, I find Q_1 – scores more frequently associated with adjustment disorders than any other diagnosis. This diagnosis is defined in DSM-III as an excessive and maladaptive reaction to an identifiable and recent psychosocial stressor, such as loss of a job or divorce or involvement in litigation—all experiences that essentially center around the need to behave in new and different ways.

Adjustment disorders in middle-aged Q_1- clients in my sample were often in response to ordinary and inevitable life transitions. When environmental situations change, behaviors and coping strategies which may have been adaptive earlier are usually no longer adaptive and need to be revised. Treatment for these individuals usually focused on circumventing them from "living in the past," which they were apt to do, either by seeking gratification from old memories rather than present experience, or by continuing to act in ways appropriate for earlier times but that do not fit their contemporary circumstances. Q_1- women whose offspring have reached adulthood are at special risk in this regard, as illustrated by the example below.

> *Example:* A 49-year-old widow came to me for psychotherapy. She reported that her husband had died two years ago. But, since her husband had been a practicing alcoholic, the marriage had not been happy. Her sorrow at his death had been tempered by relief that she was at least free from the abrasive and stormy relationship.
>
> She had recently moved away from the town in which she had lived during her marriage, and into my community. Having a good income from her husband's estate, and being personable and attractive, she had set up what should have been a pleasant lifestyle for herself. However, she felt unhappy. In exploring the reasons for her unhappiness, I discovered they centered on her strong wish to live closer to her adult children, who were still living in the same town she had just left. Since contact with her children seemed so important to her, I was nonplussed as to why she had uprooted herself. She explained she had done this because she was afraid of becoming "too dependent on them."
>
> This incident occurred several years ago, before I was aware of the validity of her insight, given her extremely low Q_1- score. Consequently, because her explanation did not make sense, I looked for some deeper, more complex, motive. Needless to say, therapy was not successful in alleviating her unhappiness and was prematurely terminated.
>
> I next saw this client two years later. She was still depressed. She reported on what had occurred in the interim since I last saw her. After terminating her first

therapy with me, she had returned to the town where her adult children lived. Shortly after having arrived there, she found herself doing exactly what she most feared she would do. She became overly involved in the lives of her children, attempting to recreate, not only the ties that had existed with her in their childhoods, but also their ties with each other. Among other things, she revived family traditions, and insisted that they spend all holidays together. In view of the children's respective spouses' having parents of their own, this caused antagonism and dissent.

Her children, annoyed at what they quite correctly perceived as her failure to recognize that their adult relationships to each other and to her were now different to what they had been in childhood, pointed out that since she could expect to live another two or three decades she might better organize her life to enjoy the years ahead instead of holding on to a dead past. Following this confrontation, she returned to my community and again entered therapy with the intention of taking her children's advice and working toward accepting change and orientating herself toward the future instead of the past. By this time, I had a better understanding of the meaning of $Q_1 -$ scores and could better appreciate her struggle to orient herself towards the future.

As I have stated before in this chapter, there is no correlation between Factor Q_1 and Factor C (ego strength). This fact challenged my earlier expectation that, since ego strength involves flexible adjustment to a changing environment, $Q_1 -$ scores would be associated with ego weakness and, hence, mental health problems. I must assume, therefore, that $Q_1 -$ people compensate for their being slow to change by using such strategies as aligning themselves with slowly changing social groups. Though $Q_1 -$ scores do not reveal an ideal response style, whether or not they reflect maladaptation rests on evaluation of the individual case. More specifically, consideration should be given to how a given examinee's conservativism combines with other traits in furthering life goals and meeting needs.

Chapter 15

Factor Q_2: Self-Sufficiency (Reliance on Self) vs. Group Dependency (Reliance on Others)

THE CONSTRUCT
Dependency as a Proximity-Seeking Response
Heredity
Self-Sufficiency
Male and Female Differences Throughout the Life Span

LOW SCORES ON FACTOR Q_2
Intrapsychic Data
Social Data
Q_2- and Childhood
Important Correlations Between Q_2- Scores
and Other 16PF Factor Scores
Clinical Relevance of Q_2- Scores

HIGH SCORES ON FACTOR Q_2
Intrapsychic Data
Social Data
Q_2+ and Childhood
Important Correlations Between Q_2+ Scores
and Other 16PF Factor Scores
Clinical Relevance of Q_2+ Scores

FACTOR Q_2: CHARACTERISTICS OF Q_2+ (SELF-SUFFICIENT) AND Q_2- (GROUP-DEPENDENT) EXAMINEES

Left Score Q_2- (GROUP DEPENDENCY)		Right Score Q_2+ (SELF-SUFFICIENCY)
(Sociably Group Dependent, a Joiner and Sound Follower)	vs.	(Self-Sufficient, Resourceful, Prefers Own Decisions)

THE CONSTRUCT

Dependency as a Proximity-Seeking Response

In this chapter I will reverse my custom and present the lower pole of this factor first. That way, we can better follow the natural progression from dependency towards self-sufficiency that occurs over the human life span. I will also, in this chapter, depart from the custom of calling its left pole "group dependency," substituting simply "dependency," because the behavior it denotes can be directed towards a single person as well as a group. Actually, though, the inclusion of Q_2+ scores in the second-order extraversion pattern shows that the latter is more frequent.

Dependency is an ambiguous term that has multiple meanings. It can imply a state of being, like being chemically dependent. Or, it can mean an interrelationship between people, wherein meeting needs requires mutual cooperation. Or, it can be an orientation that sees the source of emotional succorance and/or standards of reference as arising more from outside than from within oneself. As I refer to it here, I mean dependency of the last-mentioned kind which, according to Macoby and Masters (1970) in their extensive survey of the professional literature, is manifested this way: getting attention, seeking praise and approval, resisting separation, and asking for help. All of these behaviors express the wish to maintain contact or proximity with others.

I speculate that the proximity-seeking behaviors just described may have originated as a survival response, i.e., the so-called herding instinct, in primates and other mammals, when they were threatened. As with these other animals, it can still be readily observed in our species in its more flagrant form, as humans also tend to seek out the company of their fellows ("safety in numbers," as the expression goes) when experiencing threat. Anxiety or fear seem to be the internal states which evoke this behavior. In modern dress, Schacter's (1959) hallmark study of college women supports the existence of this relationship between proximity seeking and fear reduction. The women chose to be in the company of others, rather than to remain alone, while waiting to be subjected to what they anticipated would be painful experimental procedures, even though choosing (or seeking) company gave no tangible benefits.

Its primal origin comes not only from the evolutionary experience of our species, but from individual experience. As Gaylin (1976) notes, seeking contact with others is the earliest form of adaptation; clutch and cling, not fight and flight, are our first methods of survival. Each helpless newborn is programmed towards deriving comfort from the physical presence of its caretaker, on whom its survival relies during the time it develops necessary strengths and skills to fend for itself.

Self-Sufficiency

From the foregoing, it might logically be inferred that I am proposing that it is ideal for people to supply all their own emotional succorance and standards of reference. This is not my intention. It is true that as people gain in competency and confidence, in coping with their environments, they should gradually become less emotionally needful of the reassuring presence of others and external guidelines. However, it is important for them not to exceed reasonable limits. Thus, just as an extreme Q_2- (dependency) score may indicate a developmental failure, a Q_2+ (self-sufficiency) score of 8, 9, or 10 is not usually desirable either. As I shall discuss later, some of my high-scoring examinees had clearly travelled too far on the journey from reliance on others to reliance on themselves; their profiles showed Q_2+ scores entering into pathogenic combinations.

Heredity

The genetic component of Factor Q_2 is moderate (.37). Thus, most of what goes into determining an individual's movement along the dependency/self-sufficiency continuum is rooted in early childhood experiences. This is shown by the fact that Factor Q_2 scores in the general population change little once adulthood is reached, except in women, whose scores tend to show some increase towards the self-sufficiency pole with age. Only with therapy or some major life event are they likely to change.

Male and Female Differences Throughout the Life Span

The group mean scores are strikingly similar for both sexes (men, 18.20 and women, 18.44) as well as the standard deviations, which are 5.78 and 6.02, respectively. As noted above, women's scores do tend to increase a bit with age.

These similarities went contrary to my initial expectations, which were based on the notion that females are in all respects more dependent than males, being encouraged from childhood to act less autonomously. On reflection, however, I noted the many socially sanctioned opportunities for male proximity-seeking behavior, like fraternities, service clubs, the pool hall, and the local tavern. These opportunities have been institutionalized into the culture, and suggest that men are as reliant on these forms of social contact as women.

LOW SCORES ON FACTOR Q$_2$

Intrapsychic Data

In their test item responses, persons who score at the Q_2- (dependency) pole report that they prefer to be in the company of others rather than be alone, and that they decide on the correctness of their performance by comparing themselves to others rather than relying on their own judgment.

The self-reports that my Q_2- examinees provided in interviews followed similar lines. Their most common comments were expressed in variations of the following two statements:

"I don't like being alone."

"I feel uncomfortable when I notice that I am in some way different from others in my reference group."

These statements turned out to be closely interconnected, which became clear when they proceeded to elaborate on just what they felt when they were alone. Theirs, I discovered, was more than ordinary loneliness. These examinees felt a rudderlessness, an absence of orienting stimuli, and above all, a vague and pervasive fear. Since these were the same feelings that they reported having whenever they viewed themselves as dissimilar (hence, separate) from others, I speculate that they were describing what psychoanalysts call separation anxiety—a primal sense of vulnerability and defenselessness originally experienced in the infant when separated from its mother. Unlike most people, for whom this form of anxiety tends to only *briefly* and mildly resurge when they are removed from their significant others or familiar environments, these examinees seemed to experience it as an ever-present threat, a threat that was so ingrained in their personalities that it structured their social orientation and made them go to great lengths to avoid separations.

Social Data

The relationships of my Q_2- examinees was characterized by their overriding need to belong. Typically, they joined formal clubs or organizations, deriving satisfaction from group identification and placing much emphasis on group process. The types of clubs they preferred were usually predictable from their scores on other factors. For example, those whose profiles showed $G+$ scores, and so were strongly influenced by conventional moral values, tended to join churches. Those whose profiles showed Q_1+ (radicalness), and so were often iconoclastic and rebellious, were often staunch members of protest groups.

Their strong desire for group belonging made them susceptible to exploitation. Approximately 15% of them report that, at some time or another, they had joined cults because they were attracted to the adhesiveness of these organizations and to the opportunity they provided for strong, on-going social contact. My experience suggests that many of the persons who perished at the infamous Jonestown debacle would certainly have shown Q_2- scores if they had been tested.

Q_2- examinees were also, of course, often deeply enmeshed in more naturally formed groups, especially their families. Those of adult age who lived with their parents, and whose parents complained about their not leaving home, often turned out to be Q_2-. Their strong advocacy of togetherness led them to be overly demanding of the time and companionship of other family members, and to ignore the differences that inevitably occur among people, even in the same family, as a consequence of each human being's uniqueness. Desiring, as they did, a strong sense of solidarity in all their relationships, they were apt to feel threatened by these differences. But fearing that open confrontation and exploration would create separation, they denied that these differences existed. According to Virginia Satir (1967), and many other family therapists, this form of threat, followed by denial of the existence of the cause of the threat, results in the confusing reality distortions that contribute to severely dysfunctional family systems.

> *Example:* A family was referred to me by the children's school because two of the children were having behavioral problems. The father, although obviously not a dominant man, referred to all members of the family as a monolithic "we." Later, it became evident that he had difficulty acknowledging the differences in temperaments, reactions, beliefs, and views that existed within the family. On subsequent testing, his Factor Q$_2$ score was found to be only 2.

Q$_2$ and Childhood

It was my interviews with Q$_2$ − examinees that led me to clearly see a connection between their present behavior and a lack of childhood initiative. However, how that early behavior became translated into the proximity seeking of later adulthood is still unclear. Most salient was the frequency with which they recalled, not only their resistance to doing routine tasks unassisted, but also their failure to attempt to overcome obstacles. They were reporting resisting the classical indicators of growing self-reliance, eagerly pursued by most children as they increase in physical and mental maturity.

There are two major schools of psychological thought explaining why children fail to develop self-reliance. Behavior modification theorists argue that it results from a parental failure to reward efforts toward taking initiative and being independent. By contrast, Piaget, Freud, and structurally oriented theorists propose that this failure involves not having adequately internalized the original caretaking figures that provided support, encouragement, and instruction.

When inappropriate degrees of dependent behavior persist into adulthood, theorists of both persuasions agree, however, that there has been unsuccessful resolution during critical periods when old dependency habits meet with new urges to show initiative and experiment with autonomy. Consensus is that, generally, the most important variables involved in this outcome are parental attitudes: children will tend to remain dependent if their parents or parent figures have either *(a)* overindulged them, or, conversely, *(b)* frustrated them in their normal dependency needs by not providing sufficient care (Beller, 1955; Johnson & Medinnus, 1965).

These data coincide with what I have heard in interviews with Q_2- examinees. In the first instance, they reported that their parents were either overly protective, or had failed to reward their strivings for competence and achievement. Many reported having had parents who greeted each sign of their increasing maturity with open dismay.

> *Example:* A 27-year-old Q_2- client, who had been the youngest child in her family, and who had entered treatment because she felt she could not set appropriate goals for herself, recalled that when, as a four-year-old, she had proudly shown her mother that she could tie her shoelaces, her mother burst into tears. Interpreting her mother's reaction as disapproval, she thereupon decided to inhibit further initiative.

In the second instance, parents frustrate dependency by demanding too much, as well as by not responding to the child with adequate nurturance, warmth, or affection. Sometimes, parents actually punish the child for seeking physical contact or asking for age-appropriate help or reassurance. Children, in these instances, feel overwhelmed by the demands placed on them, and they then lose confidence. As adults, they may also want to make up for what they lacked in childhood.

My own direct observations of Q_2- youngsters revealed that they not only lacked initiative, but that they were already showing an excessive need to belong. Those whose dependency needs were being frustrated at home became overly attached to peer groups. I often discovered that those adolescents whose HSPQ profiles showed $E-$ (submissiveness) scores in addition to Q_2- scores were sometimes part of delinquent gangs where they are sound followers but never leaders or originators.

Important Correlations Between Q_2- Scores and Other 16PF Factor Scores

Table 15.1 implies that Q_2- people tend to be extraverts, since it shows correlations between Q_2- and $A+$ (affectothymia), $F+$ (surgency), and $H+$ (parmia). These factor poles join Q_2- in forming the second-order extraversion pattern, to be discussed in Chapter 18. This pattern depicts the typical extravert as someone who, in addition to being dependent, is also warmly sociable, exuberant, and adventurous.

Table 15.1

**Important Correlations Between Q_2- Scores
and Other 16PF Factor Scores**

Factor Pole	Correlation	Possible Associated Traits Indicated by Correlation
A + (Affectothymia)	.37	Outgoing, Warmhearted, Easygoing, Participating
F + (Surgency)	.36	Happy-go-lucky, Enthusiastic
H + (Parmia)	.32	Venturesome, Uninhibited, Socially Bold

Clinical Relevance of Q_2- Scores

The lives of Q_2- persons suffer from self-imposed restrictions, such as overconformity to group norms, unwillingness to take initiative, and avoidance of open disagreement or any self-assertive behaviors that threaten their social standing. These restrictions could be expected to result in the kinds of inner frustrations that eventually cause people to seek psychological treatment in the hope of discovering why they feel compelled to pay such a high price for the security of their relationships. However, in the clinical component of my sample, only seven Q_2- scorers entered treatment for this reason. The remaining 91 did so when their sense of belonging was threatened or had already been disrupted. They were seeking relief from often-crippling anxiety.

Once in treatment, the possibility is strong that the dependency of Q_2- clients will be transferred to the clinician and be expressed by emergency telephone calls, requests for extra appointments, and resistance to termination. The classical kinds of transference that ensue, in my opinion, give some credence to the theory that adult dependency is a residue of the unresolved problems in early relationships with parental figures that I alluded to earlier.

I have so far noticed three clinically revealing combinations of Q_2- and other 16PF factor scores, which I will now discuss.

1) Q_2- *(Dependency) and* $E+$ *(Dominance).* Examinees whose 16PF profiles show this combination rely on others for emotional support, while at the same time seeking to dominate them. In my experience, this is actually an uncommon combination. The Q_2- examinees in my sample avoided acting dominantly, for this behavior entails the risk of offending others and so might lead to their being rejected or excluded. Balancing these opposing tendencies takes great tact and social astuteness. When successful, it allows some people to become popular leaders, adept at moving groups to their own ends. Others who had not achieved this integration were apt to make conflicting demands on others, vacillating between dependency and controlling behaviors.

2) Q_2- *(Dependency) and* $L+$ *(Protension).* Examinees who were both dependent and protensive, as in this combination, displayed intrapsychic conflict of an approach-avoidance kind. Their suspiciousness, hypervigilance, and insecurity were at war with their yearning for dependency, since the interpersonal closeness inherent in dependent relationships exacerbated their original insecurity.

It was typical for these examinees to enter into close relationships only with a very few people. Commonly, they were part of a dyad that was one of a "can't live with or without" genre. Although in therapy they could, and usually did, quote ad infinitum a litany of injustices, which they devoutly believed had been inflicted on them by their partners, they rarely, in my experience, took the initiative to sever ties, believing either implicitly or explicitly that any relationship was better than none.

3) Q_2- *(Dependency),* $A-$ *(Sizothymia),* $F-$ *(Desurgency), and* $H-$ *(Threctia).* Q_2- scores embedded in an otherwise introverted $(A-, F-, H-)$ profile should be taken as an indication of deep insecurity, since these examinees are reporting that they are $A-$ (coolly detached from others), $F-$ (cautious and taciturn), and $H-$ (timid). In a nutshell, they are stating a preference for more social withdrawal than their dependency (as indicated by their Q_2- scores) would allow. As with anything that goes against natural predilection, continued social contact is extremely stressful for them.

Often, examinees in my sample who showed this combination were a great puzzlement to their companions, because their obvious desire for their friends' presence contrasted so strongly with their taciturnness and cool, retiring behavior when they were with friends. Spouses, in particular, found it difficult to evaluate the degree of emotional attachment between them. The truth is that these examinees' attachments were commonly superficial because they were based on dependency and not enjoyment. In other words, relationships were not ends in themselves, but served to avoid aversive feelings that occurred when they were alone.

> *Example:* A man who showed this combination of scores was involved with a woman he had met shortly after he had divorced his wife. This woman desperately wanted to end the relationship, but was afraid to do so because of the impact she feared it would have on him. She found his companionship unstimulating, as she was unable, despite the large amount of time they spent together, to share warm feelings, have fun, or have meaningful conversations with him. She reasoned, however, that this must be due to some difficulty on her part. And because he insisted that they spend all of their available time together, to the point of taking her to and from work, she saw him as being excessively in love with her.
>
> One day, she was summoned to another state because of a family emergency that required her presence for two months. For the first three weeks he called her every day. Then his calls tapered off. When she tried to call him, he was difficult to reach because he was rarely home. Finally, he wrote her to say he had returned to live with his ex-wife because he couldn't stand being alone.

HIGH SCORES ON FACTOR Q_2

Intrapsychic Data

Cattell (1973) describes persons who achieve Q_2+ scores as being self-sufficient, resourceful, and preferring to make their own decisions. Earlier (1957), he noted that these individuals prefer to study independently, to travel alone, to withdraw when stressed, and to be able to hold fast to unpopular positions. Though they are loners, he claimed that they do not avoid society because they are emotionally rejecting but because they possess "a maturity of reasoning, perhaps emotion, beginning early in childhood." (p. 211) He goes on to speculate that this characteristic may be attributed to a form of introverted thinking, i.e., thinking that is more mediated by internal structures than by reactivity to external demands, as well as by a touch of stubbornness.

Basic to the subjective experience of virtually all of the 169 Q_2+ examinees in my sample was the fact that, although they were apt to spend much time alone, they were rarely lonely. As one woman whose Q_2+ score was 10 remarked, "I enjoy my own company." This statement postulates a harmonious internal dichotomy, consisting of a part that provides and a part that receives.

Also basic to the subjective experience of my examinees was the value they placed on their privacy and freedom to choose what they will. Further, they were just as likely to respect the rights of others to do the same. Like the man in Robert Frost's poem (p. 33),[1] "Mending Wall," they believed that "good fences made good neighbors." In this respect, they differed markedly from $E+$ (dominant) examinees—with whom they were often superficially confused—as the latter are apt to encroach on the rights of others, and are counterdependent rather than independent.

Social Data

Paradoxically, in many ways Q_2+ people are the "rugged individualists," long admired in American culture, even though many in my sample were not well liked. Sometimes, and similar to $H-$ (threctic) persons, these examinees were incorrectly perceived as being shy. More often, however, since they rarely asked for help, advice, and support, they were seen as snobbish or "above it all" elitists.

In the workplace and in groups (which they usually joined for instrumental rather than affiliative purposes), they were apt to narrowly focus on the problem at hand, ignoring the interpersonal aspects of the process. It was easy, therefore, to see why others did not experience them as rewarding to be with, which, incidentally, is probably the main reason Cattell (1973) noted that Q_2+ people received fewer job promotions than their Q_2- counterparts.

Because Q_2+ individuals are not needful of reassurance, it does not mean that they are cold. Marriages in which both

---

[1]Frost, R. (1969). *The Poetry of Robert Frost.* New York: Holt Rinehart & Winston.

partners have high scores tend to be stable (Cattell & Nessel-roade, 1967). However, I found that when there was a wide difference between the spouses' Factor Q_2 scores, the low scorer tended to feel unimportant and rebuffed, especially if his or her sense of personal worth was somehow involved in meeting the needs of others. These individuals often complained that their Q_2+ spouse "can get on well without me" or "doesn't really need me."

I have noticed that Q_2+ men, but not particularly women, in my sample, placed an unusually strong emphasis on sex. I conjecture that these men find in the sexual act one of the few avenues through which they can satisfy their needs for intimacy, in a way that is congruent with their masculine ideals of self-reliance.

Q_2+ and Childhood

According to the retrospective accounts accumulated by Barton, Dielman, and Cattell (1973), Q_2+ adults typically had strong early dependency on their mothers and felt secure in their early home environments. These accounts also indicated that their parents were satisfactorily married, that they got along well with their siblings, and that they were rarely "only" children. Given the last-mentioned finding and the functional nature of their early family life, it can be assumed that they were not overly protected and that they did not have parents who discouraged healthy initiative.

Cattell and Cattell (1975) report direct observations on Q_2+ youngsters that indicate that they are mature for their age and often have older friends. At school, because they are confident about their own decisions, they do well in subjects requiring independent study, and they tend to obtain a higher level of all-around general achievement.

My own observations of Q_2+ children and adolescents have been of their social interactions. These young people are often seen as "different," occasionally labeled "weirdos" by their peers, because they do not need to conform and do the "in thing."

Important Correlations Between Q_2+ Scores and Other 16PF Factor Scores

According to Table 15.2, there is a tendency for Q_2+ scorers to show the full complement of introverted traits. This means that, in addition to being self-sufficient, a person with a high score on Factor Q_2 is somewhat likely to be A− (reserved and detached), F− (sober, taciturn, and serious), and H− (shy, timid, and threat-sensitive).

Table 15.2

Important Correlations Between Q_2+ Scores and Other 16PF Factor Scores

Factor Pole	Correlation	Possible Associated Traits Indicated by Correlation
A− (Sizothymia)	.37	Reserved, Detached, Critical, Aloof, Stiff
F− (Desurgency)	.36	Sober, Taciturn, Serious
H− (Threctia)	.32	Shy, Timid, Threat-sensitive

Clinical Relevance of Q_2+ Scores

Q_2+ scores may indicate that the examinee has been forced to become self-sufficient, either by a lack of social support or by an inability to form satisfactory human attachments. Thus, although Cattell throughout his writing has proposed that the self-sufficiency trait is *always* indicative of strength of character, my investigation of its shadow side leads me to question this proposition. The poet has said, "No man is an island," and it is contrary to the laws of nature to be so extremely emotionally self-sustaining. The price exacted by the tendency of Q_2+ people to reject help and resist self-disclosure can be seen in their high incidence of coronary heart disease, hypertension, and peptic ulcers (Sherman & Krug, 1977). In view of these findings, incidentally, it is imperative to urge anyone who has a high Factor Q_2 score to have a least one confidant.

The negative implication of a particular Q_2+ score on a profile is discernible from its combination with other 16PF factor scores. So far, I have found the following four combinations to be consistent indicators of adjustment problems.

1) *Q_2+ (Self-Sufficiency) and B− (Low Intelligence).* Below-average intelligence, as indicated by a low Factor B score, accompanied by a Q_2+ score, is seen in persons who do not seem to

learn from experience. My examinees who showed this combination were unwilling to accept guidance, and relied instead on their limited abilities. Consequently, they developed "closed minds," or cognitive systems that were incapable of generating new and better alternatives for solving their problems, dooming them to repeat the same mistakes. When this combination was further compounded by the presence of $E+$ (dominance) scores and/or $L+$ (protension) scores, indicating that the examinee was also dominant and suspicious, the system became excessively and even more dangerously closed. I have sometimes heard clinicians interpret the behavior of these individuals as self-destructive, which is patently erroneous, for their perseverance of ineffective behavior is due to an unfortunate interpersonal style and not to perverse underlying motives.

Clients demonstrating this pattern pose a strong challenge to the therapist in establishing a therapeutic alliance. Once an alliance has been achieved, the patient can best benefit by directive therapy.

2) Q_2+ *(Self-Sufficiency) and A − (Sizothymia)*. While these scores tend to go together, as they are part of the introversion pattern; when the $A-$ scores are extreme (1, 2, or 3), they indicate definite social withdrawal. As Karson and O'Dell (1976) note, the origin of the social withdrawal seems to be that the examinee was unable to form deep human attachments (as in a schizoid personality disorder) in childhood, or, less commonly, that he or she turned away from people later in life out of bitter disappointment. Persons who fall into this last category often announce that they have "given up" or are "turned off" towards people.

3) Q_2+ *(Self-Sufficiency) and L + (Protension)*. This combination conveys distrust and rejection of advice, guidance, and help from others, due to insecurities' being projected outward. Its appearance in a profile signifies that it will take much patience on the part of the clinician to win the examinee's trust.

4) Q_2+ *(Self-Sufficiency) and O + (Guilt Proneness)*. Examinees whose profiles show this pattern of Q_2+ and $O+$ scores have withdrawn out of a sense of their own unworthiness and because they believe that they would be rejected if they truly revealed themselves to others.

My clinical experience with clients whose profiles showed this combination (especially if their Factor L scores were not elevated, indicating that their social reality testing was intact), was that they responded well to Rogerian psychotherapy. This technique allowed them to experience the incongruence between their feelings of shame, guilt, and inadequacy and the therapist's acceptance of them, so that self-held distortions could be challenged and reduced. Successful therapy was accompanied by steady declines in Factor O scores, showing increased self-esteem later, reflected by decreases in Factor Q_2 scores.

Chapter 16

Factor Q_3: Investment in Maintaining a Socially Approved Self-Image

THE CONSTRUCT
The Self-Sentiment and Its Components

The Relationship Between Factor Q_3 (Self-Sentiment) and Factor O (Guilt Proneness)

Explanation of the Term "Sentiment"

Differences Between the Self-Sentiment and Other Agencies of Personal Control

Heredity

Male and Female Differences Throughout the Life Span

HIGH SCORES ON FACTOR Q_3
Intrapsychic Data

Social Data

Q_3+ and Childhood

Important Correlations Between Q_3+ Scores and Other 16PF Factor Scores

Clinical Relevance of Q_3+ Scores

LOW SCORES ON FACTOR Q_3
Intrapsychic Data

Social Data

Q_3- and Childhood

Important Correlations Between Q_3- Scores and Other 16PF Factor Scores

Clinical Relevance of Q_3- Scores

FACTOR Q_3: CHARACTERISTICS OF Q_3+ (HIGH SELF-SENTIMENT) AND Q_3− (LOW SELF-SENTIMENT) EXAMINEES

Left Score Q_3− (LOW SELF-SENTIMENT INTEGRATION)		Right Score Q_3+ (HIGH STRENGTH OF SELF-SENTIMENT)
(Uncontrolled, Lax, Follows Own Urges, Careless of Social Rules)	vs.	(Controlled, Exacting Will Power, Socially Precise, Compulsive, Following Self-image)

THE CONSTRUCT

The Self-Sentiment and Its Components

Factor Q_3 taps what Brewster Smith (1978) describes as "the uniquely human capacity to observe ourselves as objects in whose social and internal image we are emotionally invested, causing us to evaluate our behavior with forethought and afterthought and conduct ourselves accordingly" (p. 33). Cattell calls this trait the *self-sentiment.* As it is measured in the 16PF, the self-sentiment is patterned upon the cultural concept of correct behavior, and, according to my own insights, as well as the introspections shared with me by other persons, involves two major components. The first is self-concept.

(i) Self-concept. The self-concept is coextensive with Erickson's *sense of identity.* It grows out of the recognition that one's attachments, values, and beliefs tend to endure over time. Accompanying this recognition is the innate human urge to reduce cognitive dissonance, in regard to one's own behavior, which leads to the shaping and organizing of various self-perceptions into a coherent unity. This unity then comes to be experienced as "I."

Although the self-concept combines conscious and unconscious elements, only the former is measured by the 16PF. The unconscious elements are picked up by other psychological tests specially designed to tap unconscious processes, such as the Motivation Analysis Test (MAT).

The conscious self-concept can be further divided into two parts, along the lines described by Rogers (1957, 1961). One part is a *wished-for self-concept,* i.e., the socially approved concept or image one would like to have of oneself. This wished-for self-image contains the internalized standards for estimating self-worth. The second part is a *perceived self-concept,* i.e., the views one actually has of oneself and of how one is seen by others.[1]

(ii) The Evaluator. The second self-sentiment component is the *evaluator.* Unlike the self-concept, the evaluator is without content; it contains no values or standards. It is a yardstick that estimates the degree of congruence between the wished-for and perceived self-concepts. In other words, it observes how well one is living up to personal ideals. Strictly speaking, the evaluator may belong to the internal-sensing and reality-testing functions of the ego (Factor C). Rather than theorize about this point, however, let us simply include it here as part of the self-sentiment structure.

The Relationship Between Factor Q_3 (Self-Sentiment) and Factor O (Guilt Proneness)

Self-esteem follows whenever the evaluator observes that there is substantial congruence between one's wished-for and perceived self-concepts. Conversely, an observation that one is failing to live up to personal ideals results in self-degradation, shame, or anxiety. These feelings are not recorded in the self-sentiment structure, which involves only content and perceptual variables, but in Factor O (guilt proneness). As discussed in Chapter 13, Factor O measures high self-esteem at its right pole and poor self-esteem at its left pole.

A homeostatic device may be a useful analogue for visualizing the interplay between Factor O and the self-sentiment parts of Factor Q_3. Figure 16.1 shows a conception of this interplay. The conditions for self-esteem are set on the standards of the wished-for self-concept. Observations made by the evaluator that the perceived self-concept is not measuring up to these standards triggers uncomfortable feelings; these feelings are reflected in Factor O. Reducing this discomfort and restoring self-esteem requires changes in the unwanted behavior, thereby bringing the perceived self-concept into closer accord with the standards of the wished-for self-concept.

---

[1]The reader may recognize the parallel between the wished-for and perceived self-concepts and Platonic ideas. According to Plato, people carry within themselves an idea of the consummate object or situations (e.g., chair, book, vacation, friend) against which they compare their real-life counterparts.

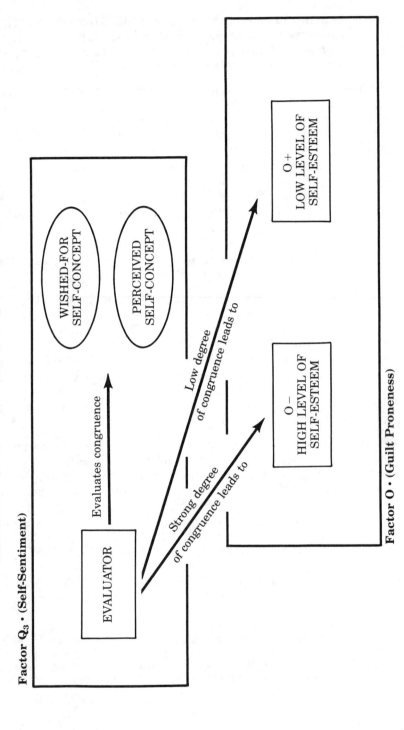

Figure 16.1 Hypothesized Relationship between Factor Q₃ (Self-Sentiment) and Factor O (Guilt Proneness), Showing Process of Self-Evaluation

Factor Q₃ · (Self-Sentiment)

WISHED-FOR SELF-CONCEPT

PERCEIVED SELF-CONCEPT

Evaluates congruence

EVALUATOR

Low degree of congruence leads to

Strong degree of congruence leads to

O+
LOW LEVEL OF SELF-ESTEEM

O−
HIGH LEVEL OF SELF-ESTEEM

Factor O · (Guilt Proneness)

The degree of discomfort that one may experience when, for some reason, one cannot or will not behave according to personal standards may threaten to overwhelm or incapacitate. In these instances, the evaluator is likely to provide protection by turning against its reality-observing function, either partially or fully blocking recognition of the incongruence from awareness. In this role, the evaluator becomes a mechanism of defense, using rationalization, denial, or repression, or other forms of self-delusion.

Explanation of the Term "Sentiment"

To complete this description of the self-sentiment, the term "sentiment," as used by Cattell, needs some explanation. Cattell uses this term identically with what psychoanalysts call "object cathexis," which means an investment. This investment may take the form of emotional attachment to a person, an animal, an object, or even an abstraction such as an idea or belief. The "self-sentiment," therefore, implies attachment to oneself, as a social being with ideals of conduct. Although this definition implies dynamic roots, the inclusion of the self-sentiment in the 16PF indicates that it also shows itself as a stylistic trait as well as a drive.

Differences Between the Self-Sentiment and Other Agencies of Personal Control

The self-sentiment is not easily recognizable as a distinct trait, as is illustrated by its failure to be found in factorings of observer ratings. Partly, this is because its operations are covert. Also, it is often unclear to observers how the self-sentiment affects behavior differently from the three other factors related to self-control, namely, Factor C (the ego), Factor G (superego), and Factor F (desurgency). Even so, each of these traits arises from underlying concerns that are as different from the self-sentiment as they are from each other.

The self-sentiment concern, as we have already stated, is for maintaining as much congruence as possible between the *perceived* and *wished-for* self-concepts and is molded out of socially approved standards. Though this concern may be commendable, it is still self-centered and, therefore, contrasts with that of the mature superego (G+), which deemphasizes preoccupation with oneself and encourages other-centeredness.

Less subtle is the contrast between the self-sentiment (Q_3+) and the ego ($C+$), since the latter's hedonistic concern for minimizing pain and maximizing long-term pleasure or satisfactions prompts behavior that avoids inner discomfort—shame, embarrassment, etc.—that comes from violation of self-sentiment ideals. The ego, however, contains none of the self-sentiment's aesthetic values of a higher self.

It is fairly easy to distinguish between Q_3+ (self-sentiment) and $F-$ (desurgency). $F-$ people control their behavior through their pessimistic and cautious outlook. They choose actions that will minimize their risk for punishment, rather than those that help maintain self-esteem.

Heredity

Even though Factor Q_3 has appreciable heritability, the fact that it is so closely tied to the wish for a socially approved self-image conveys that it is probably strongly shaped by the culture. Moreover, it has a moderate standard deviation of measurement (6.01 for men and 6.38 for women). This suggests that self-sentiment growth is influenced by exposure to schools, television, and other macrosocial institutions that impart common ideals of conduct and promote habits of self-evaluation and personal reflection.

Male and Female Differences Throughout the Life Span

Both male and female Factor Q_3 scores steadily increase through early adulthood, reaching a plateau around their 30th year, then slowly declining after the 50th year. The group mean score is 25.24 for men and 22.93 for women, a difference of over two stens.

HIGH SCORES ON FACTOR Q_3

Intrapsychic Data

Evidence from anthropological and social psychological research indicates that the proclivities for self-observation and evaluation, a desire to reduce cognitive dissonance, and a preference for maintaining self-respect and being positively regarded by others are ubiquitous. Possibly, they are innately programmed qualities, as the appreciable heritability component of Factor Q_3 suggests. It follows, therefore, that everyone has the potential for forming a self-sentiment, providing, of course, that he or she is exposed to normal learning opportunities and has attained an adequate level of cognitive and emotional development.

I have already stated that the self-sentiment's *action* occurs by evaluating the degree of congruence between the *wished-for* and *perceived* parts of the self-concept. To grasp the subjective experience of those individuals who have unusually strong self-sentiments, one need only imagine this action as continuously occupying the center of their consciousness. Therefore, even though there is a substantial correlation between Q_3+ and $O-$ (untroubled adequacy), indicating a relationship between self-sentiment strength and self-esteem in the general population, such acute self-absorption must surely be antithetical to happiness. Happiness, according to those who have studied this condition in both ancient and modern times, requires a measure of personal transcendence or lack of self-consciousness that would be difficult for persons with strong self-sentiments to achieve. The self-reports of Q_3+ examinees in my sample generally confirmed this proposition. They reported that, although they derived pride from living up to their self-ideals, it was rare for them to experience moments of joyful spontaneity. High scorers constantly monitor the correctness of their behavior; they are overly concerned about social appearance; and their standards for maintaining self-approval and respect are too high. However, they do not enjoy themselves.

In addition to their self-preoccupation, I noted two other characteristics that were integral parts of the personalities of these Q_3+ examinees. The first and foremost was a deficit of unconditional self-regard and second, its almost inevitable consequence, perfectionism.

Unconditional self-regard, which has been much discussed by Rogers (1957, 1961), is the ability to accept oneself, by the mere virtue of one's existence, as being worthy of occupying a space in the universe. Philosophically, it involves an orientation towards oneself as an essence stripped of its attributes, such as Kant described. It could also be defined as valuing oneself for *being* (a creation of nature, a child of God), rather than *doing* (working, performing) or *having* (wealth, intelligence). In a psychological sense, it is understood in terms that are more implicit than explicit and may have, according to many developmental theorists, originated in the infant's introjection of its parents' unreserved acceptance.

My Q_3+ examinees demonstrated their lack of unconditional self-regard by their strong proclivity for valuing themselves only according to the degree to which they saw themselves living up to their ideals. Thus, their regard for themselves was conditional. This had a positive outcome, in that they tended to become high achievers, obtaining standards of excellence and social recognition that would otherwise not have been possible. The less positive outcome was that, since total control over one's life is impossible, their self-worth rested on precarious conditions, i.e., being dependent on external processes such as social change or on the laws of nature, including the inevitability of aging. ("Time and circumstance happen to all"—Leviticus.)

Times when they could not realize their high ambitions, despite putting forth their best efforts, were particularly traumatic for Q_3+ examinees. However, some of these "failures" resulted from an oppressive environment that restricted their self-realization, for reasons of sex, class, or race.

It was much more demoralizing for them, however, when failures were due to their own personal inadequacies or shortcomings, which become manifested in the pursuit of unattainable goals.

> *Example:* From the point of view of the self-sentiment, it has been suggested that probably one of the most disappointed groups of individuals are those who sit in the "second fiddle" sections of major orchestras. Most have practiced their instruments for hours regularly every day since early childhood, sustained by dreams of their future glory as soloists, concert masters, or at the very least taking their place among the first violinists. But now, despite their early aspirations, they must face the limitations imposed by their modest talent, and accept the status of being second best.

People I have tested in these and other, similarly disappointing situations often had Q_3+ scores, usually accompanied by $E+$ (dominance) and $O+$ (guilt proneness) scores. This pattern indicates, in the first instance, lack of willingness to concede failure, and, in the second, poor self-esteem. Sometimes, however, the Factor O scores were in the opposite (untroubled adequacy) direction. This meant that these people were somehow blind to the incongruence between their ideals and performance, and that they were distorting reality, possibly falsely blaming their failure on external influences.

Perfectionism was the second major characteristic I frequently discovered in Q_3+ examinees. Being perfectionists, these examinees were rarely completely satisfied with their behavior. But, contrary to their belief, their problems were usually not in their behavior, which they were always attempting to improve, but in their wished-for self-concepts, which contained standards that were at best demanding, and at worst were impossible to humanly realize.

Those who were strongly perfectionist were apt to pursue their ends methodically, studiously avoiding mistakes and paying meticulous attention to details. Their efforts frequently led them to produce the best possible performances and products that they were capable of attaining. However, especially if they did not have strong reality orientations, these same behaviors could be self-defeating. Unable to discriminate the more important from the less important aspects of an undertaking, they were liable to lose sight of its purposes and myopically give equal focus to all details, some of which were irrelevant.

> *Example:* A student whom I judged as having a high Factor Q_3 score (self-sentiment) but a low Factor C score (poor reality testing) turned in fastidiously neat papers, every margin exactly measured, no trace of typographical errors, and every reference faultlessly indexed; but the material was substantively weak. I discovered that she had spent such an inordinate amount of time typing, measuring margins, and checking spelling that she did not have sufficient time to master the subject.

Despite all that has been said hitherto regarding the drawbacks of a strong self-sentiment, the obverse relationship between Q_3+ scores and the second-order anxiety pattern is evidence that Q_3+ people are usually able to bind their anxiety. Indeed, Karson and O'Dell (1976) dubbed the Q_3+ pole as the "ability to bind anxiety." "Binding anxiety" is a term used to imply a method of coping with fear and doubt. In postulating about how the self-sentiment operates in this binding process, I have noted that when persons are able to achieve congruence between their high standards and their behavior, they experience a sense of mastery and efficacy. This exercising of one's will and directing one's fate is alluded to by Cattell (1957), who quotes McDouglas's definition of will power as the self-sentiment in action. Moreover, since a sense of personal superiority can be an antidote for anxiety, anxiety binding may also result from knowledge that one's standards are higher than most people's. Many of my Q_3+ examinees felt somewhat smug when comparing themselves to their less ideal fellows.

Social Data

As with many other traits, it is the context of role relationships that determines whether persons who are highly invested in maintaining their self-sentiments will be liked or disliked, or valued or devalued, by others. According to the research findings of Cattell and Stice (1960), Q_3+ people are commonly chosen as leaders and are effective in this capacity, since they are generally viewed as trustworthy, reliable, and ethical. They are also reported to be valued in their working situations because their concern for their social reputation demands that they take the time to organize tasks, plan ahead, and avoid mistakes. As Krug (1980) notes, it is fortunate for airline passengers that commercial pilots score so highly on this trait.

Because they tended to see their homes and neighborhoods as extensions of themselves, persons whom I judged to have high self-sentiments were appreciated as neighbors. They could be expected to keep their premises in good order, not give noisy parties, and be interested in maintaining community standards. If they agreed to watch a vacationing neighbor's home, that person could be safely assured that it would be well attended in his or her absence.

However, the positive value of a strong self-sentiment does not hold for more intimate relationships and friendships. Observations of my clinical sample of Q_3+ examinees have shown that the same qualities of attentiveness to social rituals and strong task orientation, which facilitated their formal encounters and work-related activities, led them to act rigidly and compulsively at home or similar social settings, making it uncomfortable for others to be in their company. Thus, they were rarely chosen as companions with whom to relax and have fun.

While there is no statistical evidence that Q_3+ scores are indicative of either marital stability or instability, I observed that when marriage counseling was sought by couples when one spouse had a Q_3+ score and the other had a moderate or low score on Factor Q_3, contention often arose from their different standards for the comportment of the offspring. My Q_3+ clients tended to be overly concerned about their children's maintaining socially approved standards. This concern conflicted with the tolerant, relaxed attitude of their more moderately scoring partners.

Examinees whose $Q_3 +$ scores were accompanied by excessive $G+$ (moral conformity) scores were often described as "stuffed shirts" or as being "too wrapped up in themselves." Frank, in the MASH TV series, is such a caricature: status conscious, humorless in his sense of correctness, and intolerant of ambiguity, Frank perennially disowns parts of himself that do not fit with his idealized self-image.

$Q_3 +$ and Childhood

In the opening section of this chapter, I proposed that the self-sentiment develops coextensively with the capacity for reflective thought and the emerging sense of "I," and that it derives its content from what the culture regards as correct social behavior. Given what is currently known about childhood development, these conditions suggest that the most important influence the environment provides in developing self-sentiment is (a) the availability of role models that embody qualities that the growing child admires and wants to imitate, and (b) the rewards the child receives for conforming to the ideals of its reference group.

However, though frequently detectable, these childhood influences were not always revealed in the recollections of my $Q_3 +$ examinees, especially those whose profiles did not reflect the pattern of associated traits shown in Table 16.1. These individuals had often been humiliated as children and their adult preoccupation with comporting themselves correctly was to ensure that they would not have to reexperience these painful feelings. Investigations into their childhoods frequently revealed that they had suffered from a surfeit of shame, either because their parents overused "shaming" as a disciplinary or coercive technique, or because they were (or perceived themselves to be) the objects of public scorn for some deficiency within the family, like conspicuous poverty or scandalous misbehavior on the part of their parents. Adults raised by alcoholic parents were particularly likely to have this history.

The impact of experiencing shame on the developing self-sentiment not only leads to avoidance behavior but as far as I can tell, operates according to the Adlerian principle (Adler, 1957) of *overcompansation*. I discovered that Q_3+ examinees were extremely ambitious, and had been since childhood (at which time they had decided to "show them" when they grew up). Most of these examinees were extraordinarily interested in receiving admiration. Commonly, they reported having had youthful fantasies of becoming movie stars, Olympic champions, or other figures that attain fame and public adoration. Those who were fortunate enough to possess talent and opportunity had sometimes been able to realize these early yearnings, even though they were apt to pay for their overachievement with stress-related illnesses.

By contrast, a few Q_3+ examinees in my sample were markedly unambitious. Their profiles also tended to depart from the standard pattern of correlations outlined in Table 16.1, especially when $C-$ (lower ego strength) and Q_4+ (tension) scores were present. In addition, it was fairly typical for them to show $H-$ (threctic) scores also; it was their shyness and timidity that prompted them to "play it safe," and to steer clear of situations that had the potential for revealing discrepancies between their behavior and their wished-for self-concept.

Important Correlations Between Q_3+ Scores and Other 16PF Factor Scores

Table 16.1

Important Correlations Between Q_3+ Scores and Other 16PF Factor Scores

Factor Pole	Correlation	Possible Associated Traits Indicated by Correlation
$G+$ (Higher Superego Strength)	.43	Conscientious, Persistent, Moralistic, Staid
Q_4- (Low Nervous Tension)	.42	Relaxed, Tranquil, Unfrustrated, Composed
$C+$ (Ego Strength)	.40	Emotionally Stable, Mature, Faces Reality, Calm
$O-$ (Strong Self-esteem)	.37	Self-assured, Placid, Secure, Complacent, Serene
$H+$ (Parmia)	.20	Venturesome, Uninhibited, Socially Bold

Five statistically significant correlations between $Q_3 +$ scores and other 16PF factor scores appear in Table 16.1.

These correlations convey that, typically, $Q_3 +$ persons enjoy a sense of well-being. They are often relatively free from nervous tension ($Q_4 -$), manage their lives and tolerate frustration well ($C +$), and have high self-esteem ($O -$). Their high self-esteem, when viewed in conjunction with their superego strength ($G +$), suggests that they endorse and live up to conventional moral standards, in addition to their self-sentiment ideals (even though the latter relationship, for reasons explained in Chapter 13, suggest that they may have overly rigid ego defenses). Finally, as the weak though relevant $H +$ correlation shows, they may incline towards boldness rather than timidity.

The associated characteristics just delineated indicate that a $Q_3 +$ score can in most instances be interpreted as signifying good overall adjustment, even though, as noted earlier, it implies a self-regard that is highly conditional. When a $Q_3 +$ score, however, does not appear in conjunction with a configuration of 16PF scores similar to that shown in Table 16.1, it may signify disturbed personality functioning.

Clinical Relevance of $Q_3 +$ Scores

A $Q_3 +$ score that appears in a profile that fails to show more or less the standard set of correlations ($G +$, $C +$, $Q_4 -$, $O -$, and $H +$) raises questions about general adjustment. More explicitly, whenever a $Q_3 +$ score is accompanied by an $O +$ (low self-esteem) or $C -$ (low ego strength) score, for example, then the examinee's self-sentiment functions (i.e., self-evaluation, concern with self-image, and comparison of behavior with personal aspirations) are failing to promote the desired outcome. This finding suggests a number of possibilities. The examinee may be experiencing internal conflict, paying too high a price in terms of stress for trying to live up to overly high ideals, or suffering from a pathological syndrome. $Q_3 +$ scores are commonly found in the profiles of persons suffering from paranoid and narcissistic personality disorders or from early schizophrenia, all conditions marked by high levels of self-preoccupation.

$Q_3 +$ scores may also be found in the profiles of clients suffering from dissociative disorders. Although this finding has not as yet been reported elsewhere in the literature, my colleagues and I have accumulated observations demonstrating a relationship between Q_3+ scores and reactions that fit behaviors traditionally attributed to "complexes." By complexes, I am referring to the phenomena, initially recognized by Jung, wherein the person disowns sets of emotional and behavioral responses organized around specific ideas. These responses are not incorporated into the person's sense of identity because they are so contrary to his or her usual values and habits. Consequently, people refer to these behaviors as "something coming over me" or "not being myself." They are "ego dystonic," or—as it would be more technically correct to say—"self-sentiment dystonic."

My hypothesis is that complexes, as they have just been described, are particularly apt to develop when a strong self-sentiment is too tightly organized to allow for the expressions of drives, like sex or pugnacity, that are not otherwise sublimated. This is illustrated in the example below.

> *Example:* A young, unmarried, professional man, courteous, conscientious, religious, and impeccably dressed, was referred to a therapist by the local judiciary for psychological testing after having been arrested for stealing women's underwear from clotheslines. His Factor Q_3 score was 10. He revealed that his wished-for self-image sanctioned no acceptable sexual outlets for himself as an unmarried man. Unable to sublimate this drive, it was first compartmentalized and then expressed in ways contrary to his sense of self. So incompatible was this sexual expression with all other areas of his conduct that he sincerely insisted that this sexual behavior was "not me!" and that it must be attributable to his being "possessed" by some unnatural power.

Besides this more extreme example, there are many everyday instances in which people behave in ways that are strikingly contrary to their usual comportment—drinking binges, jealous reactions, and unseemly outbursts. It often turns out that these persons have overly strong self-sentiments that inhibit normal drive expressions. Clinicians, therefore, may do well to investigate for the existence of complexes or other forms of dissociation in persons whose Factor Q_3 scores are 8, 9, or 10, especially if these scores are accompanied by extreme $G+$, $C-$, or $H-$ scores. Extremely high Factor G (superego) scores indicate further behavioral rigidity. Low Factor C (ego weakness) scores indicate difficulty in satisfying needs and adapting to the demands of the environment. Finally, H − (threctic) scores indicate shyness and timidity.

LOW SCORES ON FACTOR Q_3

Intrapsychic Data

The internal experience of Q_3 − persons is revealed in their endorsement of item responses that indicate that they pay little heed to how they may appear to others and that they generally do what they feel like doing. At first glance, these responses might suggest ego weakness (as discussed earlier in Chapter 4), since they are similar to those displayed in C − scorers (especially in the disregard for consequences). Closer investigation, though, reveals that Q_3 − people simply either lack ordinary concern for maintaining a socially approved self-image, or have been unable to achieve a workable set of personal ideals upon which to pattern their behavior.

Based on the introspective reports of my Q_3 − examinees, I have been able to recognize three distinct variations of low scores on Factor Q_3.

Variant 1. $Q_3 − /C − /H − /L + /O + Q_4 +$. Low self-sentiment associated with other features of anxiety. This was by far the most frequent Q_3 − variant encountered in my sample, which is hardly surprising since $Q_3 − /C − /H − /L + /O + /Q_4 +$ scores intercorrelate to form the second-order anxiety pattern. Though they did not lack intelligence, examinees whose Q_3 − scores were particularly pronounced in this pattern were apt to appear stupid even to themselves, which further added to their feelings of inadequacy, tension, and other anxiety symptoms. They were recognizable as those individuals referred to in clinical case conferences as not having attained an adequate identity.

Upon discussion with them, it became obvious that they did not have a crystallized self-image against which they could compare their actual behavior. They revealed this failure in statements like "I don't know who I am!" Similar to adolescents, they were apt to successively try on and then discard different roles.

Variant 2. $Q_3 − /O − /Q_4 −$. Low self-sentiment associated with high self-esteem and low ergic tension. Examinees exhibiting this pattern were noticeably relaxed and self-satisfied, rather than tense and self-deprecating like Variant 1 examinees. Because their personal standards, goals, and ambitions were low, little effort was required to conform to them.

Examinees of this variant often showed an overindulgence to body narcissism.[2] For example, their preference for personal comfort, rather than for appearance, was quite marked. In fact, whenever I discovered this $Q_3 - /O - /Q_4 -$ configuration of scores on a blind 16PF interpretation, I was able to predict with about 90% accuracy that the examinee would have a sloppy or untidy appearance.

Lack of interest in maintaining a socially approved self-image left these examinees without one of the most powerful human counterforces against the urges for immediate gratification and culturally unacceptable impulsive action. This meant that they were more likely to express their wants, needs, and feelings in direct, unconventional ways.

Variant 3. $Q_3 - /A + /C + /N -$. Low self-sentiment associated with affectothymia, ego strength, and artlessness. This configuration of scores showed itself in the profiles of two examinees whose ideal was to achieve moral selflessness in the "losing of self" tradition of Western and Eastern saints.

These individuals were previously mentioned in my discussion of G scores. "Other-centered" rather than "I-centered," they had little need for self-reflection. They were what the Buddhists call "without face," giving little thought to themselves or how they appeared. I could find no explanation for their $Q_3 -$ scores other than this.

With the exception of the third variant (which, because it is based on only two examples, I will eliminate from further discussion), a general complaint among my $Q_3 -$ scorers was that they were unable to persist in achieving personal goals or realizing ambitions.

For $Q_3 -$ examinees whose profiles also showed deficits in Factor G (superego) and Factor C (ego strength) controls, it was good if they were also $F -$, even though this pattern meant control primarily through fear of punishment. Being constrained by fear,

---

[2]The relation between a low self-sentiment and narcissism is indicated by the correlation of $Q_3 -$ scores and narcissism (.37) in the 1957 study cited earlier between 16PF and dynamic scores.

while not as desirable as wishing to maximize long-term satisfactions (C +), following the promptings of conscience (G +), or wanting to live up to personal ideals (Q_3 +), is still preferable to being without any internal form of control.

Social Data

In interpersonal relationships, persons with self-sentiment deficits do not fare as well as their high self-sentiment counterparts, especially in work-related situations. For example, Q_3 − persons are overly represented among chronic seekers of vocational guidance (Cattell, 1973). It is likely that their difficulty here is explainable by research findings showing that employers do not value Q_3 − employees and pass them over for promotion. Further, because of their characteristic lack of ambition, they probably take less pride in their performance or their products than more self-respecting persons.

An exception to the relationship between low self-sentiment and producing unsatisfactory products is found among artists, who as a group have low Factor Q_3 scores (Cattell, Eber, & Tatsuoka, 1970). My hypothesis here is that their creativity occurs, not in spite of, but *because* of their low self-sentiments. Artists are generally recognized as not being much concerned by most self-sentiment kinds of rewards, i.e., prestige and public respectability. They may therefore be better able to directly focus their energies on their creations as ends in themselves. In other words, they can be object-centered rather than self-centered, in the sense that the latter term, as it is used here, implies mainstream social values.

Q_3 − examinees whom I saw in couples and marital therapy were often accused by their partners of being fickle. It is hardly surprising that there was usually credence in these accusations, since lack of self-consistency and continuity are characteristic of poorly developed self-sentiments. Consequently, it was difficult for Q_3 − people to conserve attachments over extensive periods of time. Changeable and sometimes tending to act out their ambivalences, these examinees behaved in ways that undermined their partners' confidence in the endurance of their commitments. Often they attributed their changing sense of self as being a sufficient reason for breaking promises or dissolving vows, remarking, for example: "Sure, I promised you that a year ago. But that was then. I am a different person now."

Q_3 – and Childhood

Here it can be asked, what are the early experiences that retard the self-sentiment's growth and development? Drawing from the fact that Q_3 – scores enter so prominently into the second-order anxiety pattern on the one hand and, on the other, have an *inverse* relationship to the "good upbringing" pattern,[3] they are undoubtedly of the same genre as those that produce neuroticism and undersocialization (Cattell, 1973).

In addition to these statistically based inferences, the case histories that I have accumulated suggest that low Factor Q_3 scores can be linked to three specific types of childhood experiences. In the first, the child is subjected to a surfeit of ridicule and criticism, and is afraid of being overwhelmed by feelings of shame. To protect against these painful feelings, the child avoids introspection and sets limited personal standards. The second type of childhood experience of Q_3 – scorers involved receiving so much guidance and direction that the child is discouraged from forming personal ideals or developing the habit of self-reflecting. Lacking internal representations against which to compare one's own behavior, the child continues to rely on outer cues instead of internal cues. The third, and most prevalent Q_3 – child experience according to my data, occurs when the child fails to identify with appropriate role models. In some cases, this is due to an absence of potential role models, and in other cases, though role models were available, they were not sufficiently attractive to inspire imitation, or else were regarded as being so extraordinary as to be inimitable.

> *Example:* A 45-year-old man sought therapy, saying, "I am here because I can't decide what to be when I grow up." A sensitive and intelligent man, this attempt at levity was intended to mask his inner despair at not being able to commit himself to long-term goals or attain a consistent and enduring self-concept. In taking his history, I discovered that his father was a world-renowned physicist whom he worshipped since childhood. This attitude was perpetuated by his mother's awe of his father, as well as a lack of actual father-son contact, which would have provided opportunities for demystification. Since any attempts to pattern himself

---

[3]The second-order "Good Upbringing" pattern is made up of F– (desurgency), G+ (superego strength), and Q_3+ (high self-sentiment) scores.

after his father seemed doomed to fail, they were not attempted. Not having other strong role models on whom he could draw for inspiration, he was not able to form a clear concept of a desirable and attainable self-image.

Important Correlations Between Q_3- Scores and Other 16PF Factor Scores

There is usually nothing to commend the traits indicated by the pattern indicated by the correlations in Table 16.2. They portray the Q_3- scorer as often also being $C-$ (poorly adjusted), Q_4+ (tense), $O+$ (having low self-esteem), $G-$ (probably having an underdeveloped set of moral values), and $H-$ (shy and timid). Moreover, the low scores on Factor C and Factor G indicate that Q_3- persons not only lack the benefit of a clear self-concept for directing their behavior, but they are commonly deficient in ego and superego controls also.

Table 16.2

Important Correlations Between Q_3- Scores and Other 16PF Factor Scores

Factor Pole	Correlation	Possible Associated Traits Indicated by Correlation
$G-$ (Low Superego Strength)	.43	Expedient, Disregards Rules
Q_4+ (High Ergic Tension)	.42	Tense, Frustrated, Driven, Overwrought
$C-$ (Weak Ego)	.40	Affected by Feelings, Emotionally Less Stable, Easily Upset, Changeable
$O+$ (Low Self-esteem)	.37	Apprehensive, Self-reproaching, Insecure, Worrying, Troubled
$H-$ (Threctia)	.20	Shy, Timid, Threat-sensitive

Clinical Relevance of Q_3- Scores

Because the intrapsychic and social manifestations of a poorly integrated self-sentiment are so closely tied to mental health problems, I have already entered into the clinical domain in the previous sections. In particular, I have alluded to what happens to people's behavior when they are deficient in the major sources of control provided by the self-sentiment. In addition, the common association between Q_3- and $C-$ (ego weakness), $O+$ (low self-esteem), Q_4+ (nervous tension), and $G-$ (lack of moral development) have also been noted, as well as the entry of Q_3- scores into the second-order anxiety pattern.

However, I have reserved until now mentioning the associations between Q_3- scores and certain clinical syndromes. These, according to the *Handbook for the 16PF* (Cattell, Eber, & Tatsuoka, 1970), occur most prominently in the group profiles of persons suffering from neurotic and antisocial disorders. This finding is best interpreted as indicating that these individuals have difficulty in either forming or sustaining socially approved self-images.

The *16PF Handbook* also notes the appearance of Q_3- scores in the group profile of persons who have attempted suicide. This low score on Factor Q_3 can be interpreted as reflecting a withdrawal of emotional investment in oneself as a social being, which must undoubtedly be felt when contemplating ending one's life. The extreme $L+$ (protension), $M+$ (autia), and Q_4+ (tension) scores that also enter into the profile suggest social alienation, withdrawal from external reality, and physical agitation, respectively. When added to a lowered self-sentiment, these qualities create a familiar picture to clinicians who have worked with suicidal patients. Thus, noting a configuration of Q_3-, $L+$, $M+$, and Q_4+ scores in the profiles of clients, especially in those who also appear depressed, should alert clinicians to the need to carefully evaluate the potential for suicide.

Chapter 17

---■---

Factor Q_4: Tense and Relaxed Temperaments

THE CONSTRUCT
Trait and State Forms of Tension
The Original Factor Name
Heredity
Male and Female Differences Throughout the Life Span

HIGH SCORES ON FACTOR Q_4
Intrapsychic Data
Social Data
Q_4+ and Childhood
Important Correlations Between Q_4+ Scores
and Other 16PF Factor Scores
Clinical Relevance of Q_4+ Scores

LOW SCORES ON FACTOR Q_4
Intrapsychic Data
Social Data
Q_4- and Childhood
Important Correlations Between Q_4- Scores
and Other 16PF Factor Scores
Clinical Relevance of Q_4- Scores

FACTOR Q_4: CHARACTERISTICS OF Q_4+ (HIGH TENSION) AND Q_4- (LOW TENSION) EXAMINEES

Left Score Q_4- (LOW ERGIC TENSION)		Right Score Q_4+ (HIGH ERGIC TENSION)
(Relaxed, Tranquil, Torpid, Unfrustrated, Composed)	vs.	(Tense, Frustrated, Driven, Overwrought, Fretful)

THE CONSTRUCT

Trait and State Forms of Tension

This factor measures the unpleasant sensations that accompany autonomic arousal, colloquially referred to as "nervous tension," or simply "tension." High scores (Q_4+) represent a surfeit of these sensations, and low scores (Q_4-) represent their virtual absence.

Since the 16PF is designed to measure enduring characteristics, Q_4+ on a profile usually indicates that the tension is a trait; therefore, the examinee is characterologically a tense, volatile, and easily upset individual. Less likely, but still possible, however, a Q_4+ score could indicate that the tension is a state; in this case, the examinee is reacting to some transitory situation, and his or her score will later eventually return to its former level. Likewise, a Q_4- score can also indicate either a trait or a state, but is more likely to be the former, in which case it reveals a phlegmatic temperament. It most commonly indicates a state in situations when the examinee has been tranquilized by drugs, or is deeply relaxed following strenuous exercise, for example.

Both extremes of Factor Q_4 scores, however, may be achieved by motivational distortion (See Appendix E). Not only does the transparency of the factor items make distortion fairly easy, but there are also many contexts in which some advantages can be gained by misrepresenting oneself as either tense or relaxed. For example, a person may wish to appear tense when attempting to gain entrance into a psychiatric hospital and, conversely, relaxed when trying to get discharged from it. Therefore, it is helpful to know something about the life situations of high- or low-scoring examinees when interpreting their scores, so that their possible motives for faking can be considered.

The Original Factor Name

The term "erg" is a neologism describing an internal force similar to what is usually referred to as a drive. Thus, by calling this factor *ergic tension,* Cattell (1957) was stating his hypothesis that Factor Q_4 measures the presence or absence of pressure from pent-up drives such as pugnacity or sex. However, I disagree with this hypothesis. My reasoning is that, if indeed Cattell's hypothesis were correct, there would be a *positive* correlation between Q_4+ scores and Motivation Analysis Test conflict scores, since the latter measure the attempt to repress and suppress activated drives. In looking at the correlation between the two tests (Krug, 1980), not only did I discover that this correlation did *not* occur, but that there was actually a very small, overall-negative correlation between these two sets of scores. Given this lack of experimental and statistical support for a drive pressure basis, it seems more accurate to drop "ergic" from the name of this factor, calling it simply "tension," as I shall do throughout this chapter.

Parenthetically, due to Q_4+ scores' being one of the two largest contributors to the second-order anxiety pattern, the failure to show a relationship with pent-up drive pressure supports a cognitively induced interpretation of the physical symptoms of anxiety. Cattell's initial interpretation of them as measuring pent-up drive pressure parallels Freud's first theory of anxiety, which he later discarded, replacing it with his signal theory of anxiety. This second theory attributes anxiety to the anticipation of danger.

Heredity

The heritability quotient of Factor Q_4 is moderate (.34); hence, despite its substantial environmental component, there is a definite genetic tendency towards being either tense or relaxed. Age trend data cannot be reliably discerned from the measurements that have been collected so far, probably because these data mix transitory state fluctuations with stable trait characteristics.

Male and Female Differences Throughout the Life Span

The group mean for Factor Q_4 is 20.61 for men and 25.96 for women. This is a large and statistically significant difference that conveys women as being more tense than men. The wide standard deviation, however, is similar for both sexes—men, 9.41 and women, 8.93.

HIGH SCORES ON FACTOR Q$_4$

Intrapsychic Data

The physical symptoms that Q$_4$+ scores signify are known to anyone who has experienced strong arousal of the autonomic nervous system. Feeling "jittery," "nervous," "on edge," or "pressured" are familiar, everyday expressions used to describe these sensations.

That Q$_4$+ scores measure a decidedly unpleasant subjective condition receives support from their strong negative correlations (Krug, 1980) with scales from other psychological tests measuring psychological comfort and personal control. These include the "Sense of Well Being," "Self-Control," "Tolerance," "Good Impression," and "Intellectual Efficiency" scales of the CPI; the "Number of Favorable Adjectives" scale of the ACL; the "Personal Integration" scale of the OPI; and the "Composed" scale of the EPS scales.

Because of the transparency of the items and because people are often too proud to admit that they are so distressed, especially in nonclinical situations, Karson and O'Dell (1976) recommend interpreting Q$_4$+ scores as possibly conveying either a cry for help or a signal that the examinee is too overwhelmed to give socially desirable answers. They also recommend, however, that the test interpreter should be mindful that, because the scores can represent an acute reaction or state, they may fluctuate excessively. Therefore, it is not uncommon for an examinee to answer the questions and obtain a Factor Q$_4$ score of 8, 9, or 10 on one day, and to have moderate scores the following day when tension is reduced. Having observed this occurrence myself, my policy is to have high-scoring examinees retake the test after a short time.

Most Q$_4$+ examinees in my sample were able to discern whether their tension was due to a passing state, or to an enduring part of their personalities. In the first instance, examinees reported that they found themselves overreacting to negative stimuli that might not bother them at other times. In addition, they reported such things as "not being themselves," "feeling shaky," or having unaccustomed stiffness and soreness in their shoulder and neck muscles.

By contrast, characterologically tense examinees were likely to describe themselves as persons who habitually had trouble relaxing or even just sitting still for extended periods, because they "always need to be doing something." Most recognized the "nervous" quality of their energy and that it did not come from a surplus of healthy vitality. They also usually recognized that they were impatient or accident prone and irascible. Many feared becoming incapacitated or losing control.

Inexperienced interpreters of the 16PF may confuse tension —as measured by Factor Q_4 scores and as described by the examinee apart from the test situation—with low ego strength $(C-)$ and low self-esteem $(O+)$. Factor Q_4, however, differs fundamentally from these two traits in that it is associated with physiological arousal rather than cognition. For example, while persons with low ego strength often react impulsively, they do so out of low frustration tolerance rather than to provide a physical outlet. Tense (Q_4+) persons are likely to tap their fingers, pace floors, fidgit, or do some spur-of-the-moment thing, simply to release tension. Likewise, the person suffering primarily from low self-esteem $(O+)$ is more plagued by self-denigrating ideas than by the physical symptoms, like sleeplessness or gastric upsets, that the tense person shows.

Actually, the 16PF trait most similar to tension is $H-$ (threctia), for it, too, involves hyperactivity of the autonomic nervous system. $H-$ springs from *oversensitivity* to stimuli and is manifested in avoidance behavior. Tension, on the other hand, is the aftermath of overstimulation. Thus, whereas the $H-$ examinee complains of shyness and diffidence, and expresses the desire to ward off exposure to threatening situations, the tense person complains of being overwrought and nervous.

Social Data

The fact that Factor Q_4 is frequently not reliably revealed in the ratings of observers presumably is due to the social desirability of presenting a cool, calm exterior, which causes people in most ordinary circumstances to appear less tense than they are. Their success in this regard depends largely upon their ability to deal effectively with reality and their degree of social poise and sophistication. These traits are discernible, in the first instance, from the person's Factor C (ego strength) scores and, in the second, from their Factor N (shrewdness) scores.

When my Q_4+ examinees showed their discomfort by appearing ill at ease or restless, other people tended to respond according to their own particular personality makeup. For the most part, however, others are either annoyed by the tense person or are sympathetic.

Other people tend to respond negatively to a tense person who discharges tension extrapunitively. The 16PF profiles of extrapunitive Q_4+ examinees in my sample showed either $E+$ (dominance) or $L+$ (protension) scores. Both types falsely blamed others for their short tempers, impatience, and distractability. Moreover, those who happened to be in positions of authority were inclined to make quick, irrational decisions or explode into anger and, as a result, were strongly disliked by their subordinates. Fortunately, they were few in number, reflecting Cattell and Stice's (1960) finding that it is rare for Q_4+ persons (whose tension is characterological) to assume positions of leadership and authority.

Q_4+ and Childhood

Cattell (1957) described the typical Q_4+ 11-year-old as a child who "feels scared, shakes, sweats without reason, worries, gets tense and excited when thinking over events, and often gets much annoyed over small things." These responses resemble another behavioral pattern associated with the high pole of another factor, Factor D (excitability). This factor is found mostly in children, as I mentioned previously, in Chapter 5. Although excitability, like tension, is characterized by restlessness and tension-reducing activity, excitability has an attention-getting, demanding, acting-out quality not always present in Q_4+ (tense) children.

Because tension is so highly determined by situational influences, a high score in a child's profile should cause the examiner to wonder what is going on in the child's life to cause the tension. Sometimes the child is obviously responding to some recent trauma, like the birth of a sibling or the divorce of parents. In these cases, unless the trauma is particularly strong or complicated, the tension will subside once the crisis is resolved, whereupon the Factor Q_4 scores will be of a more moderate level on repeated testing. When it is not possible to link an extreme score to some definite situation, and especially if it persists in future testings, the child may be experiencing protracted stress, and the examiner should find out more about what is happening in the child's life.

My person investigations into the lives of Q_4+ children has on several occasions led to the uncovering of ongoing physical, sexual, and emotional abuse. More commonly, however, the children disclosed less florid stresses, in the form of being subjected to anxious or overly strict parents.

My adult Q_4+ examinees whose tension turned out to be characterological typically recollected stressful childhoods. Like their youthful counterparts, their stresses had varied origins.

Important Correlations Between Q_4+ Scores and Other 16PF Factor Scores

Table 17.1 shows the important correlations between Q_4+ scores and other 16PF factor scores.

Table 17.1

Important Correlations Between Q_4+ Scores and Other 16PF Factor Scores

Factor Pole	Correlation	Possible Associated Traits Indicated by Correlation
O + (Guilt Proneness)	.61	Apprehensive, Self-reproaching, Insecure, Worrying, Troubled
C − (Low Ego Strength)	.59	Affected by Feelings, Emotionally Less Stable, Easily Upset, Changeable
Q_3 − (Low Self-sentiment)	.42	Undisciplined Self-conflict, Lax, Follows Own Urges, Careless of Social Rules
L + (Protension)	.38	Suspicious, Hard to Fool
H − (Threctia)	.33	Shy, Timid, Threat-sensitive

Table 17.1 shows that Q_4+ scores are correlated with the full complement of other factor poles that make up the second-order anxiety pattern. This pattern conveys that it is common

for Q_4+ examinees, not only to feel tense, but to experience other anxiety-related symptoms. Specifically, they are low in self-esteem $(O+)$, are lacking in ego strength $(C-)$, are shy and timid $(H-)$, feel alienated, mistrustful, and insecure $(L+)$, and do not maintain socially approved self-concepts (Q_3-).

Clinical Relevance of Q_4+ Scores

Karson and O'Dell (1976) call the "+" pole of Factor Q_4 *free-floating* anxiety, meaning pervasive, generalized fears that are not attached to any particular idea, object, or event. In only 28 instances was I able to attribute the scores of Q_4+ examples in my sample to this form of anxiety. In other instances, examinees showed other elements of the second-order anxiety pattern $(C-,\ H-,\ L+,\ O+,\ Q_3-,\ Q_4+)$, for their anxiety was linked to some identifiable fear, anticipation of some dreaded event or encounter, or to self-doubt or self-denigrating thought.

As a state rather than trait measurement, Factor Q_4 scores have been found to increase in response to disappointments and frustrations. The most common situations evoking these responses are cited in the *16PF Handbook* as unhappy love affairs, failures to get promotion, unstable marriages, and chronic invalidism.

The *16PF Handbook* also reports Q_4+ scores in the group profiles of alcoholics, psychopaths, manic-depressives, and persons attempting suicides. My clinical findings, in addition to reflecting these trends, have also reliably found a disproportionate number of Q_4+ clients showing a propensity for unpremeditated violent behavior. These individuals became easily agitated and acted out aggressively with little or no provocation.

> *Example:* A receptionist politely asked a waiting patient who had been pacing the floor for 15 minutes if she could help him. He responded by punching a wall and verbally abusing her. The 16PF I had obtained several hours earlier showed his Factor Q_4 score to be 10.

Skidmore (1977) and others have noted that Q_4+ scores go down after therapy is successfully directed toward other traits in the anxiety constellation. Helping clients increase their self-esteem, develop internal controls, or recognize their distortions about being harmed or tricked are examples of these interventions. Though I sometimes use these indirect modes of reducing uncomfortable levels of tension, I am more likely to attempt to reduce the clients' tension by interventions that are directly aimed at reducing autonomic nervous system arousal. My rationale is that the tension can be in itself so demoralizing as to cause people to make negative self-evaluations, project fears, and act in other maladaptive ways, thereby setting up a vicious cycle that further escalates the original tension. To achieve this goal, I have suggested anti-anxiety medications, biofeedback, and vigorous exercise routines. Overall, I have found meditation techniques less helpful, since Q_4+ scorers usually find it difficult to sit still. However, the results of an unpublished pilot study that I conducted, in which a group of anxious clients were trained to meditate twice daily, showed statistically significant decreases in their Factor Q_4 scores over a three-week period. Factor Q_4 scores of clients in the control group, who received only supportive and insight therapy, did not decrease significantly.

LOW SCORES ON FACTOR Q_4

Intrapsychic Data

"Relaxed, tranquil, torpid, unfrustrated, and composed" are the adjectives used at the beginning of this chapter to describe this pole. They combine to create what Galen, in the second century A.D., described as the phlegmatic temperament. As a *state,* they describe what most people have experienced, even though fleetingly, as the languorous sensation that follows strenuous exercise, meditation, or a deep, restful sleep. That this state is enjoyable is evident by the frequency with which tranquilizing drugs are abused to achieve it. Certainly, none of my Q_4- examinees complained about their subnormal tension level.

The negative side of being underreactive is that it leaves an individual lacking in vigor and drive. I noted that these qualities were conspicuously absent in many of the Q_4- examinees in my sample. They were contented with their lots in life; they tended to live in the present and did not project themselves too much into the future. Like Q_3- people, they were apt to be unambitious or underachievers, but obviously for different reasons, since Q_4- scorers usually maintained adequate self-images.

Q_4- scores may be obtained falsely when the person is so motivated, and in instances when examinees are out of touch with their bodily sensations. They may also be attained when their anxiety is bound in a physical symptom to which they show "La Belle Indifference."

Social Data

$Q_4 -$ individuals are described by others as "easygoing," or, more colloquially, "laid back." Slow to take offense, easy to get along with, and undemanding, they are rated as comfortable companions by relatives, coworkers, friends, and other acquaintances. Their unruffability is often soothing, sometimes contagious.

Since $Q_4 -$ individuals are difficult to motivate, they can be frustrating to partners and spouses who are worldly and ambitious. Among my clinical sample were several women who were annoyed by their husbands' complacency and unwillingness to exert effort to achieve social or economic success. Conversely, I have noted, as Barton and Cattell (1972) observed, that $Q_4 -$ women as a rule seem quite happily married. Since I conjecture that this may be at least partly due to their acceptant natures, I find it hard to hypothesize about why a similar association between $Q_4 -$ scores and happy marriages was not found in men.

Teachers complained to me about their difficulty in motivating $Q_4 -$ students, as did employers and supervisors about $Q_4 -$ employees. However, even though these persons were lacking the optimal level of anxiety considered necessary for attaining good performance standards, they were not usually lackadaisical or inclined to turn in sloppy work unless they were also lacking in superego $(G -)$ or self-sentiment $(Q_3 +)$ development.

$Q_4 -$ and Childhood

As yet I have not discovered any reliable connections, either in my observations or in the literature, between childhood experiences and low tension scores in later adulthood. It remains an open question, therefore, as to what predisposes the acquisition of a relaxed temperament. Some $Q_4 -$ children whom I have observed could be described as lethargic rather than relaxed. While the lethargy of some resulted from poor physical health, in others I could find no environmental or physical explanations for their behavior.

Important Correlations Between Q_4- Scores and Other 16PF Factor Scores

Table 17.2 portrays typical Q_4- persons as also having, above all, high self-esteem $(O-)$ and strong ego $(C+)$—a combination that, as I have proposed in previous chapters, bespeaks of overly strong defense mechanisms. The pattern of correlations indicates that Q_4- individuals are also apt to have socially approved self-concepts (Q_3+), to be trusting and secure $(L-)$, and to underreact to threatening stimuli $(H+)$.

Table 17.2

Important Correlations Between Q_4- Scores and Other 16PF Factor Scores

Factor Pole	Correlation	Possible Associated Traits Indicated by Correlation
O – (Untroubled Adequacy)	.61	Self-assured, Placid, Secure, Complacent, Serene
C + (High Ego Strength)	.59	Emotionally Stable, Mature, Faces Reality, Calm
Q₃ + (High Self-sentiment)	.42	Controlled, Exacting Will Power, Socially Precise, Compulsive
L – (Alaxia)	.38	Trusting, Accepting Conditions
H + (Parmia)	.33	Venturesome, Uninhibited, Socially Bold

These associated characteristics provide an image of the typical Q_4- scorer as someone who has a positive and relaxed self-attitude. The sense of well-being he or she enjoys, however, may be based somewhat on maintaining strong ego defenses.

Clinical Relevance of Q_4- Scores

Gautama Buddha is probably the quintessence of the relaxed, tranquil, unfrustrated, characteristics that Q_4- scores measure. The Buddha, in his own life, extinguished desire and proposed that others should do the same, to avoid suffering. He reasoned that inasmuch as desire leads to emotional attachments to objects and people, which are all transitory because by nature they are inevitably subject to loss (thus leading to pain), it is better not to have the desire that puts this melancholy wheel in motion.

If my Q_4- examinees—here I am referring to those whose lack of tension was a trait—seemed not to have extinguished their desires, they seemed at least to have dampened them. Although they did not experience the exuberance and joy that accompanies the gratification of strongly felt desires, neither did they suffer the corresponding level of disappointment, grief, or loss when they were not satisfied. Whether or not one opts to live this way is a value judgment best left to personal predilection. From a clinical perspective, I have found a link between Q_4- scores and psychological disturbance, *only* when they are combined with other scores. When these combinations, of which I have noted three, are found in a profile, they merit the clinician's further inquiry.

Q_4- *(Low Tension) and O− (High Self-Esteem)*. Although Q_4- and O− scores are often found together on the same profile, due to their intercorrelation in the general population, it is always useful to consider them in terms of a given examinee's life situation.

O− scores (stens of 1, 2, or 3) indicate strong defensive mechanisms. When these scores appear in profiles of examinees in difficult or stressful situations, these individuals may be dangerously distorting reality to the point that they are failing to protect themselves or to take necessary precautions. When Q_4- scores also appear in the profile, this possibility merits even further suspicion, because of the inappropriateness of their low tension levels.

Q_4- *(Low Tension) and L+ (High Protension)*. Usually, high scores on Factor L are seen with high scores on Factor Q_4. L+ scores indicate suspiciousness, jealousy, hypervigilance, and insecurity—feelings and responses that are sharply inconsistent with physical relaxation. It is likely that persons whose profiles show this combination are unaware of their body sensations, as I have discovered from observations of examinees in my sample. Their attention was so riveted on the outer world that they failed to pay sufficient attention to their own physical clues to be able to interpret them correctly.

Q_4- *(Low Tension) and O+ (Guilt Proneness)*. Examinees whose profiles show this combination are reporting, on the one hand, that they are plagued by self-doubt, worry, disturbed sleep, and apprehension $(O+)$. On the other hand, their Q_4- scores reveal that their level of autonomic arousal is abnormally low. This combination suggests the psychomotor retardation that frequently accompanies depression.

My policy, therefore, upon discovering Q_4- and $O+$ scores in a profile is to administer the Clinical Analysis Questionnaire (CAQ) to the examinee. Without exception, all 27 examinees tested by this method had some elevation on the Factor D_4 scale, indicating depressive fatigue and weariness.

Chapter 18

The Second-Order Factors:
The Underlying Organizers of Temperament

OVERVIEW OF THE SECOND-ORDER FACTORS IN THE 16PF

Extraversion vs. Introversion

High Anxiety vs. Low Anxiety

Tough Poise vs. Emotionality

Independence vs. Subduedness

High Control vs. Low Control

OVERVIEW OF THE SECOND-ORDER FACTORS IN THE 16PF

Since traits tend to fall into certain predictable patterns, a factor analysis of the correlations of the 16 primary factors discussed in Chapters 2 through 17 reliably reveals a number of second-order factors, though only the five largest are included in the 16PF. These are: extraversion, anxiety, tough poise, independence, and control.[1]

As with the primary factors, second-order factor scores utilize the sten scale (1-10). After converting the raws to corrected stens, the score for each relevant primary factor is weighted and added together to obtain the second-order factor sten score. Worksheets for this purpose are available from the test publisher.

A quick glance at the second-order factor stens on any given profile provides the interpreter with an immediate overall insight into the examinee's style. Specifically, they indicate whether the examinee is, on the whole, outgoing or reserved, anxious or comfortable, primarily emotional and intuitive or unemotional, dependent or independent, and high or low on self-control.

Consequently, when interpreting a profile, it is useful to note the second-order factor scores before continuing at an examination of the primary factors. I have come to see them as analogous to the first broad outline created by an artist's brush *before* the canvas is filled in with the details, contrasts, and highlights that give the picture its final form. This outline, though rough, foreshadows the particulars to come. The outline also provides a general framework for organizing pieces of information as they are gleaned from each primary factor interpretation.

The remainder of this chapter is broken into five sections, each of which describes a specific second-order factor.

Extraversion vs. Introversion

The largest second-order factor is the familiar extraversion vs. introversion pattern. Though generally recognized as closely matching Jung's construct by the same name, what is less obvious is that it is also in accord with Freud's subject (self)/object (external) polarities. Freud's polarities are based on the observation

---

[1]When originally named, Cattell used Roman numerals for the second-order factors. Readers not familiar with the 16PF may confuse these symbols with the primary factor symbols, Q_1, Q_2, Q_3, and Q_4, which use Arabic numerals. For that reason, I shall refer to the second-order factor right pole in naming these factors.

that pleasure can be obtained from one's own reverie, ideas, and imagination, as well as by interacting with the environment. In terms of individual differences, the empirical evidence from research on this factor is that most people come to prefer one of these modes of gratification over the other.

As it has been mentioned in preceding chapters, a person's score on extraversion strongly influences how various other traits are expressed. Thus, in addition to indicating the examinee's level of expressiveness and tendencies toward being either outwardly or inwardly focused, the second-order extraversion score provides an illuminating backdrop for interpreting primary factor scores. For instance, in Chapter 11 it was noted that when an M+ (autia) score appears with extraversion, it can be assumed that the examinee will be inclined to freely share personal insights, ideas, and thoughts with other people. Similarly, an introverted examinee with exactly the same M+ score will almost certainly be less communicative.

Table 18.1

Primary Factor Poles Contributing to Extraversion and Introversion

EXTRAVERSION

Primary Factor Pole[1]	Characteristics Involved in Extraversion
Q_2 − (Group Dependency)	Joiner of Groups, Sound Follower
H + (Parmia)	Venturesome, Uninhibited, Socially Bold
F + (Surgency)	Happy-go-lucky, Enthusiastic
A + (Affectothymia)	Outgoing, Warmhearted, Easygoing, Participating

INTROVERSION

Primary Factor Pole	Characteristics Involved in Extraversion
Q_2 + (Self-sufficiency)	Self-sufficient, Resourceful, Prefers Own Decisions
H − (Threctia)	Shy, Timid, Threat Sensitive
F − (Desurgency)	Sober, Taciturn, Serious
A − (Sizothymia)	Reserved, Detached, Critical

[1]All tables in this chapter present the relevant factors in the order of the importance of their contribution to the second-order factor score.

Whether one becomes an extravert or introvert depends upon having the genetic disposition and learning experiences that are particular to the primary factors that make up the wider extraversion pattern. The poles of these primary factors are presented in Table 18.1. Each is listed in order of the weight of its contribution to the extraversion-introversion pattern.

From Table 18.1 it will be seen that typical extraverts are not only oriented towards their environments in both their interests and satisfactions, but that they also have a certain effusive quality. Usually, they are Q_2+ (like to feel a sense of belonging), $F+$ (happy-go-lucky, enthusiastic, and stimulus seeking), $H+$ (venturesome, uninhibited, and socially bold), and $A+$ (outgoing, warmhearted, easygoing, and participating).

On the other hand, introverts tend to show more restraint than extraverts, are less involved with their surroundings, and have fewer social contacts. They are likely to be Q_2- (self-sufficient), $F-$ (sober, cautious, and taciturn), $H-$ (shy and easily intimidated), and $A-$ (emotionally and socially reserved).

There are certain ways that the primary factor scores can be different from both the extraverted and introverted patterns shown in Table 18.1. First, a person can get an extreme score on a factor that does not contribute as much to a second-order score as another factor might be expected to contribute. For example, in the extraverted pattern, the person may get a higher score on Factor A—normally the lowest contributor to extraversion— while getting a more moderate score on Factor Q_2—normally the largest contributor when the score is at the left extreme. Thus, the rank order contribution of each of these two primary factors to the second-order factor is reversed. An examinee whose primary scores show this transposition will be more genuinely social and less dependent on support from others than the usual extravert.

Another way that primary scores depart from the standard pattern occurs when the relevant primary scores reflect both the extraverted and introverted camps. There are common combinations of this kind, and I have found them to indicate socially ambivalent attitudes. One combination shows *extraverted* $A+$ (affectothymia) and Q_2- (group dependence), with *introverted* $F-$ (desurgency) and $H-$ (threctia) scores. Examinees whose profiles show this configuration are gregariously inclined and enjoy the physical presence and support of others, while at the same time feeling socially inhibited, timid, and shy. They frequently report that they would like more companionship.

Another relevant combination reverses the above pattern. It combines *introverted* A− (sizothymic) and Q_2+ (self-sufficiency) scores with *extraverted* F+ (surgent) and H+ (parmia) scores. Examinees with these scores lack warmth and have a low need for social belonging, but are attention getting and bold. Sometimes they are exploitive in their interpersonal relationships.

High Anxiety vs. Low Anxiety

Not only do people differ in the *intensity* of the discomfort they experience when presented with external threat, but they also differ in the internal noxious stimuli that they generate for themselves, in the form of worry and tension, for example. These differences are measured by the second-order anxiety factor.

Table 18.2 below presents the six primary factors that typically make up this factor. Here again, and throughout this chapter's tables, each factor is listed in order of the contribution it makes to the second-order pattern.

What is measured by the high pole corresponds to anxiety, both as it is commonly understood and with factor-analytic research findings (Cattell & Scheier, 1961; Rickels & Cattell, 1965). The primary factors that contribute to anxiety convey the usual complex of dysphoric feelings, with unpleasant thoughts and sensations, that anxious people report. When the entire pattern is present in a profile, it contains $O+$ (being beset by worry, apprehension, and self-reproach), Q_4+ (physical tension), $C−$ (being easily upset and having poor tolerance for frustration), $Q_3−$ (self-image problems), $L+$ (alienation and mistrust), and $H−$ (feeling oversensitive to environmental stimuli).

Anxiety can be characterological (a trait), but it can also be a passing reaction (a state). While it is not possible to confidently discern which of these conditions is reflected in a given examinee's second-order anxiety factor score, some clues can be gained from the magnitude of the individual scores from which it is composed. When $C−$ (lower ego strength) and $Q_3−$ (low self-sentiment) scores are prominent contributors, it is more apt in my experience to reflect characterological anxiety, as ego strength and self-sentiment strength are unlikely to fluctuate in response to changes in mood. Of course, it is also helpful, when attempting to decide if the score reflects a trait or state, to know if the examinee is presently facing an anxiety-provoking situation.

The low anxiety pattern in Table 18.2 shows a complex of feelings, thoughts, and sensations opposite to anxiety. Examinees who score at this pole typically are Q_4- (relaxed and composed), $O-$ (self-assured and complacent), $C+$ (in control of their emotions and tolerant of frustration), and $L-$ (secure and accepting). They are also $H+$ (bold) and Q_3+ (are maintaining socially approved self-images).

Table 18.2

**Primary Factor Poles Contributing to High Anxiety
and Low Anxiety**

HIGH ANXIETY

Primary Factor Pole	Characteristics Involved in High Anxiety
$O+$ (Guilt Proneness)	Apprehensive, Self-reproaching, Insecure, Worrying Troubled
Q_4+ (Ergic Tension)	Tense, Frustrated, Driven, Overwrought
$C-$ (Lower Ego Strength)	Affected by Feelings, Emotionally Upset, Changeable
Q_3- (Low Self-sentiment)	Lax, Follows Own Urges, Careless of Social Rules
$L+$ (Protension)	Suspicious, Hard to Fool
$H-$ (Threctia)	Shy, Timid, Threat Sensitive

LOW ANXIETY

Primary Factor Pole	Characteristics Involved in Low Anxiety
$O-$ (Untroubled Adequacy or Low Guilt Proneness)	Self-assured, Placid, Secure, Complacent, Serene
Q_4- (Low Ergic Tension)	Relaxed, Tranquil, Unfrustrated, Composed
$C+$ (Higher Ego Strength)	Emotionally Stable, Mature, Faces Reality, Calm
Q_3+ (Higher Strength of Self-sentiment)	Controlled, Exacting Will Power, Socially Precise, Compulsive
$L-$ (Alaxia)	Trusting, Accepting Conditions
$H+$ (Parmia)	Venturesome, Uninhibited, Socially Bold

Although what has just been described seems to be a highly desirable psychological condition in terms of emotional comfort, it also has a down side. It can be associated with lack of motivation, as is noted in the following quotation from the *Administrator's Manual for the 16PF* (1986).

> People who score low on this factor tend to be those whose lives are generally satisfying, and those who are able to achieve those things that seem to them to be important. However, an extremely low score can mean lack of motivation for difficult tasks, as is generally shown in studies relating anxiety to achievement. (p. 26)

In interpreting a second-order anxiety score, it can be particularly useful to look for relevant primary factor scores that are not consistent with the standard pattern detailed in Table 18.2. One inconsistency I look for, in particular, is omission of a Q_4+ (ergic tension) score from an anxiety constellation. This failure to report tension even though the other symptoms of anxiety are present may indicate that the examinee is out of touch with physical sensations. Occasionally, it means that he or she is becoming catatonic.

Tough Poise vs. Emotionality

The main practical value that comes from knowing a person's tough poise/emotionality score is that it conveys what is likely to be meaningful to that person and how he or she processes information. This is particularly useful for clinicians when predicting the kind of approach to which a given client is apt to be most responsive. In building a therapeutic alliance, for example, clients high on tough poise respond best when they are told about established facts and presented with practical solutions that make sense. Clients who lean more to emotionality, however, are usually more influenced by a sympathetic and imaginative approach that acknowledges their feelings and appeals to their intuitive understanding.

Tough poise has been shown to align with another expression of the same factor—U.I. 22 Cortertia in the Objective-Analytic Battery, from which this 16PF factor originally got its name. (See Appendix C for a description of the Objective-Analytic Battery.) Cortertia is an abbreviation of "cortical alertness," indicating a high level of cortical activation as manifested by alertness to environmental stimuli. Tough poise has been experimentally demonstrated to exist by Hundleby, Pawlik, and Cattell (1965) in tests linking it to short flicker fusion and high electroencephlogram alpha waves. In the same research, repeated testing of the subjects over a three-month period has shown tough poise to have a stability coefficient of .80, which establishes it as an enduring personality characteristic rather than a passing state.

Persons who score at the low pole (emotionality) lack cortical acuity. Less responsive to external stimuli, they are attuned to their subjective responses, especially their feelings. They therefore tend to have contemplative temperaments, leading them to be aware of the vagaries and subtleties of life. These qualities place them in marked contrast to their "tough-poised" opposites, who incline more toward a "readiness to operate and handle problems at a dry, cognitive level" (Cattell, Eber, & Tatsuoka, 1970).

These differences between tough poise and emotionality are discernible from Table 18.3 below, which depicts the typical high-scoring person of both sexes as primarily someone who is $I-$ (realistic and unemotional), $A-$ (coolly detached from people), $M-$ (practically oriented toward the environment), and $F+$ (exuberant). By contrast, the low scorer is depicted as $I+$ (sensitive and emotionally responsive), $M+$ (imaginative and reflective), $A+$ (warmly involved with people), and $F-$ (serious).

Table 18.3 differs from the two preceding tables in this chapter in that it shows the contribution of primary factors separately for men and women. It shows that the tough poise pattern includes $I-$, $A-$, and $F-$ for both sexes. In addition, however, the male pattern involves Q_1-. For females, $E+$ and $L+$ also contribute. These differences indicate that tough poise and emotionality do not follow parallel lines in men and women. High-scoring men tend towards a conservative way of thinking (Q_1-) not typically present in high-scoring women. Although Q_1+ scores do not enter into the female pattern, women who score high on tough poise are inclined to be $E+$ (dominant) and $L+$ (suspicious). This means they may have a certain defensive, possibly aggressive, quality not shared by their male counterparts. Maybe this is because handling problems at a dry, cognitive level (tough poise) goes against the cultural feminine stereotype.

Along the same lines, the low-scoring emotionality pattern in women is augmented by $E-$ (submissiveness) and $L-$ (alaxia).

Table 18.3
Primary Factor Poles Contributing to Tough Poise and Emotionality

TOUGH POISE

Primary Factor Pole	Characteristics Involved in Tough Poise
Males	
I – (Harria)	Tough-minded, Self-reliant, Realistic
M – (Praxernia)	Practical, "Down to Earth," Concerned
A – (Sizothymia)	Reserved, Detached, Critical, Aloof, Stiff
Q_1 – (Conservatism)	Conservative, Respecting Traditional Ideas
F + (Surgency)	Happy-go-lucky, Enthusiastic
Females	
I – (Harria)	Tough-minded, Self-reliant, Realistic
M – (Praxernia)	Practical, "Down to Earth," Concerned
E + (Dominance)	Dominant, Assertive, Aggressive, Stubborn, Competitive, Bossy
F + (Surgency)	Happy-go-lucky, Enthusiastic
L + (Protension)	Suspicious, Distrustful, Skeptical
A – (Sizothymia)	Reserved, Detached, Critical, Aloof, Stiff

EMOTIONALITY

Primary Factor Pole	Characteristics Involved in Emotionality
Males	
I + (Premsia)	Tender-minded, Sensitive, Overprotected
M + (Autia)	Imaginative, Absent-minded
A + (Affectothymia)	Outgoing, Warmhearted, Easygoing, Participating
Q_1 + (Radicalism)	Experimenting, Liberal, Free Thinking
F – (Desurgency)	Sober, Taciturn, Serious
Females	
I + (Premsia)	Tender-minded, Sensitive, Clinging, Overprotected
M + (Autia)	Imaginative, Absent-minded

Table 18.3 concluded on next page.

Table 18.3 *(Concluded)*

Primary Factor Pole	Characteristics Involved in Emotionality
E – (Submissiveness)	Humble, Mild, Easily Led, Docile, Accommodating
F – (Desurgency)	Sober, Taciturn, Serious
L – (Alaxia)	Trusting, Accepting Conditions
A + (Affectothymia)	Outgoing, Warmhearted, Easygoing, Participating

These unassertive and self-effacing qualities undoubtedly under-score these women's emotionality. The low-scoring pattern in men, instead of E – and L –, includes $Q_1 +$ (radicalism).

Independence vs. Subduedness

Table 18.4 below shows the primary factor correlations contributing to high and low poles for men and women separately. Again, the pattern seems to be largely similar, but somewhat different for men and women.

Independent males and females are E + (dominant and unac-commodating), $Q_1 +$ (radical in their thinking and nontraditional), H + (venturesome and bold), G – (morally nonconforming), and $Q_2 +$ (self-reliant). Women who show this pattern of independence have an added tendency for being more M + (involved with their ideas and inner ponderings than with practical matters). Moreover, they do not necessarily manifest the N – (straightforwardness), L + (suspiciousness), and O – (high self-esteem), which are typical of independent men.

Given the traits listed above, a high score suggests a picture of examinees of both sexes who operate by their own internal guidelines and rely less than most others on conventional standards. If they embrace the prevailing zeitgeist, the probability is that their conclusions were not made by default.

According to its label, low-scoring examinees are subdued as well as dependent. Both male and female examinees who follow the typical low-scoring pattern will be E – (unassertive), $Q_1 –$ (conventional and conservative of temperament), H – (shy and timid), G + (morally conforming), and $Q_2 –$ (needful of the support and presence of others). Women with low scores derived from the constellation in Table 18.4 are also M – (practical and

Table 18.4

Primary Factor Poles Contributing to Independence and Subduedness

INDEPENDENCE

Primary Factor Pole	Characteristics Involved in Independence
Males	
E + (Dominance)	Assertive, Aggressive, Stubborn, Competitive
H + (Parmia)	Venturesome, Uninhibited, Socially Bold
Q_1 + (Radicalism)	Experimenting, Liberal, Free Thinking
L + (Protension)	Suspicious, Hard to Fool
O − (Untroubled Adequacy)	Self-assured, Placid, Secure, Complacent, Serene
N − (Artlessness)	Forthright, Unpretentious, Genuine but Socially Clumsy
G − (Weaker Superego Strength)	Expedient, Disregards Rules
Q_2 + (Self-sufficiency)	Self-sufficient, Resourceful, Prefers Own Decisions
Females	
E + (Dominance)	Assertive, Aggressive, Stubborn, Competitive
Q_1 + (Radicalism)	Experimenting, Liberal, Free Thinking
H + (Parmia)	Venturesome, Uninhibited, Socially Bold
M + (Autia)	Imaginative, Absent-minded
G − (Weaker Superego Strength)	Expedient, Disregards Rules
Q_2 + (Self-sufficiency)	Self-sufficient, Resourceful, Prefers Own Decisions

SUBDUEDNESS

Primary Factor Pole	Characteristics Involved in Emotionality
Males	
E − (Submissiveness)	Humble, Easily Led, Docile, Accommodating
H − (Threctia)	Shy, Timid, Threat Sensitive

Table 18.4 concluded on next page.

Table 18.4 *(Concluded)*

Primary Factor Pole	Characteristics Involved in Emotionality
$Q_1 -$ (Conservatism)	Conservative, Respecting of Traditional Ideas
$L -$ (Alaxia)	Trusting, Accepting Conditions
$O +$ (Guilt Proneness)	Apprehensive, Self-reproaching, Insecure, Worrying, Troubled
$N +$ (Shrewdness)	Polished, Socially Aware
$G +$ (Stronger Superego Strength)	Conscientious, Persistent, Moralistic, Staid
$Q_2 -$ (Group Dependent)	Group Dependent, A "Joiner" and Sound Follower
Females	
$E -$ (Submissiveness)	Humble, Mild, Easily Led, Docile, Accommodating
$Q_1 -$ (Conservatism)	Conservative, Respecting Traditional Ideas
$H -$ (Threctia)	Shy, Timid, Threat Sensitive
$M -$ (Praxernia)	Practical, "Down to Earth" Concerns
$G +$ (Higher Superego Strength)	Conscientious, Persistent, Moralistic, Staid
$Q_2 -$ (Group Dependence)	Group Dependent, "Joiner" and Sound Follower

disinterested in abstractions). Though not $M -$, their male counterparts are $N +$ (socially shrewd), $L -$ (trusting), and $O +$ (self-reproaching).

Thus, given that it is derived from these primaries, the designation of "subduedness" for the left pole makes sense. Together, these qualities suggest a temperamental willingness to submit to societal control out of a need for interpersonal support and external guidelines. This means that, in sharp contradistinction to their independent opposites, examinees who score at the subdued pole need a fair amount of outside structure and feedback in most areas of their lives. In clinical situations, they usually respond well to directions and feel most confident with therapists and counselors who are somewhat authoritarian.

High Control vs. Low Control

The control factor is a recent addition to the set of second-orders routinely scored in the 16PF. Its practical value to the test interpreter is that it conveys how well a given examinee is able to both inhibit impulses and persist in directing his or her behavior along *socially desirable* lines. The social desirability element is what separates the control pattern's primary factors—Factor G (superego strength) and Factor Q_3 (self-sentiment strength)— from the other two 16PF indicators of self-control, namely C + (ego strength) and F − (desurgency). In the first instance, the ego aids self-control by curbing emotional reactivity and by evoking cause-and-effect thinking. It is concerned, however, only in furthering personal gratification. Desurgency likewise is also not necessarily concerned with social rules and values, but rather with avoidance of punishment and personal safety. As a cautious, serious outlook, it exerts self-control primarily by inhibiting impulses.

Table 18.5

**Primary Factor Poles Contributing to High Control
and Low Control**

HIGH CONTROL	
Primary Factor Pole	**Characteristics Involved in High Control**
G + (Superego Strength)	Conscientious, Persistent, Moralistic Staid
Q_3 + (Self-sentiment Strength)	Controlled, Exacting Will Power, Socially Precise, Compulsive
LOW CONTROL	
Primary Factor Pole	**Characteristics Involved in Low Control**
G − (Weaker Superego Strength)	Expedient, Disregards Rules
Q_3 − (Weaker Self-sentiment Strength)	Lax, Follows Own Urges, Careless of Social Rules

High Control. As already discussed, the high control pattern arises from a combination of high scores on Factor G (superego strength) and Factor Q_3 (self-sentiment strength). Consequently, examinees achieving high control scores base their morals and personal standards on mainstream values. Typically, they show interest in maintaining a respectable public image—persistence, staidness, strong will power, and conscientiousness. Compulsivity and rigidity are also characteristics commonly encountered in those individuals.

Low Control. A low score requires more care to interpret than a high score, since the lack of socialization into the cultural mainstream that it indicates may occur for more than one reason, and therefore may have quite different implications. Thus, a low-scoring examinee may or may not be without moral restraint, and may be either concerned or unconcerned about personal standards. He or she may just simply hear and march to a different cultural drum.

In evidence of this fact, the reader may remember from previous chapters (Chapters 7 and 16) that the "$-$" poles of Factor G (superego strength) and Factor Q_3 (self-sentiment strength), from which the low control pattern is derived, tap various psychological conditions. A G$-$ score does not necessarily mean poor superego development, for it can be achieved by people who have strong but unconventional morals. Similarly, although a Q_3- score usually indicates social identity problems, it may sometimes be achieved by persons who are quite simply not self-centered.

Even when a given examinee's low score does indeed mean lack of self-sentiment and superego strength, it does not mean he or she is without self-control. If the profile also shows C$+$ (ego strength) and/or F$-$ (desurgency) scores, then it can be assumed that the examinee is able, in the first instance, to act rather than react and in the second, to exercise caution.

However, a low score accompanied by a C$+$ score can occasionally point to sociopathic tendencies. The example below illustrates sociopathic behavior by a woman who showed this pattern. She achieved her objective precisely because she was able to use her ego strength to solve the problem on hand and did not experience shame and guilt associated with a normally developed superego or self-sentiment.

> *Example:* The woman, Ms. Z, explained how she had gotten a salesperson to violate store policy by refunding her money for a garment she had bought and worn. Initially the salesperson refused to accept the garment,

pointing out that only unworn merchandise could be returned. Ms. Z then considered various strategies to get the salesperson to change her mind, and decided that embarrassing her by causing a scene would probably work best. She thereupon burst into loud, pitiful sobs, arousing the attention of other customers, who flocked around her to see what her distress was about. She explained, between sobs, to all who would listen, that she was being treated rudely, that she was a single parent and needed the refund money to feed her children, and that she had never worn the garment (all lies). The red-faced salesclerk quickly handed Ms. Z the refund money and hurried her out of the store.

Appendixes

APPENDIX A

The Discovery of the Sixteen Personality Factors
by Factor-Analytic Techniques
and the Subsequent Development of the 16PF

APPENDIX B

Factor Analysis

APPENDIX C

Major Psychological Tests Based on Cattell's
Multivariate Experimental Research

APPENDIX D

Determining Heredity by Multivariate Abstract Variance
Analysis (MAVA) Methods

APPENDIX E

Motivational Distortion/Validity Scales

APPENDIX A

The Discovery of the Sixteen Personality Factors by Factor-Analytic Techniques and the Subsequent Development of the 16PF

The 16PF (Sixteen Personality Factor Questionnaire) purports to measure the full complement of temperament traits rather than just a few of them. Prior to its development, therefore, the human temperament had to be completely mapped out. This ambitious task was undertaken by Cattell and his coworkers at the University of Illinois in 1943. After following Allport's lead of listing all dictionary descriptions of human behavior and deleting synonyms, they empirically tested the correspondence of these adjectives with actual behavior by asking observers to rate a sample of subjects on them. A factor analysis was then performed on the results.

This first factor analysis revealed only 12 factors. These were indexed A through O. But later, when questions were made up for these factors and administered, not as ratings, but as a self-report questionnaire to a group of subjects, an additional four factors were found in the subsequent factor analyses. These were indexed Q_1, Q_2, Q_3, and Q_4. Since they appeared only from subjective data, it was obvious that these factors were measuring internal, covert responses that were without obvious external manifestations.

The existence of all sixteen factors, and the seven second-order factors which can be calculated from them, was repeatedly replicated in later factorings of new data obtained from other samples of subjects. These findings and several refinements of questions led to the final construction and publication of the 16PF in 1949. Translated into numerous languages, such as German, Chinese, Italian, Spanish, and French, the structure of the 16PF factors has been confirmed in over 20 different cultural groups. Cattell also created the High School Personality Questionnaire (HSPQ) for adolescents, and the Children's Personality Questionnaire (CPQ) for children.

Meanwhile, a considerable array of everyday life criteria is becoming increasingly available from weighted combinations of 16PF scores. This makes it possible to use an examinee's test results to predict his or her suitability for a particular career or compatibility with other types of persons, to name just two examples. The 16PF can be used for many other purposes, therefore, in addition to its use as a test for clinical assessment.

Suggested Reading:

Cattell, R. B., Eber, H. W., & Tatsuoka, M. M. (1970). *Handbook for the Sixteen Personality Factor Questionnaire* (16PF). Champaign, IL: Institute for Personality and Ability Testing, Inc.

APPENDIX B

Factor Analysis

For an introduction to factor analysis for those who are not too knowledgeable about mathematics, readers might like to try *The Essentials of Factor Analysis* by Child (1970). For those who want more depth, I recommend the texts of either Cattell (1978) or Gorsuch (1974). Here, I will give only a thumbnail sketch, based largely on the explanation and examples put forth by Cattell and Child (1975).

The basic premise of factor analysis is that when several variables consistently intercorrelate (i.e., when their magnitudes grow, diminish, or disappear together), there is an underlying reason. For example, when plants begin to sprout in the spring, trees show their leaves, and hibernating or migrating animals return and propagate, these simultaneous events are caused by the underlying factor of the sun's position relative to that region on the earth.

Using oxygen deficiency as another example, a reduction in the oxygen supply to human organisms brings about corresponding or "concomitant" changes in body functions. Mental and physical activities degenerate, the hemoglobin level in the blood drops, respiration rate increases, and fatigue develops. While one or several of these symptoms might occur in response to other abnormal conditions, some *unique* blend of these symptoms will be characteristic of oxygen deficiency.

The purpose of factor analysis, therefore, is to show which variables do, in fact, interrelate—and the extent of this interrelationship. Consequently, it can be defined as a search for the hidden, deeper variables underlying, causing, or influencing an observed concomitant variation of more observable or superficial variables, and an estimate of the degree of each one's involvement.

Suppose we observed six variables in a particular situation—there is a great advantage in taking several when we want a more rounded notion of how phenomena interact in a real life situation. Let's label the variables A to F, as seen in the table below. This table is a *factor matrix,* which is the first result of a factor analysis that tries to identify factors that underlie these six variables.

Variables (tests, devices, items, etc.)	Factors		
	I	II	III
A	.52	.12	.08
B	.40	.02	.02
C	.35	− .10	.11
D	.35	.15	.71
E	.10	.45	.50
F	.05	.70	.00

Notice that three factors, Factors I, II, and III, are found in this example. Using well-defined criteria, it is possible to specify the number of factors which will tell us all we want to know about the interrelationships of the variables. This process is called *extracting* factors.

The figures within the table are, in effect, correlations, called *factor loadings*. These loadings can have either positive or negative values between + 1 and − 1, as correlation coefficients do. Numbers closer to + 1 or − 1 reflect a greater degree of relationship between the variable and the factor than do numbers closer to zero.

It is important to determine how big a loading must be for it to be considered statistically significant. Sample size, or the number of subjects in the experiment, is a consideration; but as a rough guide, values less than .15 are rarely entertained; and, more commonly, values should be greater than .25.

Looking again at the example, it will be seen that all the high values have been blocked off for the three factors. Variables *A, B, C,* and *D* have something in common and contribute to Factor I (we ignore *E* and *F* in discussing Factor I, except to say that they do not figure in it). Observe in Factor III the inclusion of two variables, *D* and *E,* already involved in the other factors, showing that it is quite possible for a variable to be related to more than one factor. Using the oxygen deficiency example again, suppose that *D* was a measure of respiration rate and *E* a self-rating of fatigue. If the first factor were, shall we say, the factor containing the symptoms of oxygen deficiency, then D and E would certainly correlate with Factor I. But, should we label the third factor *Anxiety,* it is understandable why D and E would also load on that factor. This is an illustration of the way in which factor analysis subtly teases out dual functions that might never have appeared in bivariate analysis.

There are two methods for doing factor analysis: in one, the factors may be unrelated, and in the other, partly correlated. The former, i.e., unrelated, procedure is called an *orthogonal solution* and the latter, an *oblique solution*. Cattell's method is always to seek oblique solutions. He claims that, while orthogonal solutions have their uses, they do tend to ignore the fact that most aspects of human behaviors are related to some extent.

Suggested Readings:

Cattell, R. B. (1978). *The Scientific Study of Factor Analysis.* New York: Plenum.

Child, D. (1970). *The Essentials of Factor Analysis.* London: Holt Rinehart & Winston.

Gorsuch, R. L. (1974). *Factor Analysis.* Philadelphia: Sanders.

APPENDIX C

Major Psychological Tests,* Based on Cattell's Multivariate Experimental Research

Clinical Analysis Questionnaire, CAQ

Although hypotheses about pathological syndromes (especially anxiety, neurosis, and effects of poor socialization) can be suggested from certain combinations of its scores, the 16PF does not clearly identify psychosis or depression. Thus, to discern these features, 12 scales from factor-analytically identified traits were added to the existing 16PF scales to create the CAQ, Clinical Analysis Questionnaire.

These additional scales resulted from factoring items from reliable and valid depression assessment questionnaires. The resulting 12 scales appear in the CAQ as D_1, Hypochondriasis; D_2, Suicidal Depression; D_3, Agitation; D_4, Anxious Depression; D_5, Low Energy Depression; D_6, Guilt and Resentment; and D_7, Boredom and Withdrawal; Pa, Paranoia; Pp, Psychopathic Deviation; Sc, Schizophrenia; As, Psychasthenia; and Ps Psychological Inadequacy.

The clinical advantage to be gained by combining pathological and normal personality scales into a single test is that it shows how symptoms interact with basic personality structure. In this context, examinees, rather than being defined by diagnosis, can be understood as individuals who have different strengths and shortcomings, cognitive styles, and ways of relating to people—all of which is important information for clinicians developing individualized treatment plans.

Like the 16PF, the CAQ is constructed as a questionnaire with one or two responses available for each question. It has the same scoring procedures, and also uses the sten scale. However, unlike the 16PF, the pathology scales do not have quite the same bipolar nature. *On the whole,* high scores on Part II of the CAQ signify presence of psychic discomfort.

Figure C.1 shows the profile of a 26-year-old schizophrenic woman.

*All test materials available, to qualified professionals, from Institute for Personality and Ability Testing, Inc., P.O. Box 188, Champaign, Illinois 61824-0188. Tel: (217) 352-4739.

STANDARD TEN SCORE (STEN)

FACTOR	Raw Score Form A	Raw Score Form B	TOTAL	STEN	LOW SCORE DESCRIPTION	HIGH SCORE DESCRIPTION
A				4	Reserved, detached, critical, aloof, stiff (Sizothymia)	Warmhearted, easygoing, outgoing, participating (Affectothymia)
B				6	Less intelligent, concrete-thinking (Lower scholastic mental capacity)	More intelligent, abstract-thinking, bright (Higher scholastic mental capacity)
C				3	Affected by feelings, emotionally less stable, easily upset (Lower ego strength)	Emotionally stable, mature, faces reality, calm (Higher ego strength)
E				2	Humble, mild, accommodating, conforming (Submissiveness)	Assertive, aggressive, stubborn, competitive (Dominance)
F				2	Sober, prudent, taciturn, serious (Desurgency)	Happy-go-lucky, enthusiastic, impulsively lively (Surgency)
G				5	Expedient, disregards rules, feels few obligations (Weaker superego strength)	Conscientious, persistent, moralistic, staid (Stronger superego strength)
H				1	Shy, timid, threat-sensitive, restrained, diffident (Threctia)	Venturesome, uninhibited, socially bold (Parmia)
I				7	Tough-minded, self-reliant, realistic (Harria)	Tender-minded, sensitive, overprotected (Premsia)
L				7	Trusting, adaptable, free of jealousy, easy to get on with (Alaxia)	Suspicious, hard to fool, self-opinionated (Protension)
M				8	Practical, "down-to-earth" concerns, regulated by external realities (Praxernia)	Imaginative, absent-minded, careless of practical matters (Autia)
N				5	Forthright, unpretentious, genuine but socially clumsy (Artlessness)	Shrewd, polished, socially aware, calculating (Shrewdness)
O				7	Self-assured, placid, secure, complacent, serene (Untroubled adequacy)	Apprehensive, self-reproaching, insecure, worrying, troubled (Guilt proneness)
Q1				5	Conservative, respecting traditional ideas (Conservatism of temperament)	Experimenting, liberal, analytical (Radicalism)
Q2				7	Group-dependent, a "joiner" and sound follower (Group adherence)	Self-sufficient, resourceful, prefers own decisions (Self-sufficiency)
Q3				3	Undisciplined self-conflict, lax, follows own urges, careless of social rules (Low integration)	Controlled, exacting will power, socially precise, compulsive (High strength of self-sentiment)
Q4				7	Relaxed, tranquil, unfrustrated, composed (Low ergic tension)	Tense, frustrated, driven, overwrought (High ergic tension)

PART II

	Score	Part I (Low pole)	Part II (High pole)
D1	6	Is happy, mind works well, does not find ill health frightening (Low hypochondriasis)	Shows overconcern with bodily functions, health, or disabilities (High hypochondriasis)
D2	8	Is contented about life and surroundings, has no death wishes (Zestfulness)	Is disgusted with life, harbors thoughts of acts of self-destruction (Suicidal disgust)
D3	4	Avoids dangerous and adventurous undertakings, has little need for excitement (Low brooding discontent)	Seeks excitement, is restless, takes risks, tries new things (High brooding discontent)
D4	7	Is calm in emergency, confident about surroundings, poised (Low anxious depression)	Has disturbing dreams, is clumsy in handling things, tense, easily upset (High anxious depression)
D5	9	Shows enthusiasm for work, is energetic, sleeps soundly (High energy euphoria)	Has feelings of weariness, worries, lacks energy to cope (Low energy depression)
D6	6	Is not troubled by guilt feelings, can sleep no matter what is left undone (Low guilt and resentment)	Has feelings of guilt, blames himself for everything that goes wrong, is critical of himself (High guilt and resentment)
D7	9	Is relaxed, considerate, cheerful with people (Low bored withdrawal)	Avoids interpersonal contact, shows discomfort with people (High bored withdrawal)
Pa	7	Is trusting, not bothered by jealousy or envy (Low paranoia)	Believes he is being persecuted, spied on, poisoned, controlled, mistreated (High paranoia)
Pp	4	Avoids engagement in illegal acts or breaking rules, sensitive (Low psychopathic deviation)	Complacent towards own or others' anti-social behavior, is not hurt by criticism (High psychopathic deviation)
Sc	9	Realistically appraises himself and others, shows absence of regressive behavior (Low schizophrenia)	Retreats from reality, has uncontrolled and sudden impulses (High schizophrenia)
As	8	Is not bothered by unwelcome thoughts and ideas or compulsive habits (Low psychasthenia)	Suffers insistent, repetitive ideas and compulsive habits (High psychasthenia)
Ps	9	Considers himself as good, dependable, and smart as most others (Low general psychosis)	Has feelings of inferiority and unworthiness, timid, loses his head easily (High general psychosis)

Copyright © 1975 Institute for Personality and Ability Testing
Reproduced by permission.

Figure C.1
CAQ Profile of Schizophrenic Woman

Motivation Analysis Test, MAT

The Motivation Analysis Test, or MAT (Cattell, Horn, Sweney, & Radcliffe, 1964), though derived from the same principle of objective performance measurements upon which the O-A Battery is based, differs from that instrument by using only subtests that specifically assess *incentive* for achieving gratification.

The 10 factors that compose the MAT were selected because they represent the most common foci of motivation experienced by persons in contemporary Western society. Five factors refer to what Cattell has named "ergs," which he proposes are inborn propensities to seek biological goals. These are toward sex (Ma), pugnacity (Pg), assertiveness (As), body narcissism (Na), and security seeking (Fr). The other five factors, which Cattell calls "sentiments," refer to acquired attachments, towards career (Ca), parents (Ho), marital partner (Sw), oneself, especially as a social being (SS), and superego values (SE).

Each of the 10 factors consists of two separate but interconnected parts: an Unintegrated Component and an Integrated Component. The former represents motivation that is subjectively not well recognized, is often preconscious, and is measured by subtests for autistic thinking and naive projection. By contrast, the latter is synonymous with conscious recognition, as manifested in acknowledged interests or intentional goal-seeking behavior, and is measured by subtests for intentional thought screening and for assessing the amount of information acquired in relation to the factor. All subtests are administered by paper and pencil and use the sten scale.

The MAT is not used only for assessing both potential and realized incentive for achieving gratification in the 10 areas delineated above. It is also used for detecting conflict, either in the form of incompatible motivations, e.g., career ambition vs. a liking for rest and relaxation, or conflict towards pursuing a specific goal. The last-mentioned instance is revealed by the appearance of a higher ratio of unintegrated over integrated component scores on the associated factor. Figure C.2 below illustrates the MAT profile of a 41-year-old male alcoholic following medical detoxification but prior to receiving psychological treatment.

The IPAT Culture Fair Intelligence Test, CFIT

The IPAT Culture Fair Intelligence Tests (Cattell & Cattell, 1965) were developed out of the research of Horn and Cattell. The

Figure C.2. MAT Profile: U, I, and Total Scores on All Ten Factors

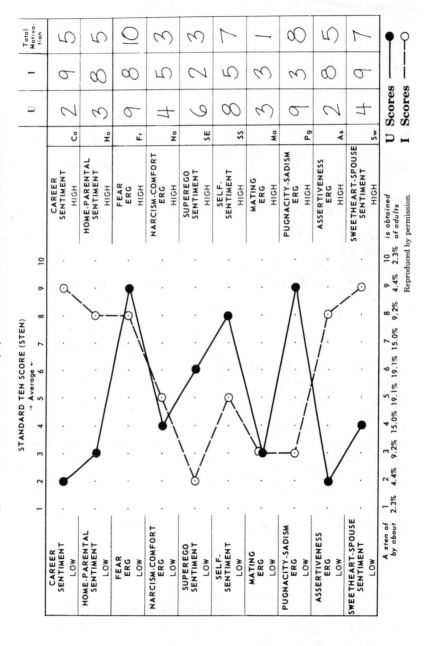

U Scores ●——
I Scores ○---

research is summarized in Cattell's *Intelligence: Its Structure, Growth, and Action* (1987). Cattell and Horn propose that standard tests like the WAIS, WISC, and Binet measure two forms of intelligence: *fluid intelligence* and *crystallized intelligence*. The former is a general, nonspecific, relation-perceiving and understanding capacity, whereas the latter is the product of learning.

In tests that measure both intelligences, because crystallized intelligence is strongly influenced by cultural enrichment, the scores on the subtests which measure it may in some instances inaccurately estimate actual intellectual capacity when computed into the final overall score. On this basis, educationally advantaged people may be assigned a somewhat inflated intelligence quotient. And, more importantly, others who are poorly educated may be assigned an intelligence quotient that seriously underestimates their ability to understand and comprehend.

The purpose of the Culture Fair Intelligence Test (CFIT), as the name implies, is to measure intelligence as free as possible from cultural bias. These scales, therefore, eliminate crystallized intelligence, concentrating only on the fluid intelligence factor. CFIT scales present the examinee with tasks that do not draw on stored information or acquired skills.

There are three forms, or levels, of the CFIT. Scale 1 is intended for children 4 to 8 years of age and is unlike the other scales because it includes some verbal items. Scales 2 and 3 contain four subtests involving different perceptual tasks: completing series, classifying, solving incomplete designs, and evaluating conditions. Since age norms have been developed for Scale 2, it is suitable for use with children 8 years or older, adolescents, and adults. For those exceptionally bright individuals who are anticipated to obtain ceiling scores on Scale 2, Scale 3 may be substituted, for the difficulty level of its items makes it possible to measure intelligence quotients of 140 and above.

All three scales are normally given under timed conditions and can be administered to groups as well as individuals.

Objective-Analytic (O-A) Batteries

In contradistinction to the 16PF and the CAQ, which are founded on data obtained from self-reports and observational ratings of subjects in uncontrolled situations, the O-A batteries (Objective-Analytic Batteries) are derived from experiments that occurred in standardized laboratory situations wherein subjects were presented with tasks and their performances recorded. In one test, typical of others in the experiments, the subjects' GSR rates were recorded while they viewed threatening stimuli, and their memory for details of what they had seen tested later. As this example illustrates, the tests were designed to tap responses outside of conscious control and to eliminate self-evaluations so that subjects were unable to fake, at least in a socially desirable way. This led Cattell to name these tests as "objective."[1]

Factor analysis of these test results yielded numerous factors. Some could be aligned with first- and second-order 16PF factors, while others corresponded to familiar, everyday behavior. Ten factors that Cattell and Schuerger (1978) finally incorporated into the O-A Battery were selected because they could be measured by paper-and-pencil tests rather than by relying on complex or unusual apparatus. These factors are U.I. 16, Ego Standards; U.I. 19, Independence vs. Subduedness; U.I. 20, Evasiveness; U.I. 21, Exuberancy; U.I. 23, Realism vs. Tensidia (Tense Resistance); U.I. 28, Asthenia (Lassitude) vs. Assurance; U.I. 32, Exvia (Extraversion); U.I. 33, Discouragement.

The U.I. which precedes each factor's label stands for *Universal Index,* which is a term borrowed from the physical sciences. Originally, it was used for identifying the O-A factor patterns until such time as appropriate names could be found for them.

Suggested Readings:

Cattell, R. B. (1987). *Intelligence: Its Structure, Growth and Action.* New York: North-Holland.

Cattell, R. B., & Child, D. (1975). *Motivation and Dynamic Structure.* London: Holt Rinehart & Winston.

Cattell, R. B., & Schuerger, J. M. (1978). *Personality Theory in Action: Handbook for the Objective-Analytic (O-A) Test Kit.* Champaign, IL: Institute for Personality and Ability Testing, Inc.

---

[1]The term *objective,* as in a multiple-choice test, could be more precisely called *conspective scoring,* since it refers only to availability of specified, outside criteria which allows different test graders to assign the same scores.

Krug, S. E. (1980). *Clinical Analysis Questionnaire Manual.* (1980). Champaign, IL: Institute for Personality and Ability Testing, Inc.

Schuerger, J. M. (1986). Personality assessment by objective tests. In R. B. Cattell & R. Johnson (Eds), *Functional Psychological Testing.* New York: Brunner/Mazel, pp. 260-287.

APPENDIX D

Determining Heredity by Multivariate Abstract Variance Analysis (MAVA) Methods

Starting with Galton in the 19th century, the method for estimating the influence of heredity on a trait has been by what is called the *twin method,* which compares the difference between identical twins with that between fraternal twins or siblings. The rationale for this method rests on the fact that, since the latter have only 50% of their genes in common, they differ by heredity as well as environmental effects. In contrast, identical twins, who have identical genes, differ only by their exposure to environments. By measuring differences between these paired differences, therefore, it is possible to estimate how much genetics plays a part in personality development.

In the 1960s, however, Cattell developed a more comprehensive method, called Multiple Abstract Variance Analysis (MAVA), which has since been used in analysis of 16PF traits. This method divides the variance (differences from various family groupings) of 16PF scores into abstract genetic and environmental components. Some of the equations are listed below:

$$\sigma_{ITA}^2 = \sigma_E^2 \ ,$$
$$\sigma_{ST}^2 = \sigma_E^2 + \sigma_H^2 \ ,$$
$$\sigma_{UT}^2 = \sigma_H^2 + \sigma_{BFM}^2 + \sigma_E^2 \ .$$

By juggling with such simultaneous equations in which the variable on the left is always directly measurable, one can solve for the abstract variables on the right.

ITA = identical twins raised apart, ST = siblings raised together, UT = unrelated children raised together, BFM = hereditary variance between family members, σ_H = hereditary variance between children in the same family, σ_E = all environmental variance.

APPENDIX E

Motivational Distortion/Validity Scales

Because the 16PF uses the questionnaire method to assess personality, it is potentially subject to sabotage (deliberate attempts by a test-taker to make the test useless) and to motivational role distortion.

Described in the *16PF Handbook,* motivational distortion occurs when the test-taker presents a picture that may be distorted, consciously or unconsciously, by his or her own personality, and by a given testing situation. Motivational distortion refers both to responses that reflect socially desirable behavior as well as to a response set to present a negative picture.

With the 16PF, because Forms C and D were commonly used in occupational selection work, a scale to detect socially desirable responding was included in these forms at the time of their initial development. Scales to measure both types of distortion in Form A were developed by Winder, O'Dell, and Karson (1975). Many objective tests include scales that try to discern whether the test-taker's responses reflected motivational distortion. Often, in other tests as well as in the 16PF, responses in the socially desirable direction have been referred to as "faking good." Presenting a negative picture of oneself has been referred to as "faking bad."

Even though these scales were labeled "faking good" and "faking bad," the reader is encouraged to read further about these 16PF validity scales, because high scores do not necessarily mean that the person consciously "faked" their responses to the test. (See explanations for high scores below.)

For Form A, the faking good and faking bad scales were developed by contrasting groups of people who had completed the 16PF under instruction to fake good or fake bad with people who had completed the test under normal instructions. A Random Scale was also developed, which identifies infrequently chosen responses.

In subsequent research, Krug (1978) developed a sten conversion table for raw scores on the faking good and faking bad scales. He also examined correlations between the primary scales of the 16PF and scores on the validity scales. He found that people tended to get higher scores on extraversion-related factors and lower scores on anxiety-related factors when they got high scores on the faking good scale. Similarly, people with high scores on the faking bad scale seemed to respond in ways that reflected more introversion and anxiety. Given these patterns, Krug then developed a system of modifications to sten scores, based upon scores on the validity scales. Sten scores of 7 or greater on the faking good and faking bad scales will result in modifications of selected primary factor scores. These changes, outlined on the scoring key, are typically not large—never more than two sten-score points, and usually only one.

High Faking Good: Means that the person responded to the questionnaire much like people who were instructed to present a desirable image in responding to the questionnaire.

- High social desirability in responses may be a realistic self-appraisal:

    It may be that, even though the person's score on "faking good" is elevated, the person wasn't "faking" at all. He or she responded to the questions in such a way as to indicate socially desirable behavior, because he or she actually behaves in these ways. In fact, members of the clergy tend to get high scores on this scale.

- Answers may have been deliberately, consciously distorted (sabotage):

    The person may have deliberately answered in a socially desirable way. This is most commonly seen in situations where the person is taking the test in a job-application.

Obviously, then, a high faking good score in itself does not indicate an invalid profile. When the score is high, one should look at the profile to see if there are any elements that are less than desirable. In particular, one should look at the scales most affected by motivational distortion—Factors A, C, F, G, H, L, O, Q_3, and Q_4. For example, if the person admits some self-doubt, tension, social timidity, etc., then the evidence for dismissing the profile as an invalid (all "faked-good") description of the test-taker is greatly reduced.

- Socially desirable answers may reflect the test-taker's self-image, but may or may not reflect behavior:

    The person was answering so as to portray how they actually think they would behave; however, responses that reflect his or her self-image may or may not be in line with actual behavior. Usually, if the self-image is more positive than actual behavior, this type of responding is not a conscious distortion of responses, as the person is not aware of the existence of any discrepancy between their self-perceptions and their actual behavior. It is true that some high-scoring people are very aware of the image they would like to present. This does not mean that their 16PF profile is an inaccurate or invalid picture. Depending on the setting, this quality might actually be positive; some managers, for example, get elevated scores on this scale, but this may contribute to their success (IPAT Staff, 1987).

High Faking Bad: Means that the person responded to the questionnaire much like people who were instructed to present a negative image in responding to the questionnaire.

When elevated faking bad scores are present, the test-taker's answers indicate a significant willingness to be self-critical, sometimes to the point of appearing less than adequate for some life situations. The main reasons for the high degree of socially undesirable responding are:

- a plea for help or an indication of experiencing subjective distress (this may follow the onset of depression or other major disorder);
- an overly critical judgment of oneself, or negative self-evaluation;
- deliberately misleading answers (for instance, to support a claim of psychological disability).

High Scores on Both Scales: On rare occasions, both the faking good and faking bad scales may be elevated. This may be due to careless responding or failure to understand the administration instructions (Walter, 1979). A high random score would tend to confirm the first inference, while the second might be supported by a very low score on Factor B. It also may be that the test-taker does not speak English, or cannot read the questions. When these two scales are both elevated, it would be good for the professional to pursue the matter with the test-taker. Modifications made to the sten scores will largely cancel out when both sets are applied.

High Random Score: Means that the person chose responses that are not usually chosen by people who are taking the questionnaire.

The initial Winder, O'Dell, and Karson research indicated that a raw score of 5 or greater on the Random Scale is significantly high. Krug (1981) points out that elevations on the Random Scale can indicate careless responding to the questionnaire. However, the person may be choosing infrequently endorsed responses because of severe disturbance accompanied by increased anxiety and impaired cognitive functioning.

A practical note: The keys for scoring Form A include a separate key for scoring faking good and faking bad. However, the key does not include the Random Scale. Readers should consult Karson and O'Dell (1976) for instructions on scoring the Random Scale.

Part I of the Clinical Analysis Questionnaire also measures the 16 primary normal personality scales of the 16PF, but Part II of the CAQ adds 12 additional, pathology-oriented scales. In measuring the normal personality scales, however, CAQ Part I does so with 128 items instead of the 187 of the 16PF. Part I of the CAQ contains a validity scale, the "V" scale, that consists of 10 items found to have very infrequently endorsed alternatives (Krug, 1979, 1980). Like the Random Scale for Form A, one explanation of an elevated score (a raw score greater than 3 is considered high) is that the person answered the test in a careless or random manner. However, an elevated score may indicate psychological upset at the time of answering the test. One can also use the 16PF Form A in combination with the Part II of the CAQ (the 12 pathology scales). In this case, one can also score all three of the 16PF Form A validity scales. Again, though, for Part I of the CAQ (128 items), faking-good and faking-bad scores are not available; it contains only the V validity scale.

This material prepared by Mary Russell, 1989.

References:

Cattell, R. B., Eber, H. W., & Tatsuoka, M. M. (1970). *Handbook for the 16PF*. Champaign, IL: IPAT.

IPAT Staff. (1987). *Human resource development report user's guide*. Champaign, IL: IPAT.

Karson, S., & O'Dell, J. W. (1976). *A guide to the clinical use of the 16PF*. Champaign, IL: IPAT.

Krug, S. E. (1978). Further evidence on 16PF distortion scales. *Journal of Personality Assessment, 42*(5), 513-518.

Krug, S. E. (1979). The development of a validity scale for the Clinical Analysis Questionnaire. *Multivariate Experimental Clinical Research, 4*(4), 125-131.

Krug, S. E. (1980). *The Clinical Analysis Questionnaire manual.* Champaign, IL: IPAT.

Krug, S. E. (1981). *Interpreting 16PF profile patterns.* Champaign, IL: IPAT.

Winder, P., O'Dell, J. W., & Karson, S. (1975). New motivational distortion scales for the 16PF. *Journal of Personality Assessment, 39*(5), 532-537.

Walter, V. (1979). *Personal Career Development Profile manual.* Champaign, IL: IPAT.

Bibliography

Adler, A. (1957). *Understanding human nature*. Greenwich, CT: Fawcett.

American Psychiatric Association. (1980). *Diagnostic and statistical manual of mental disorders* (3rd ed.). Washington, DC: Author.

Anthony, E. J. (1975). *Explorations in child psychiatry*. New York: Plenum.

Aronson, E. (1976). *The social animal* (2nd ed.). San Francisco: Freeman.

Aronson, E. (1980). *The social animal* (3rd ed.). San Francisco: Freeman.

Bandura, A. (1977). *Aggression: A social learning analysis*. Englewood Cliffs, NJ: Prentice-Hall.

Barrie, J. M. (1978). *Peter Pan, or the boy who wouldn't grow up*. New York: Scribner's & Sons.

Barton, K., & Cattell, R. B. (1972). Marriage dimensions of personality. *Journal of Personality and Social Psychology, 21*, 369-375.

Barton, K., & Cattell, R. B. (1972a). Real and perceived similarities between spouses: Test of likeness vs. completeness theories. *Psychological Reports, 31*, 15-18.

Barton, K., & Cattell, R. B. (1972b). Personality before and after a chronic illness. *Journal of Clinical Psychology, 28*(4), 464-467.

Barton, K., Dielman, T. E., & Cattell, R. B. (1972). Personality and I.Q. measures as predictors of school achievement. *Journal of Educational Psychology, 63*, 398-404.

Barton, K., Dielman, T. E., & Cattell, R. B. (1973). Child-rearing practices related to child personality. *Journal of Social Psychology, 124*, 293-302.

Beach, F. A. (1948). *Hormones and behavior*. New York: Paul B. Hoeber.

Beller, E. K. (1955). Dependence and independence in young children. *Journal of Genetic Psychology, 87*, 25-35.

Berne, E. (1960). *What do you say after you say hello?* New York: Grove.

Birkett, H. (1980). An experimental study of ego components. In preparation.

Bloom, L. Z., Colburn, K., & Pearlman, J. (1975). *The new assertive woman*. New York: Dell.

Bowlby, J. (1946). *Forty-four juvenile thieves: Their character and home life*. London: Bailliere, Tindal & Cox.

Bowlby, J. (1952). *Maternal care and mental health*. Geneva: World Health Organization.

Bradford, B. T. (1979). *A woman of substance*. New York: Avon Books.

Brewster Smith, M. (1978). Perspectives on selfhood. *American Psychologist, 33*, 1053-1062.

Burdsal, C. A., & Cattell, R. B. (1974). A definitive second order factor analysis of the personality structure in high school age children. *Journal of Genetic Psychology, 124,* 173-177.

Byrne, D. (1969). Attitudes and attraction. In L. Berkowitz (Ed.), *Advances in experimental social psychology: Vol. 4.* New York: Academic Press.

Cameron, N. (1963). *Personality development and psychopathology: A dynamic approach.* Boston: Houghton Mifflin.

Carlsyn, D. A. (1979). Non-pathological personality characteristics of low back pain patients. Doctoral dissertation, University of Washington.

Cattell, H., Tomakawa, S. A., DeRego, F., & Cattell, R. B. (1985). An enquiry into a personality test for overactive children. *Multivariate Experimental Clinical Research, 7,* 103-111.

Cattell, R. B. (1957). *Personality and motivation structure and measurement.* New York: World Book.

Cattell, R. B. (1972). The nature and genesis of mood states: A theoretical model with experimental measurements, concerning anxiety, depression, arousal and other mood states. In C. D. Spielberger (Ed.), *Anxiety: Current trends in theory and research, Vol. 1* (pp. 115-183). New York: Academic Press.

Cattell, R. B. (1973). *Personality and mood by questionnaire.* San Francisco: Jossey-Bass.

Cattell, R. B. (1978). *The scientific use of factor analysis.* New York: Plenum.

Cattell, R. B. (1979). *Personality and learning theory.* (Vol. 1). New York: Springer.

Cattell, R. B. (1982). *The inheritance of personality and ability.* New York: American Press.

Cattell, R. B. (1987). *Intelligence: Its structure, growth and action.* Amsterdam: North Holland Publishers.

Cattell, R. B., & Barton, K. (1975). Changes in personality over a 5-year period: Relationship of change to life events. *JSAS Catalog of Selected Documents in Psychology, 5,* 283. MS #1018.

Cattell, R. B., Barton, K., & Vaughn, G. M. (1973). Changes in personality as a function of college attendance or work experience. *Journal of Counseling Psychology, 20*(2), 162-165.

Cattell, R. B., & Butcher, J. (1968). *The prediction of achievement and creativity.* Indianapolis: Bobbs-Merrill.

Cattell, R. B., & Cattell, A. K. S. (1950). *The IPAT Culture Fair Intelligence Test, Scales 2 and 3.* Champaign, IL: Institute for Personality and Ability Testing.

Cattell, R. B., & Cattell, M. D. (1975). *Handbook for the Junior and Senior High School Personality Questionnaire.* Champaign, IL: Institute for Personality and Ability Testing.

Cattell, R. B., & Child, D. (1975). *Motivation and dynamic structure.* London: Holt, Rinehart & Winston.

Cattell, R. B., Eber, H. W., & Tatsuoka, M. M. (1970). *Handbook for the 16PF.* Champaign, IL: Institute for Personality and Ability Testing.

Cattell, R. B., Horn, J. L., Sweney, A. B., & Radcliffe, J. A. (1964). *Handbook for the Motivation Analysis Test (MAT).* Champaign, IL: Institute for Personality and Ability Testing.

Cattell, R. B., & Nesselroade, J. R. (1969). Likeness and completeness theories examined by Sixteen Personality Factor measures on stably and unstably married couples. *Journal of Personality and Social Psychology, 7,* 351-361.

Cattell, R. B., & Pawlik, K. (1965). The relationship between certain personality factors and measures of cortical arousal. *Neuropsychologia, 3,* 129-151.

Cattell, R. B., & Scheier, I. H. (1962). *The meaning and measurement of neuroticism and anxiety.* New York: Ronald.

Cattell, R. B., & Schuerger, J. M. (1978). *Personality theory in action: Handbook for the Objective-Analytic (O-A) Test Kit.* Champaign, IL: Institute for Personality and Ability Testing.

Cattell, R. B., & Stice, G. F. (1960). *The dimensions of groups and their relation to the behavior of members.* Champaign, IL: Institute for Personality and Ability Testing.

Cattell, R. B., & Wenig, P. (1952). Dynamic and cognitive factors controlling misperception. *Journal of Abnormal & Social Psychology, 47,* 497-809.

Cattell, R. B., Young, H. B., & Hundleby, J. D. (1964). Blood groups and personality traits. *American Journal of Human Genetics, 16,* 397-402.

Checkley, H. (1964). *The mask of sanity.* (4th ed.). St. Louis: Mosby.

Child, D. (1970). *The essentials of factor analysis.* London: Holt, Rinehart & Winston.

Cronbach, L. J. (1970). *Essentials of psychological testing* (3rd ed.). New York: Harper Bros.

Ellis, A. (1975). *How to live with a neurotic* (rev. ed.). New York: Crown.

Erickson, E. (1968). *Identity, youth and crisis.* New York: Norton.

Evans, B. (1968). *Dictionary of quotations collected and arranged.* New York: Delacorte Press. p. 94.

Farley, F. H. (1981). Basic process individual differences: A biologically based theory of individualization for cognitive, affective and creative outcomes. In F. H. Farley & N. J. Gordon (Eds), *Psychology and education. The state of the union.* New York: McClutchan.

Farley, F. H. (1985). Psychology and cognition. In J. Strelau, F. H. Farley, & A. Gale (Eds)., *The biological bases of personality and behavior: Theories, measurement techniques, and development* (Vol. 1). New York: Hemisphere.

Freud, A. (1946). *The ego and the mechanisms of defense.* New York: International Universities Press.

Freud, S. (1946). Some psychical consequences of the anatomical distinction between the sexes. In J. Strachey (Ed.), *Standard edition of the complete works of Sigmund Freud* (Vol. 21). London: Hogarth. (Originally published 1925)

Freud, S. (1961). The outline of psychoanalysis. In J. Strachey (Ed.), *Standard edition of the complete works of Sigmund Freud* (Fol. 23). Lonson: Hogarth. (Originally published 1940)

Frost, R. (1969). *The poetry of Robert Frost.* New York: Holt, Rinehart & Winston.

Garmenzy, N. (1976, August). Master lecture on developmental psychology, American Psychological Association, New York.

Gaskell, E. (1984). *Cranford.* Harmondsworth, England: Penguin.

Gaylin, W. (1976). *Caring.* New York: Avon Books.

Gaylin, W. (1979). *Feelings.* New York: Harper & Row.

Gilligan, C. (1982). *In a different voice.* Cambridge, MA: Harvard University Press.

Gillis, J. S. (1982). *Too tall, too small.* Champaign, IL: Institute for Personality and Ability Testing.

Guinouard, D. E., & Rychlak, J. F. (1962). Personality correlates of sociometric popularity in elementary school children. *Personality and Guidance Journal, 40,* 438-442.

Guilford, J. P. (1967). *The nature of human intelligence.* New York: McGraw-Hill.

Gorsuch, R. L. (1974). *Factor analysis.* Philadelphia: Saunders.

Hartman, H. (1939). *Ego psychology and the problem of adaptation.* New York: International Universities Press.

Herriot, J. (1976). *All things bright and beautiful.* London: Pan Books.

Horn, J. L. (1968). Organization of abilities and the development of intelligence. *Psychological Review, 75,* 242-259.

Hundleby, J. D., Pawlik, K., & Cattell, R. B. (1965). *Personality factors in objective test devices.* San Diego: Knapp.

Institute for Personality and Ability Testing. (1970). *Tabular Supplement No. 1 to the 16PF Handbook: Norms for the 16PF Forms A and B (1967-68 Edition).* Champaign, IL: Author.

IPAT Staff. (1986). *Administrator's manual for the 16 Personality Factor Questionnaire.* Champaign, IL: Institute for Personality and Ability Testing.

IPAT Staff. (1987). *Human Resource Development Report user's guide.* Champaign, IL: Institute for Personality and Ability Testing.

James, W. (1968). In J. J. McDermot (Ed.), *The writings of William James.* New York: The Modern Library, Random House.

James, W. (1958). *The varieties of religious experience.* New York: A Mentor Book, American Library. (Originally published 1902)

Jellinek, J., & Williams, T. (1984). Post traumatic stress disorder and substance abuse in Vietnam combat veterans. *Journal of Substance Abuse Disorders,* (1), 87-97.

Johnson, R. C., & Medinnus, G. R. (1965). *Child psychology, behavior and development* (2nd ed.). New York: Wiley.

Jung, C. J. (1928). *Psychological types.* New York: Harcourt & Brace.

Karson, S., & Haupt, T. D. (1968). Second-order personality factors in child guidance clinical patients. *Multivariate Behavior Research, 3,* 99-106.

Karson, S., & O'Dell, J. W. (1976). *A guide to the clinical use of the 16PF.* Champaign, IL: Institute for Personality and Ability Testing.

Kelly, E. L. (1967). Attribution theory in social psychology. In D. Levine (Ed.), *Nebraska symposium on motivation. Vol. 15.* Lincoln, NE: University of Nebraska Press.

Kesey, K. (1975). *One flew over the cuckoo's nest.* New York: New American Library.

Kretchmer, E. (1925). *Physique and character.* London: Kegan Paul.

Kiley, D. (1983). *The Peter Pan syndrome.* New York: Avon Books.

Kipling, R. (1940). *Rudyard Kipling's verse. Definitive edition.* New York: Doubleday.

Kohlberg, L. (1964). Development of moral character and moral ideology. In M. L. Hoffman & L. W. Hoffman (Eds), *Review of child development research* (Vol. 1). New York: Russell Sage Foundation.

Kohlberg, L., & Kramer. (1969). Continuities and discontinuities in child and adult moral development. *Human Development, 12,* 93-120.

Krug, S. E. (1978). Further evidence on 16PF distortion scales. *Journal of Personality Assessment, 42*(5), 513-518.

Krug, S. E. (1979). The development of a validity scale for the Clinical Analysis Questionnaire. *Multivariate Experimental Clinical Research, 4*(4), 125-131.

Krug, S. E. (1980). *Clinical Analysis Questionnaire manual.* Champaign, IL: Institute for Personality and Ability Testing.

Krug, S. E. (1981). *Interpreting 16PF profile patterns.* Champaign, IL: Institute for Personality and Ability Testing.

Jrug, S. E., & Sherman, J. L. (1977). Psychological trait analysis in preventive medicine. *Journal of the International Academy of Preventive Medicine, 4*(2), 48-56.

Levine, S. (1982). *Who dies? An investigation into conscious living and conscious dying.* New York: Anchor Books, Doubleday.

Longsteth, L. E. (1974). *Psychological development of the child* (2nd ed.). New York: Ronald.

Macoby, E. E., & Masters, J. (1970). Attachment and dependency. In P. Mussen & L. Carmichael (Eds), *Carmichael's manual of child psychology* (pp. 73-146). New York: Wiley & Sons.

Markham, B. (1983). *West with the night.* San Francisco: North Point Press.

Maugham, W. S. (1984). *The moon and sixpence.* New York: Penguin. (Originally published 1919)

Menninger, K. (1938). *Man against himself.* New York: Harcourt & Brace.

Michenbaum, D. (1977). *Cognitive behavior modification.* New York: Plenum.

Michener, J. (1953). *Hawaii.* New York: Random House.

Monat, A., & Lazarus, R. (1979). *Stress and coping.* New York: Columbia University Press.

Myers, I. (1962). *The Myers-Briggs type indicator: Manual.* Princeton, NJ: Educational Testing Service.

Osborn, A. F. (1963). *Applied imagination.* New York: Scribner.

Peck, M. S. (1978). *The road less travelled.* New York: Simon & Schuster.

Piaget, J. (1965). *The moral judgement of the child.* New York: The Free Press. (Originally published 1932)

Porter, R. B., Cattell, R. B., & IPAT Staff. (1985). *Handbook for the Children's Personality Questionnaire (CPQ).* Champaign, IL: Institute for Personality and Ability Testing.

Pumfrey, P. D., & Ward, I. (1971). A four-year follow up of maladjusted and normal children. *Bulletin of the British Psychological Society, 24,* 83.

Rieke, M. L., & Russell, M. T. (1987). *Narrative Score Report. User's guide.* Champaign, IL: Institute for Personality and Ability Testing.

Rickels, K., & Cattell, R. B. (1965). The clinical factor validity and trueness of the IPAT verbal objective batteries for anxiety and regression. *Journal of Clinical Psychology, 21,* 257-264.

Rogers, C. R. (1957). A theory of therapy: Personality and interpersonal relationships as developed in the client-centered framework. In S. Koch (Ed.), *Psychology. A study of a science. Formulation of the person and the social context, Vol. 3.* New York: McGraw-Hill.

Rogers, C. R. (1961). *On becoming a person.* Boston: Houghton Mifflin.

Rosenthal, S. V., Aitken, R. C., & Zealley, A. K. (1973). The Cattell 16PF personality profile in asthmatics.*Journal of Psychosomatic Research, 17,*(1), 9-14.

Rothman, A. I., & Flowers, J. F. (1970). Personality correlates of first year medical achievement. *Journal of Medical Education, 45,* 901-905.

Sandler, J., & Freud, A. (1985). *The analysis of defense: The ego and the mechanisms of defense revisited.* New York: International Universities Press.

Satir, V. (1967). *Conjoint family therapy* (rev. ed.). Palo Alto, CA: Science and Behavior Books.

Schachter, S. (1959). *The psychology of affiliation.* Stanford, CA: Stanford University Press.

Schuerger, J. M. (1986). Personality assessment by objective tests. In R. B. Cattell & R. Johnson (Eds), *Funcltional psychological testing*. New York: Brunner/Mazel, pp. 260-287.

Seward, J. P. (1941). The hormonal induction of behavior. *Psychology Review, 48,* 302-315.

Shapiro, D. (1965). *Neurotic styles*. New York: Basic Books.

Sherman, J. L., & Krug, S. E. (1977). Personality-somatic interactions: The research evidence. In S. Krug (Ed.), *Psychological assessment in medicine*. Champaign, IL: Institute for Personality and Ability Testing.

Skidmore, S. (1977). Translating psychological profiles into treatment procedures. In S. E. Krug (Ed.), *Psychological assessment in medicine*. Champaign, IL: Institute for Personality and Ability Testing.

Sperry, R. W. (1968). *Mental unity following surgical disconnection of the cerebral hemispheres*. New York: Academic Press.

Terkel, S. (1972). *Working*. New York: Ballatine Books.

Thurstone, L. L. (1938). *Primary mental abilities*. Chicago: Chicago Universities Press.

Tyler, A. (1986). *The accidental tourist*. New York: Berkley Books.

Walter, C. (1979). *Personal Career Development Profile manual*. Champaign, IL: Institute for Personality and Ability Testing.

Watson, J. D. (1969). *Double helix*. New York: New American Library.

Watts, A. (1972). *The book: On the taboo against knowing who you are*. New York: Random Books.

Wheelwright, J. (1964). *Manual for the Jungian type survey Gray-Wheelwright test* (16th rev.). Palo Alto, CA: Society of Jungian Analysts of N. California.

Whitman, W. (1959). Song to myself. In J. E. Miller (Ed.), *Complete poetry and selected prose*. Boston: Houghton Mifflin.

Winder, P., O'Dell, J. W., & Karson, S. (1975). New motivational distortion scales for the 16PF. *Journal of Personality Assessment, 39*(5), 532-537.

Winnicott, D. W. (1964). *The child, the family and the outside world*. Baltimore: Penguin Books.

Witkin, H. A. (1962). *Psychological differentiation: Studies of development*. New York: Wiley.

Yankalovich, D., & Barrett, W. (1970). *Ego and instinct. The psychoanalytic view of human nature*. New York: Random House.

Zigler, E., & Glick, M. A. (1986). *A developmental approach to adult psychopathology*. New York: Wiley & Sons.

Author Index

Subject Index